Book Publishing
Career
Directory

Book Publishing Career Directory

Second Edition

The Career Directory Series

Editor-In-Chief: Ronald W. Fry

The Career Press Inc.
PO Box 34,
Hawthorne, NJ 07507
1-800-CAREER-1

Copyright ©1987 by The Career Press Inc.

"The Structure And Functions of the Book Business" by Chandler B. Grannis copyright ©1985 Westview Press, Inc., Boulder, CO and reprinted with permission. Originally published in The Business of Book Publishing, edited by Elizabeth A. Geiser and Arnold Dolin, with Gladys S. Topkis.

"Book Clubs: An (Unexpected?) Area of Opportunity" by Jessica Weber, copyright ©1986 Jessica Weber. Written for this Series, revised and updated for this edition.

"Planting Inflammatory Ideas in the Garden of Delight: Reflections on Editing Children's Books" by Ann Beneduce copyright ©1962, 1985 by Gerald Gross and reprinted with the permission of Harper & Row Publishers Inc. Originally appeared in Editors on Editing, revised edition, edited by Gerald Gross.

The Career Directory Series

Book Publishing Career Directory
ISSN 0882-8261

Text edition (Paperback)   ISBN 0-934829-13-6
$26.95

Text edition (Cloth)   ISBN 0-934829-19-5
$34.95

Text editions of this Directory may be ordered by mail or phone directly from the publisher. To order by mail, please include price as noted above, $1.50 handling per order, plus $1.00 for each book ordered. (New Jersey residents please add 6% sales tax.) Send to:

The Career Press Inc.
62 Beverly Rd., PO Box 34,
Hawthorne, NJ 07507

Or call Toll-Free 1-800-CAREER-1 to order using your VISA or Mastercard or for further information on all books published or distributed by The Career Press.

Trade Paperback edition   ISBN 0-934829-07-1
Available only to bookstores and only from Williamson Publishing, Charlotte, VT.

TABLE OF CONTENTS

SECTION III: OPPORTUNITIES IN MARKETING & SALES

SECTION IV: OPPORTUNITIES IN ADVERTISING & PUBLICITY

SECTION VIII: APPENDICES

ACKNOWLEDGEMENTS

In February, 1986, we published the first edition of the <u>Book Publishing Career Directory</u>, the last of the four volumes in our newly-christened <u>Career Directory Series</u>. At that time, I wrote: "A major resource work like this first <u>Book Publishing Career Directory</u> cannot be compiled, edited, designed and published without the input, help and contributions of many professionals. Collecting and codifying the data has been a herculean task. So, not surprisingly, we have many people to thank."

The task *had* been a daunting one, but it had also clearly been a worthy and important project. And all our efforts were amply rewarded by the overwhelmingly positive response to the first edition of this volume -- and, eventually, to the whole <u>Career Directory Series</u> -- from industry professionals, students, teachers, counselors and librarians.

Then we had to sit down and confront the work necessary to bring out this second edition. . .and the five others in the now *six*-volume <u>Career Directory Series</u>.

I used "herculean" before, so I'm not sure what word (*Samsonian???*) could connote the difficulties we encountered and the efforts necessary to overcome them and "exceed our own success." Yet I felt that goal was paramount -- to ensure that this volume would continue to be viewed as *the* book unhesitatingly recommended <u>to anyone</u> considering a career in book publishing <u>by anyone</u> who knew anything about the publishing business.

We asked many friends and colleagues to help us again. . .and to help us more.

We made a lot of new friends. . .then asked *them* for help.

They all made this new effort possible. So, again, our thanks to our friends:

-- First and foremost, to Parker Ladd, Chuck McMahon and the rest of the staff of the Association of American Publishers, the primary industry trade association for book publishers (to which, you'll find, many of our authors refer). They were instrumental in the earliest stages of this project, helping with advice, information and recommendations for contributing authors. Without their help, it would have been far more difficult to attract the top professionals who donated their time, experience and advice to this (and the first) edition.

-- The many contributors who, while fulfilling their own significant job responsibilities, somehow found the time to write the articles -- those invaluable bits of advice -- we believe are the core of this <u>Directory</u>. We commend them for the concern they've shown for you -- the aspiring professionals some of them may even eventually hire!

Our most heartfelt thanks to: Herb Addison, Ann Beneduce, Don Burden, Gary Craig, Bob Ewing, Josephine Fagan, Chandler Grannis, John Holland, Julia Knickerbocker, Diane Kuppler, Chet Logan, Lyman Louis, Ken McCormick, Zlata Paces, Mike Pratt, Fred Schilling, Bob Stewart, Sam Vaughan, and Jessica Weber.

-- And special thanks to their staffs, who often helped with the research, dealt with our editors to make sure all the materials arrived on time, and handled the many details endemic to such an undertaking.

-- Diane Moore, executive director of the Art Director's Club, who recommended the professionals who wrote the chapters on art and design in both editions of this volume (plus those who contributed to our Advertising and Magazines volumes, as well). Details of the ADC's many student-related programs are included in Appendix A.

-- Many other top executives were unable, because of time constraints or other pressing commitments, to add articles to this year's edition, though many then worked with us to get other authors, looked over galleys, or suggested important new topics. In no particular order, our thanks to: Andrew Neilly, Jr., Elizabeth Gordon, Charlotte Zolotow, Scott Marsilio, Larry Kirschbaum, Joni Evans and Anne Durrell.

-- Thanks to the many publishing companies that provided the detailed information on internships, training programs, employment contacts, and, most important, entry-level job opportunities. (See the Job Opportunities Databank for this exclusive data.) We thank each of them for helping us gather this information for you.

-- The many people at The Career Press and our supplier companies who worked long hours compiling this data, editing articles, proofreading and doing all the other things necessary to complete a volume of this size and complexity. We thank all of them for their time, efforts and invaluable contributions: Dick Start, Harvey Kraft, Scott Zipper, Abby Whitlan, Roberta Kopper, Tam Mossman, Tom Stein, Joe Zipper, Carol Start, Bill Killpatrick, Cy Chaiken, Michelle Gluckow, and all the folks at Words at Work, Book Mart Press, L'Escape Artistes, and the staff of the New York Public Library.

-- Penultimately, to Bob Martin, ex-creative writing instructor at Princeton University, who 20 years ago warned me I'd "starve" if I dared ever think I could write professionally. Here's looking at you, Bob.

Last, but only in this section, my wife, Gretchen. I keep telling her it *will* get easier and I *will* slow down. I know *she* knows it won't and I won't. But I love her for pretending -- most of the time -- that it's OK anyway.

Thank you -- all of you -- my friends.

Ronald W. Fry
President
The Career Press Inc.

Getting The Most Out Of Your Directory

Despite its notorious reputation for underpaying the editors, salespeople, advertisers, promotors and producers who toil in its vineyards, the book publishing industry is, nevertheless, what employment counselors call a "glamour" industry. Consequently, there is usually an ample supply of qualified candidates willing to work for pennies and a shortage of actual entry-level jobs.

This <u>Book Publishing Career Directory</u>, now in its second edition, was specifically created to help *you* break out of the pack hunting for one of those jobs. It won't just tell you how to get a first job in book publishing -- because*how* to get a job is only one aspect of the complex learning process you will need to go through, a process that includes learning about yourself, the book publishing business in general (it *is* radically different from newspapers or magazines), and key publishers and job specializations in particular.

It's a process of discovering *what* you want to do, *where* you want to do it and then, and *only* then, *how* to break down the publisher's front door. This <u>Directory</u> is, therefore, a compendium of *all* the resources you'll need to make the *series* of decisions necessary to get that first job. . .or to give you a better understanding of the book publishing business so you can move on from your first job.

And it's written by the <u>pros</u> -- nearly two dozen of the top people in book publishing. Articles and advice written specifically for this volume and directed specifically to *you*.

But why shouldn't we include information on magazines and newspapers, too? Aren't they all involved in "publishing?" Doesn't that make them pretty similar? Not by a long shot. Although some of the departments and job descriptions *sound* similar, these publishing worlds are as different as any other industries, despite their all having "publishing" in their names. Being a book editor at Random House has little in common with editing *The New York Times* , and won't prepare you very well for editing *Good Housekeeping*, either. Even given these differences, some have tried to lump all three industries into a single "publishing career guide." The result, unfortunately, is a book that gives short shrift to all three industries. (The other problem in virtually all such volumes we've seen is that they're invariably written by a freelance writer who's never worked for a book publisher, magazine or newspaper!)

So, in the first edition of this <u>Directory</u>, we made the decision to limit all of the information and articles to book publishing. For those interested in the world of magazines, we prepared the <u>Magazine Publishing Career Directory</u>, a new edition of which (under the shortened title <u>Magazines Career Directory</u>) is also now available.

And, in response to the many students who wrote us asking about opportunities in newspaper publishing -- those of you interested in becoming the next Hildy Johnson -- we've added a new volume to our <u>Career Directory Series</u> -- the all-new <u>Newspapers Career Directory</u>. If you're sure you want to be in "editorial," but don't know the differences between the editorial functions at a magazine, newspaper and publishing house, these three volumes will help you explore all three industries before you make the mistake of breaking into the wrong one! <u>There is not significant movement between these industries</u>, so knowing the differences and moving in the right direction from the very start of your career is extremely important.

HOW TO USE THIS DIRECTORY

Anyway, to return to those of you interested in *book* publishing. We've attempted to organize this <u>Directory</u> in such a way that reading it is a logical, step-by-step, educational progression.

The Introduction by Ken McCormick, former Editor-in-Chief at Doubleday, and Section I (chapters 1-5) offer an overview of the industry and a look at some specialized areas of publishing you may not have considered as areas of opportunity -- university presses, book clubs, scientific/technical publishers, and the world of electronic publishing.

Sections II through V offer more detailed discussions of the major areas of job specialization -- Editorial (Trade, college, elhi and children's books), Marketing & Sales (for Trade, college or elhi publishers and subsidiary rights sales); Advertising & Promotion (advertising and publicity/public relations) and Production (art & design, manufacturing). The twelve chapters in these sections were written by some of the top leaders in each field.

After studying these sections, you should be well on your way to deciding exactly <u>what</u> you want to do -- Section VI will help you figure out <u>how</u> to go about getting your first chance to <u>do</u> it. It includes a detailed Job Search Process that will take you through evaluating yourself and potential employers, preparing resumes and cover letters, the interview process and, finally, sifting the job offers. It also features a new article by Chet Logan, Vice President Personnel at Harper & Row, on internships and training programs. . .and, not incidentally, what to do to catch *his* eye (and the eyes of other top recruiters at the major houses).

Section VII is your Job Opportunities Databank, including listings of publishing houses throughout the United States and Canada. Many of these listings include information on internships, training programs, key contacts, even actual and expected entry-level job listings. This information is exclusive to this <u>Directory</u>, gathered through our own surveys of these publishers.

Finally, Section VIII consists of three appendices -- (A). industry trade organizations; (B). trade publications; and (C). the best-known publishing courses -- more important information to make sure you get exactly the right first job in book publishing.

DISAGREEMENTS AND REDUNDANCIES

You'll discover as you read through the many articles in this volume that <u>the authors don't agree on everything!</u> In fact, you'll find certain instances where they rather vehemently *dis*agree, including their basic advice on breaking into the business, whether New York really is "where it's at," and more.

What's going on here? How do you know who to listen to? Frankly, no one has all the answers, let alone all the *right* answers. Such occasional disagreement is only to be expected given the varied career paths and experiences our contributors have gone through in so many different departments at so many varied houses. We also think it's important that *you* realize there isn't always one way in, one way to do a job, one place to work, one way to think. We have occasionally inserted "Editor's Notes" into the body of articles to refer you to other chapters or sections where you can find related, though perhaps contradictory, advice or information.

On the other hand, you will occasionally find repititious advice -- on interviewing techniques, how to break in, etc. -- from article to article. (Reviewers especially please note!) <u>We are aware of this duplication and have purposefully not edited out such repititious advice.</u> Why?

Not everyone will read every page of this book -- the young man who's always wanted to be an editor might never make it through the Production Section. Someone just "thumbing through" may entirely miss an important piece of advice if it's in only one section or chapter.

And second, although we believe the extensive job search process included in our staff-written Section VI "covers all the basics," if the advice is sound and correct, we're sure it can't be repeated often <u>enough</u>.

S/HE, HIS OR HER, ETC.

As we noted in the first edition of this volume, finding gender neutral terms that don't totally disrupt each article's particular style -- in a book with so many different styles -- was virtually impossible. We personally find contractions like "s/he" strange, having to use "his or her" four or five times in a single sentence awfully awkward.

We have attempted to refer to a title, function, etc. wherever possible to avoid such gender identification. When unable to do so, we have been inconsistent -- using "his or her" the first couple of times so you know we're aware of the importance of such nonmasculine identification, but then reverting to the single masculine pronoun for simplicity's sake. We suspect you'll understand that we don't think all our readers are men.

THE GOAL WE SET. . .AND ACCOMPLISHED

When we began this project, students we queried indicated an intense need for a guide to resources -- articles and advice on every aspect of the book publishing business by the practitioners out there doing the work, listings of major houses (with then unavailable information like who to talk to, potential openings, educational requirements, etc.), the trade organizations to contact, the magazines to read.

The overwhelmingly positive reaction to the first edition of this volume proves that we achieved our initial goal: To produce the most comprehensive, all-inclusive guide to book publishing for entry-level people ever published.

We feel confident that with this second edition we have succeeded in the more difficult goal we set for ourselves this time: To make the best book on getting into book publishing even better.

Most of all, we hope it helps *you* get exactly the job you want in this exciting business.

Good luck!

INTRODUCTION

Have I Got A Career For You!

By

Ken McCormick, Senior Consulting Editor
Doubleday & Co.

Let's start at the very beginning. You've come to New York City to get a job in publishing. You know one fellow/girl from college whose been in New York for a year, but they work in a totally different business. You can count on your friend to teach you how to get around town, but he/she knows *NOTHING* about publishing. What do you do *now*?

I know a man -- let's call him "Joe" -- who came to New York years ago under similar circumstances. He's now a veteran in the business, even something of an institution, but back then he was just another scared kid from out of town trying to break into the big-time world of New York publishing. One night not so long ago, we started talking about how bleak it must be for someone starting out in this business without any connection to anyone in publishing. We traded stories of how *we* had gotten our starts in the business. While I thought Joe was romanticizing his tale then, I now suspect his story happens more often than any of us think. Perhaps hearing his experiences will make *you* feel a little less alone as you start trodding the cold streets of Manhattan, hoping that someone, *some*where, will introduce *you* to some publishing guru.

"It was terrible," he began. "I'd come to New York -- with a brand-new diploma from the University of Texas -- to get into publishing. I didn't know a soul in New York. But I had heard of *Publishers Weekly* at school, so I went to the library and read a couple of current issues. There was one piece about a big guy in the business -- Alec Blanton of MacMillan. His picture made him look like a human being and, it turned out, he was a graduate of my *alma mater*."

"I marched to his office on Madison Avenue and told his secretary I had a message for him. (I didn't *really* have a *message* as much as some news I hoped would establish some tentative connection between us: A rather legendary journalism professor at Texas had just had quite an honor bestowed on him. I hoped that he knew, or at least *had heard of*, this professor. It wasn't the greatest connection ever invented, but I hoped it would at least get me in the door and give me a chance to talk with him.)

"The secretary took my name. Minutes later, a big, jovial man came out, looked me over, and asked, 'So what happened to Professor Franklin? I don't read the alumni news as much as I should.'

"It turned out that Professor Franklin was one of his idols. Connection established!. He invited me into his office. It wasn't a big or showy place, but from the papers, half-read manuscripts and books strewn around -- and the picture of Maxwell Perkins prominently centered on one wall -- you got the distinct sense that a lot of important work went on there. . *publishing* work.

"My 'pre-planning' had consisted of creating the story to get in the door. Now that I was actually in his office, I wasn't sure how to get the conversation going. In literature class, I'd read quite a bit of Thomas Wolfe, who had, as it turned out, just died. So I took the chance and asked if he had known him. He had. In fact, he felt Wolfe was one of our great novelists. So we talked about Wolfe. Eventually, the conversation returned to Professor Franklin. By the time we talked about *him* for a while, my new 'friend' was virtually glowing.

"The phone rang. 'I'm with someone now,' he said. 'I'll call you back in a few minutes'. A few minutes! -- it was time to take the bull by the horns. So, as he hung up, I told him why I had *really* wanted to see him: I wanted him to give me a *job*.

"Mr. Blanton leaned forward and smiled, 'You want a job, and I don't have one for you. But go and see George Shively at Stokes. He's a good guy, and he likes young people'. I asked him if I could use his name. He said I could, shook my hand, and was reaching for the phone (to call Mr. Shively???) as I left the office.

"George Shively was a doll, though he was working for a publishing house I'd never heard of. Unfortunately, I got the same story -- No jobs open. But *he* referred me to a lady at Simon & Schuster. And *she* referred me to someone else. . .who referred me to yet another editor. And so it went. No one had a job for me, but everyone passed me on to someone else. Within a week, I had seen *seven* people.

"The last conversation took a slightly different turn. 'Get right up to the Colony Bookshop,' this editor advised. 'They called me yesterday looking to hire somebody.' I practically ran uptown. . .and got the job. It wasn't exactly what I had hoped for. But in a single week, I *had* met seven people -- seven big-time professionals who turned out to be friendly and helpful -- and landed my first job in publishing. Seven people whom I hadn't known at all seven days before."

Joe and I continued to reminisce for the greater part of an evening. But that story is the one most pertinent to those of you who are trying to emulate Joe's success and get a first job in publishing. What does it all mean? None of the people Joe spoke with had known him before he walked in the door. And few of them knew many of the others with whom Joe had spoken. But each of them had *heart*. Each of them had been willing to take the time to speak with a newcomer and offer his or her help and advice. It says, I think, some nice things about the nice people who work in this business of book publishing.

HOW TO START A SUCCESSFUL PUBLISHING CAREER

In the Job Search section of this volume, you'll find detailed advice on writing resumes and cover letters, interviewing, following up, and more. Read them carefully. In addition, once you have a better idea of the area of publishing or specialization you want to get into, you can study the pertinent chapter(s) by the top professional who's written about that area for this Career Directory. Each of them discusses the requisite educational and/or extracurricular preparation you need to land that first job. (One piece of advice with which my colleagues may or may not agree: you might not be able to get that perfect first job, the one doing what you always wanted to do. I suggest you take *any* responsible job offered you by a good, respectable house and then work within the company to get to the job/area/ specialization you want. There's a lot of competition out there -- people are looking for jobs and publishers are always seeking talented job candidates. So get in the door -- you have a better chance of moving around once you're already part of the company.

Once you've landed a job -- no matter how lowly -- it's important to realize that your publishing education *has just begun*. Borrow *Publisher's Weekly* (or subscribe to it yourself) and read it every week, the ads as well as the articles. Learn the difference between Trade publishing (books you can buy in a bookshop) and Educational publishing (books which are primarily textbooks). Scientific publishing is another field, religious publishing another, and so on. All special fields All important areas to learn about.

In 1928, when I started in publishing, there were 5,000 different titles published. In the past year, there were about 42,000 titles published. 5,000 was too few, and 42,000 is too many. Help find ways to enable the publisher you are working for do the best possible job on the fewest number of books and still make money. Remember: You are in business; no one is subsidizing your house -- it must make money to survive.

How to help your house

Whether you're at the top of the employment ladder or have just taken a first job as a clerk or a secretarial assistant (it pays you a salary that pays the rent!), you should be looking for ways to help your house. . .a search that will often, not incidentally, wind up helping *you* and *your* career, too.

Read magazines. When you see a story or an article by someone who hasn't been published in the book field, write to the author. Tell him or her how much you enjoyed the piece and ask if they have an idea for a novel or non-fiction book.

If they are any good, they *will* have an idea, possibly lots of them. Ask them to send you copies of whatever they've written that might work as a book. Or just synopses of their ideas. Read everything and start corresponding with the author. Encourage them. Keep copies of every such letter. Why do all this? Because sooner or later, you'll find a Joy Cowley.

My wife read *Short Story International* and came across a short story by a Joy Cowley, a writer from New Zealand. My wife had never heard of her before, but wrote her a letter and, in return, got part of a novel. She read it, liked it, and encouraged the editorial board at Doubleday to offer Joy a book contract. As a result of my wife's aggressive search for ways to help Doubleday, we eventually published four books by Mrs. Cowley. This kind of editorial sleuthing is going on all the time at any good publishing house.

When do you stop your publishing education? The answer is: never. Even if you've reach the "top of the ladder" and no longer attend courses or seminars for yourself, you'll still attend Denver or Radcliffe. . .but as a teacher. It's essential to *pass on* what you've learned.

When is it time to move on?

Most publishers give a raise every six months -- a nominal raise, that is. You may not see a big increase for a while, so if a job that looks interesting opens up at another publisher, you may want to consider it. But think about the <u>house</u> you're currently working for, not just the job you currently have. Make sure you want to change <u>houses</u>, and not just jobs. If you do decide to leave, ask your potential employer for a reasonable increase, but don't price yourself out of the market. And before you make the switch, ask someone whose advice you trust whether *they* think you should.

When I was a young man in publishing I seemed to be surrounded by tall trees. I saw no possibility of getting anywhere. I went to our sales manager (Frank Henry, a wonderful guy with a hearty laugh) and asked "Is there any future for me at Doubleday?" He suddenly became very serious "Stay," he advised. "In about two years, the whole climate here will change, and there really will be a job for you -- one a lot better than you have now." Now he was the sales manager and I was in the editorial department, but I sensed that I could trust his advice and that he knew what he was talking about. I stayed.

Now, unbeknownst to *me*, a mere toiler in the editorial vineyards, two red hot people at Doubleday were in the wrong jobs One, Dan Longwell, went to *Time* magazine and helped start *LIFE*. The other, Malcolm Johnson, was really a scientific publisher. He left for a very good house where his knowledge of scientific publishing would push him along. Those two moves opened up two "holes" and gave me an unexpected chance (we *were* in the depths of the Depression, and there weren't a lot of openings). Good houses -- and Doubleday was and is one of those -- usually look to their own people to fill an opening before searching "on the outside." I was promoted.

Every once in a while, I shiver when I think of the mistake I would have made if I'd given in to my small pessimism about my future. In two years everything *did* change and I got a break. (And I eventually became editor-in-chief!) Thank God for the Frank Henrys of this world.

Use this <u>Book Publishing Career Directory</u> to expand your current knowledge of publishing and, perhaps more importantly, to expand the areas of possibilities you're able to consider. Look at the chapter on working for a *university press*. What incredible changes have taken place there in the last few years! More and more of their books are competing with Trade publishing houses. The University of Nebraska Press, for example, has a very hot paperback line. Many of Wallace Stegner's best books are in that series. Learn more about what university presses are doing *now,* as opposed to what they *used* to do.

Think about <u>scientific publishing,</u> especially if you're technically-inclined or trained. Or working for a <u>book club</u> or in the fast-growing area of <u>religious publishing.</u> Or for one of the many <u>educational publishers.</u>

And even if you are hoping to break into Trade publishing, you can find*lots* of opportunities in areas besides editorial! Consider marketing, sales, promotion. . .or subsidiary rights, advertising, public relations, production. You'll find interesting and informative articles on all these areas of specialization (and more) in the pages that follow. Don't pass them by -- you might learn about an area you never even considered before and find a totally unexpected career opportunity.

Don't think your search is confined to New York. Regional publishing has grown wildly, if not always profitably. When I was a high school and college student in Oregon, there was one struggling book publisher in Portland, another in San Francisco. But that was *it* for West Coast publishing. Now there are book publishers in Seattle, Portland, a number around San Francisco and Los Angeles, and many more all over the country.

So "Happy Publishing." If you want a career in book publishing, it's out there for you. Learn to type well, have a ravishing appetite for books, and be endlessly aggressive about not stepping on other people's hands (or toes).

Good luck. And smile. . .no matter *how* apprehensive you are.

* * *

In his nearly 60 years in book publishing, Mr. McCormick has worked with a group of famous authors far too numerous to list in full, among them: Sir Rudolph Bing, Noel Coward, William O. Douglas, Edna Ferber, Arthur Hailey, W. Somerset Maugham, Lowell Thomas, Leon Uris, Louis Nizer, Pierre Salinger, Irving Stone, Robert F. Kennedy, and many others.

Beginning his career at the Doubleday Bookshop in New York's Pennsylvania Station in 1930, he worked at a number of their book outlets before being appointed promotion manager in 1933. He joined the Editorial department in 1935, becoming associate editor in 1937, editor-in-chief in 1942, and vice president in 1948. Since 1971 he has been a senior consultant editor with the company and, since 1973, has fulfilled similar responsibilities at the Franklin Library.

Mr. McCormick has been active throughout his career in numerous industry organizations. He is a former director of the American Book Publishers Council, served several years as chairman of their Committee on Reading Development, and has taught creative writing at Columbia University.

Mr. McCormick is married to the former Anne Hutchens, who works in the subsidiary rights department of Alfred A. Knopf publishers. They live in New York City.

SECTION I

The
Book
Publishing
Business

CHAPTER 1

The Structure And Functions Of The Book Business

By

Chandler B. Grannis, Former Editor-In-Chief
Publishers Weekly

"Structure" may be too static a term for such a variegated, fluid endeavor as book publishing. Nevertheless, the actions necessary to get any book published follow a fairly natural pattern that applies to all books, and publishing houses generally fall rather easily into groups according to the kinds of books published, the constituencies served, the markets sought, and the styles of business or institutional structure involved.

"Business," too, may be a not quite sufficient term to describe an enterprise in which the commodity is the product of human thought and creativity. Publishing assuredly is a business in the full sense, but it is also something more, because it concerns all the responsibilities and opportunities of communication.

Many publishing operations are recognized as "commercial"; many are considered "noncommercial." Some firms seek to "maximize profit" as a primary goal; many feel fortunate to achieve what could be called reasonable profits; and some exist not primarily (or at all) to make a profit, but to meet some defined need (social, scholarly, or religious, for example) on a break-even or subsidized basis. But whether they are "in business" or not, all publishers, if they are to carry out their chosen purposes, have to be business-like.

Writers about the book industry (including this one) have said over and over that the publishing of books can be a business, a profession, a gamble, or all three, and that for many people it is a vocation or calling. Herbert S. Bailey, Jr. suggested another choice of terms to describe the industry by calling his book The Art and Science of Book Publishing. Still another term -- "the accidental profession" -- was used by Samuel S. Vaughan (who wrote the excellent introduction to the first edition of this volume and is represented in the Editorial section of this edition) for his contribution to To Be a Publisher, the Association of American Publishers' (AAP) book about education for publishing. I strongly suggest you obtain a copy of this booklet.

THE MANY "STRUCTURES" OF BOOK PUBLISHING

One can notice all these characteristics at different points and with different intensities throughout the publishing industry.

The common publishing procedures

First, there is the basic structure or common procedure that brings all books into being: a sequence of creating, producing, and disseminating them, along with financial management and administration. Accordingly, in publishing houses large, medium, or small, the functions are those of:

(1) planning a program, commissioning or selecting manuscripts and book projects, evaluating the material, and editing it for printing;

(2) designing, specifying, and overseeing manufacture;

(3) marketing in all its aspects; and

(4) managing and coordinating these activities.

Currently reshaping arrangements in every department of publishing -- in editorial, production, marketing, financial, and administrative operations and even in authorship -- is the electronic factor, most obviously manifested by the swiftly proliferating use of in-house data processing and word processing equipment. The essential functions of publishing are the same as before, but the procedures and order of events are being sharply changed. Mastery of the many new technological tools is vital. (*See Gary Craig's chapter on Electronic Publishing for more on this important area -- Ed.*)

The types of books published

A second aspect of book industry structure can be unearthed by studying the categories into which the industry divides itself by types or broad fields of publishing. In 1982, the aggregate net receipts of all U.S. publishers from domestic and foreign sales came to about $7.999 billion. The divisions accounting for this sum are as follows (the percentages are derived from the annual report compiled by the Association of American Publishers to show each division's approximate share of the total net receipts):

Adult Trade (general books of fiction and nonfiction of the kinds sold in most bookstores and circulated in public libraries): Hardcover - 8.4%; Paperbound (not including mass market) - 5.7%.

Juveniles (children's books): Hardcover - 2.3%; Paperbound - 0.6%.

Religious: 4.9% (including Bibles - 2.3%)

Technical and Scientific: 5.4%

Business and Other Professional: 6.7%

Medical: 3.4%

Book Clubs (sales to subscribers): 7.4%

Mail Order Publishing (other than clubs): 7.6%

Mass Market Paperbounds (pocket or "rack size" only): 10.3%

University Presses: 1.2%

Elhi Texts: 13.2%

College Texts and Materials: 14.3%

Standardized Tests: 0.9%

Subscription/Reference (encyclopedias and so forth sold by subscription): 5.0%

Audio/Visual and Other Media (primarily for schools): 1.9%

Other Sales (unbound printed sheets, miscellaneous merchandise): 0.3%

Overall, publishers' receipts in the middle 1980s are increasing at a rate of about 9% to 10% per year.

From the standpoint of dollars received, therefore, the biggest divisions of publishing are Trade (Adult, Juvenile, and some Religious combined), about 22%; Professional (Technical, Scientific, Business, and Medical combined), almost 15.5%; College, 14%; Elhi Texts, 13%; and Mass Market Paperbound, 10%. So much for publishers' sales in dollars.

The total numbers of copies that account for those dollars divide up rather differently. The figures have been estimated by the Book Industry Study Group (BISG), a nonprofit industry service organization. John P. Dessauer, for BISG, sets the 1982 unit sales by U.S. publishers at about 1.901 billion books. Calculations made from the BISG report suggest that Adult and Juvenile Trade books accounted for about 23.7% of all units sold; Religious - 5.7%; all Professional - 3.5%; Book Clubs - 9.7%; Mail Order - 2.9%; Mass Market Paperbounds - 34.9%; University Presses - 0.6%; Elhi Texts - 13.3%; College Texts - 5.7%; Subscription/ Reference - less than 0.1%. High-priced categories often involve fewer books; for example, compare dollars and unit ratios of the Mass Market category with those of the Professional group.

Subject categories of books published

Still another aspect of the structure of publishing can be seen by examining the total numbers of titles published in major subject classifications. Title counts and estimates of average prices are made in cooperation with the Library of Congress by the R.R. Bowker Co., primarily. The Bowker reports, appearing in a spring annual summary issue of *Publishers Weekly* (the primary trade magazine for the book publishing industry, to which I strongly suggest you consider subscribing) and in a reference book, the Bowker Annual of Library and Book Trade Information, show a yearly output of over 50,000 titles in the middle 1980s. Roughly 85% of these are brand-new books; the rest are new, revised, or specially reprinted editions. Probably about a third of the 48,000-odd new titles are in paper covers of one kind or another. Bowker reports the numbers under 23 topical headings selected through consultation with library and publishing people.

Publishing from a marketing and sales standpoint

One very important way to view the structure of publishing is to look at its markets. In fact, the processes of editing and producing books all point to the final step: making the book public. How publishers identify and develop their markets, how these efforts are structured, and how they affect the pattern of the publishing house are topics described in detail in at least three books: Nat Bodian's Book Marketer's Handbook (for scientific, scholarly, medical, and other professional books and journals): Robert Carter's Trade Book Marketing Handbook; and the American Booksellers Association's (ABA) updated Manual on Bookselling, edited by Robert Hale, Allan Marshall, and Jerry Showalter.

What proportions of publishers' sales are made to what markets? Each firm, group of books, or title calls for its own analysis, but in the overall structure of book publishing, some idea of the proportions in very broad areas can be gained from studies made by AAP and BISG. From the latter's reports it is possible to calculate the following rounded-off estimates of sales ratios in U.S. book publishing in the 1980s: General Retailers -- 25% of all the sales; College Stores - 15%; Libraries and Institutions - 8%; Schools - 16%; Direct to Consumers - 26%; Other Domestic Sales (unbound sheets and miscellaneous merchandise) - 1%; Export - 9%. Widely different ratios appear, of course, in the reports of the individual divisions -- Adult Trade, Professional, College, and so on. The same holds true for estimates of the proportion of sales that go through wholesalers to the above markets; for the industry overall, 22% of the sales pass through wholesalers.

The marketing role of related associations

An important marketing role is played by associations related in one manner or another to the book industry. Large annual meetings (accompanied by domestic and foreign book exhibits and important regional meetings) are held by the big umbrella group of book retailers, the ABA (American Booksellers Association); by the NACS (National Association of College Stores); and by the evangelical CBA (Christian Booksellers Association). The great annual conferences and exhibits of the American Library Association (ALA) are opportunities to present trade and professional books. The many academic and professional

professional association conferences also present book displays and, in addition, facilitate contacts with authors and experts in many fields.

Important industry reference tools

It goes almost without saying that the industry's reference tools are essential in its book marketing structure. They also give an idea of the industry's size and scope: The 1986 edition of <u>Books in Print</u> (BIP), Bowker's multivolume annual index, lists more than 650,000 books. In the annual <u>Subject Guide to Books in Print</u>, the BIP listings are rearranged under more than 60,000 topical headings and subheadings. In 1986, BIP named some 15,000+ publishers of the listed books.

The number of consistently active publishers is much smaller, however -- more like the approximately two thousand U.S. publishers named, with departments and personnel, in Bowker's <u>Literary Market Place</u> (<u>LMP</u>). This annual directory also cites great numbers of service firms, agents, manufacturers, suppliers, reviewers, associations, and other categories of book-related activity. In addition to the important entry-level job information contained in this <u>Career Directory</u>, <u>Literary Market Place</u> should be considered an important tool in your search for a first job in book publishing.

The changing business structures of book publishers

The business structures within which all these book publishing functions exist are of many kinds. And the activities of any publishing house are, of course, influenced by the specific type of business structure that's adopted, which may determine whether a department has close or distant relations with management, what levels of costs and profits are demanded, and the policies toward risk taking, cost controls, author relations, and overall goals. Business changes in recent years have certainly altered some traditional publishing structures: Control has shifted in many cases from book-oriented to financially-oriented people; mergers have proliferated; publishing companies and their parent companies have grown in size and complexity.

On the other hand, there have been divestitures, cutbacks and some countertrends. Some editorial imprints have survived, at least for a time, by working within a large house that performs the non-editorial functions. Some writers and editors have formed cooperatives that prepare and produce projects that are handled under a publisher's imprint. Most important, hundreds of small partnerships and individual or family-owned enterprises have sprung up nationwide over the past two decades; and scores of them have survived. These small houses have built their own structure of cooperative service devices, including wholesalers and trade associations that give practical advice and assistance and hold their own book fairs.

A proliferation of clubs and associations

For the more established publishers, industry associations have long been important in the structure of the industry. The booksellers' associations, as noted, are vital to trade publishing. For the publishers themselves, the AAP represents the broadest spectrum of publishers of all kinds. The Association of American University Presses (AAUP) represents most of the scholarly publishing houses on university campuses. The Society for Scholarly Publishing is made up primarily of individuals in academic, scientific, governmental, and other presses and institutions. The Children's Book Council brings together the people in "juvenile" publishing for the exchange of professional and business information and for cooperative promotion. *(Important industry associations are listed in Appendix A -- Ed.)*

Local and special-interest clubs abound in the book field. Some have national membership, many hold instructional programs, and all present discussions of industry problems and opportunities. There are groups made up of literary agents; women in publishing; people in small firms; young publishers; and people who work in religious publishing, publicity, advertising, library marketing, domestic sales, foreign sales, translating, editing in specialized areas, illustration, typography, and design.

There are peripheral groups whose interests range from reading and literacy to book collecting and the history of printing and publishing. Many people in publishing work with or in organizations of authors: the important national societies, such as the Authors Guild and the American Center PEN, the international literary society of poets, playwrights, editors, essayists, and novelists, as well as smaller or regional groups devoted to specific genres (e.g., science writers, science fiction writers, mystery writers, romance writers, etc.). Consult LMP for a complete list of all the many organizations associated in some way with the book publishing industry.

The book publishing industry's emphasis on education

Education for publishing has been increasingly recognized as a needed element in the industry. Local workshops and university extension programs are held in many places, and the important summer institutes, especially the pioneering Radcliffe program and the even more intensive University of Denver program and the New York University courses, have produced valuable recruits for the industry. The AAP has assisted many programs and has held traveling seminars. *(For a list of the most important book publishing courses, see Appendix C -- Ed.)*

These, then, are the principal structures that make up the book publishing industry. Most of the people in it are concerned most of the time with the operational structures. But it is interesting, rewarding, and sometimes very important to have a view of the entire scene, especially for students or others seeking their first jobs in our exciting profession. This book should help serve that purpose.

* * *

A graduate of Columbia University, Class of 1934, Mr. Grannis joined Publishers Weekly in 1936, was editor-in-chief (1968 to 1971), and has since remained an active contributing editor. He is editor and co-author of What Happens in Book Publishing (Columbia, 1957, 1967), editor of Heritage of the Graphic Arts (Bowker, 1952) and editor and co-author of Banned Books 387 B.C. to 1978 A.D. (Bowker, 1978).

He has served recently as a trustee of the American Printing History Association and was the first president of its New York chapter.

8

CHAPTER 2

Electronic Publishing: What Is It? And Is It For You?

By

Gary Craig, Program Director
Electronic Publishing Division
John Wiley & Sons, Inc. Publishers

"ELECTRONIC PUBLISHING DEPARTMENT, PLEASE"

If you walk into a publishing house and ask for the "electronic publishing" department, you'll get a variety of responses. Sometimes you'll be referred to the production department, sometimes to the data processing department, sometimes to a software product group. Most often, they won't even know what you're talking about!

I guess that qualifies electronic publishing as a "leading edge" area of publishing. And if that's the case, there is a very big question any potential job applicant must ask: What is my tolerance for interruption, uncertainty, and rapid change of direction?

"Regular" publishing is fairly predictable: When you accept a position, at any level, you will enter a functioning environment. The major activities have an operational structure, and the people already there will have little difficulty in passing on to you the details of "how we do it here." (You may immediately want to change "how we do it here", but that's standard -- every new employee is expected to contribute to improving the process.)

But when you join an "electronic publishing" area, you will be conducting business and, at the same time, inventing the way that business is done. In the course of doing so, you will frequently have to abandon many procedural approaches that, it turns out, do not work -- not because they don't get your own work done, but because they are in conflict with other in-house systems, financial reporting requirements, or even the company's long-term view of itself.

You will find, even if you enter at an administrative level, that you are expected to help "sell" your own department's operations to the rest of the company; in fact, how well you do that may determine how long your job exists.

If you are motivated by work alone, if you believe you would be uncomfortable in a position where you must simultaneously keep the work moving and keep a company-wide perspective, if you are happiest when you come to work at nine, leave at five, and erase the job from your mind 'til the following morning, please read no further -- electronic publishing is too exciting to be treated that way. It needs people who are excited by its potential to change the way people think about knowledge and information. It requires a commitment, not only of labor but of ideas, plus a generalist's vision of where our society as a whole is going.

ELECTRONIC PUBLISHING AT WILEY

We see electronic publishing as a piece of the company's philosophy, an affirmation that a traditional company (we have been in business since 1807) can respond to change. It is not, therefore, an activity or even a department, but rather an idea against which a whole spectrum of activities and opportunities are tested.

If we accept a book manuscript on a diskette, rather than on paper, we have made a decision to change the company -- handling that project will demand different kinds of people and different procedures.

If we have been publishing, for decades, a standard handbook, whose main audience is now using computers to do the majority of their work, we have to decide whether we should offer them that same information in a form which lives in the machine, instead of in a dog-eared book on the shelf.

If we have an opportunity to publish a reference work that is extremely valuable to the marketplace, but only if it can be updated very frequently, we know in advance we cannot approach it conventionally -- it takes a long time to make a "regular" book. If we decide to do the book at all, we'll have to seriously consider publishing it electronically.

If we want to publish a reference work that is simply too large to squeeze into a book, we must look at electronic publishing as the only way we can deliver the information to the customers.

If we are publishing some information that is invariably used in conjunction with a computer program, it is probably not reasonable for us to print that information in a book; we should provide the information in the form which integrates directly with that program.

Internally, electronic publishing is how we streamline our publishing process and shorten, as much as possible, the interval between when we receive an author's original material and when we can get it into the hands (or machines) of our customers. And externally, it offers us dozens of options for matching our product -- very exactly -- to our customers' needs; the more we can do *that*, the more solid will be our position in the markets we serve.

BUT WHAT ABOUT THE COMPUTERS?

Yes, we do depend on computers. In fact, some of us even use them. But please don't get the idea that electronic publishing jobs are computer jobs.

Do you like to work on a computer? Good -- you will be able to identify with the customers for electronically-delivered products.

Do you like to write programs? Good -- you are probably a very logical thinker, and electronic publishing requires some very systematic activities. But if you come to my department, you'll never write a BASIC program (although you'll be a big help when we have to buy some programming outside).

Are you motivated by disorder? Good -- electronic publishing offers so many design and implementation options that every project begins by looking like utter chaos; the computer is a frighteningly powerful tool which, in fact, can do anything you ask -- it requires considerable mental discipline to decide *what* you should ask it to do.

WHY DOES ELECTRONIC PUBLISHING EXIST?

Is it just a novelty? After all, publishing is publishing; it just means getting some kind of information from its author to some other person. *How* that is done never did matter very much -- nailing information to doors of churches, writing it on scrolls, even writing letters -- all these things accomplished the desired result.

For more than five hundred years, we've been doing it in these packages called books. Books are perfectly nice products, and they should be -- the book as a delivery vehicle has been evolving during those hundreds of years, with refinement after refinement contributing to the design in response to customer needs. It's probably your own positive feelings about books which have led you to consider publishing as a career in the first place.

Books, however, have some limitations as all-purpose, information delivery packages:

1) *Size* -- you can only glue so many sheets of papers together in a binding.

2) *Weight* -- have you ever tried to lift an unabridged dictionary?

3) *Timeliness* -- information is often two or three years old by the time it is finally published in print.

4) *Labor-intensiveness* -- human labor is about the most expensive commodity around; building this cost into the price of the product sometimes places the publication beyond the reach of its audience.

5) *Non-transferability* -- if you have information in print and you want to use it in a computer or word processor, you will probably have to type it all over again.

On the other hand, information -- considered in machine-readable form -- can take on a great variety of forms:

1) It can be created by the author using his or her own computer, sent to the publisher, edited and otherwise manipulated, and then sent -- again in machine-readable form -- straight to a compositor who will convert it into typographic-appearing output that can be used as the "mechanical" (original) for a book.

2) It can be keyboarded once and then "loaded" onto a large computer, where customers access it by hooking their own computers to telephones and issuing commands. In this form, portions difficult to find in the printed form can be readily located in seconds.

3) It can be updated as often as needed, right up to the time manufacturing (or "loading") begins. Often, this last-minute updating capability adds considerable value to the product.

4) It can be delivered to a customer in exactly the machine-readable format the customer needs, possibly for use in the customer's own computer or electronic "workstation."

5) It can be easily merged with information from other publications to create new or enhanced products.

6) It can be made more valuable by combining it with a software product that gives the customer the ability to manipulate and rearrange it in various ways.

And on and on, limited only by imagination and marketplace acceptance!

ELECTRONIC PUBLISHING PRODUCTS

Here are some specific products you'll find:

A <u>directory</u> of a certain body of names and addresses, accompanied by descriptive information about those contacts. The same information may exist in print, but online it can be searched, manipulated ("all the addresses with CHEMISTRY in their names," for example), and labels ordered containing just the names you want.

References to all articles in nearly a thousand different journals and magazines. These "bibliographic" databases are the mainstay of the industry -- they have been around for a long time, and many people think they are the only kind of online product.

The full text of entire magazines or journals. Not only are the references available, but the entire article as well. Portions or the entire text can be easily inspected, extracted or printed. Printing is also sometimes done "offline" and mailed later, at a lower cost.

Financial databases, containing details of a company's structure and business activities -- its sales, locations, management names, information about branch offices, stock prices, credit status, etc. These are among the most expensive databases, because they support some decision-making which has the potential for very high profit.

Scientific data collections, sold online as databases, but also licensed to the manufacturers of laboratory equipment for integration with the software delivered to the purchaser of the instrument. Industry has always sold hardware combinations; the idea of selling a data collection (or "library") as part of an installed equipment sale is a newer but growing area.

Consumer databases of things like hotel accommodations, airline flight schedules, games, and other general interest databases, usually sold at reduced prices during the host systems' off-peak time (evenings, weekends). These online offerings are usually more "user friendly." The search and retrieval options are more limited, presented through Chinese restaurant-like "menus" of selection options (one from column A, one from column B, etc.).

Data collections from printed works such as handbooks. Often the data is sold integrated with software that not only delivers the data to the user but also offers various graphic display and manipulation options (chemical drawings, x/y axis charts, graphic displays specific to particular technical professions). This field is just getting started and is one of the more technical areas, since graphics are generally more complex than plain text. It is also one of the most exciting areas.

Estimates vary, but there are around 4,000 online products now, a ten-fold increase in the last five years or so.

THE KINDS OF JOBS AVAILABLE IN ELECTRONIC PUBLISHING

While looking at specific jobs, you should also be aware of the several different kinds of companies involved in the chain of events we are calling "electronic publishing". You will also need to know a few terms:

Publishers

The traditional book publisher is often still distributing in printed form the information that is electronically published. In fact, many or all of each product's expenses are often charged to the printed version, with the additional "electronic" income being regarded as "other income" -- nice to have, of course, but not the driving reason for the existence of the publication.

Program director/publisher/acquisitions editor: Built on the similar position in conventional publishing, this is the person who negotiates contracts, does strategic planning, has bottom-line responsibility for the department or division, and, in general, is responsible for the business decisions. Previous experience in performing the same job for printed publications would, of course, be relevant, but so would an extremely broad exposure to many publishing areas -- remember, electronic publishing is important because it takes new looks at traditional publishing.

Product manager: This person may have a variety of titles. The role usually includes primary responsibility for awareness of the marketplace (or marketplaces) where the product's audience is found. The skills are the same basic ones used by all marketers -- knowledge of mailing lists, attendance at trade shows, cultivated networks of personal contacts, etc. Product management usually includes ultimate responsibility for the success or failure of the product, including negotiations with others (in-house and outside) whose actions may affect that success. At this stage of the game, libraries and major corporations are the most important customers, so having been a user of databases or computer systems in one of those environments would be a big help in identifying customers' needs and in relating to those customers.

Technical administrator/database administrator: This person is the main "computer type" in the group. Databases must be designed, host system capabilities must be understood, and, with the help of the product manager and others, translated into functional products. In addition, databases that are already "online" (that is, currently available through host systems) must be supported -- tapes must be shipped out periodically, online data must be inspected, quality of the information must be sustained, and some means must exist for keeping track of the numerous magnetic tapes, documentation, and other odds and ends. Usually the technical administrator either does or supervises this activity.

Customer support (aka "hotline") person: This person is frequently the main customer contact, or at least is responsible for administering customer support. This is a critical position, and one in which the right person can gain considerable personal acclaim and gratitude by performing it well. The problem with online databases is that they don't actually exist -- there is nothing you can show the customer, nothing to which the customer can react at the personal level. Rather, you are selling the potential of answering questions, of finding information. You can only succeed through continuous contact with the customers, thoughtful analysis of their specific needs and problems, and the cultivation of their personal loyalty to both yourself and your product. Interpersonal skills, obviously, are the key ingredient; teaching experience helps, too.

<u>Sales manager.</u> Just as in other fields, the sales manager has one main responsibility -- to bring in sales dollars. To do this, the sales manager must devise just the right combination of tactics and personnel to ensure that sales forecasts are met. Often, the sales manager's compensation is directly related to the sales dollars which come in. There is little credit for "trying hard" -- results are the key criterion. In the case of databases, this is a difficult assignment, because sales in growth areas are very difficult to forecast, and there is little past experience that is applicable to this particular sort of product. The customers' learning curve is also a factor -- you cannot bring in real sales until the customers understand the product sufficiently to know when it meets their needs, and there are few proven tactics for speeding up this learning curve.

Host systems

A host system is simply a company that operates a huge computer facility, one which not only stores large masses of information (databases), but also maintains hundreds of incoming telephone lines, and supports the programs which allow the customers at the other ends of those telephone lines to access particular databases. In effect (though the actual business arrangements vary), the publisher rents a part of the host system's computer in order to give its customers a place to use the publication (database). The host system also owns the software that lets customers make inquiries against the database; part of the cost of using the information is shared with the host as a fee for that software.

<u>Producer contact/producer liaison</u>: This function is critical. The publisher is the source of a specific database, but the host system is selling a service consisting of its own unique combination of databases and system capabilities that distinguishes it from its competitors. The producer liaison constantly balances the sometimes conflicting needs of the publishers with those of the host system. Typically, one such person is responsible for a group of publishers whose products are complementary. His or her role includes the packaging of those databases into a coherent "product family" to be marketed as part of the host system's package.

<u>Sales manager.</u> Very similar to the publisher's sales manager. In this case, the product being sold is the host system's package of services.

<u>Customer support</u>: Even more important -- and considerably more difficult -- than at a publishing house. The publisher only has to answer questions about one or two databases -- the host system's customer support person must be knowledgable about hundreds of databases, each with its own quirks. This person is an extremely skilled online "searcher," a skill usually learned in a school of library science or through years of experience in searching databases at, for example, a busy corporate or university library. The more frequently a person searches, the better his or her online support skills. In general, technical search questions come to the host system, while questions about the content of a database are directed to the publisher.

Networks

Though computers can easily "talk" to each other over standard, voice grade telephone lines, it is expensive to use standard long distance lines for this purpose.

Therefore, this type of communication is usually done via a separate system, one that transmits only digital information between computers. The network is usually reached by dialing a local "node" (really just a local telephone number) that connects to the larger network. Usually the user of an "online" database pays a single charge to the host system; the host system then pays out a portion of this money to the publisher and to the network.

The positions available in network firms are beyond the scope of this article; networks are really a specialized kind of computer service bureau, not a deliberate part of the publishing process.

Other positions at publishers

Publishers operate offices in which they must employ an army of secretaries, receptionists, administrative assistants, and other support staff. The electronic publishing group is no exception. However, in the case of electronic publishing, you will find that these positions offer a greater than average potential for either career advancement or job enhancement. Aptitudes for handling customer questions, using databases, helping with trade show arrangements, handling unconventional record keeping assignments, etc., are quickly recognized and supported by managers -- there is simply too great a variety of work needed in this field to expect that it will fall cleanly into standard "job descriptions".

WHAT I LOOK FOR IN APPLICANTS

As in any job, previous experience is always an advantage. But since electronic publishing is brand new, few applicants come in with really relevant experience.

On the other hand, an applicant's handling of the interview itself is critical. Any staff member will spend a great deal of time explaining things -- design ideas to other staff, product features to customers, what work we need done to outside contractors. So I am always looking for people who have a full command of the language, who can express not only general ideas, but can develop an idea using specific, relevant examples, and have the knack of choosing exactly the right word. Electronic publishing extends the power of words geometrically, so someone in the field must have a healthy respect for it.

I also look for a person who gets excited about doing something new. *I* still get excited about electronic publishing, and I want people in the group who share that enthusiasm.

I also look for at least minimal computer literacy, especially in a work context. I want people who regard the computer as a helpful appliance, not as a number cruncher or data handling machine. The ability to relate to an inanimate device through a keyboard should feel very natural -- in an odd way, I feel that a pianist has this same sense of inter-action, giving selected instructions through a keyboard and producing something amazing by doing so.

I would be impressed by someone who has been a project leader. Any kind of project -- community service, school, scientific research -- that requires managing a large number of events over a fairly long time span. Electronic publishing projects tend to get rather complicated -- I want people who are stimulated by projects of this scale.

HOW TO FIND THE OPPORTUNITIES

1) Take a look at the journals where database products are advertised (*Online, Online Review*, and *Database* are good starting places). Look at the ads and the articles -- you will get a feel for the kinds of issues which are important to our customers.

2) Review the catalogs of the major host systems (DIALOG, BRS and MEAD DATA are some of the main ones serving libraries; also look at THE SOURCE, COMPU-SERVE, and GENIE -- these host systems are more consumer-oriented).

3) Do some reading about the various electronic mail systems. These systems are increasingly being used as the distribution means (directly or through connections to other systems) for online information of many kinds.

4) Go to your librarian, specifically the reference librarian. Librarians are currently the primary market for online databases, and they know all about them. Ask the librarian how databases are used, which ones are important, why they are important, how they handle the charges they have to pay for using them, how they deal with the clients whose questions require the use of a database, and any other questions you can think of. Not only will you learn a great deal about databases, but the ease with which you are able to do such an interview will be a test of your aptitude for dealing with this kind of customer.

5) Be an online client yourself -- ask the librarian if you can request a "search" on some part of the online database world. See how it feels to be a client. (There may be a charge for this -- think of it as a career investment).

6) Get yourself a password to one of the easier systems (see above for the list). Browse around in the system, see how much information you can discover. If you find you are able to do it instinctively, without looking at the instructions very often, you probably have a very good feel for using online information. If you enjoy the experience, electronic publishing may be the very thing for you!

* * *

Gary Craig is program director of Wiley's electronic publishing group, under the company's corporate development area. He joined the company in 1978 as library sales manager, and his initial exposure to online information was his work in developing the database containing all of Wiley's product information, supporting catalogs, newsletters, and other marketing needs. When he learned in 1981 that an electronic publishing group was being formed, he eagerly volunteered to handle the marketing for that unit, and a few years later was given the job of running the group.

Before coming to Wiley, he worked at McGraw-Hill and Harcourt Brace Jovanovich in several areas, including management of domestic and foreign sales and as director of international advertising. He majored in both English and journalism and did additional graduate work in dramatic arts.

Mr. Craig is active in several industry associations, and speaks frequently on subjects related to the development and marketing of electronic publications. He is also the author of several published articles in these areas.

CHAPTER 3

Working For A University Press

By

Herbert J. Addison, Vice President and Executive Editor
Oxford University Press

University presses differ from each other almost as much as commercial publishers differ from each other. But all university presses have the same basic publishing mission: to search out and publish works of scholarship that will contribute to the world of knowledge. Some presses do only such "scholarly" books. Others, however, publish a wide range of titles -- some indistinguishable from those produced by the commercial houses -- but still reserve some portions of their lists for scholarly books.

Many university presses began as vehicles for publishing the works of the faculties of their associated universities. As time passed, however, they began to reach beyond their own campuses in an effort to publish the best works they could find, wherever they were written. Today, it is not unusual for a local university press to compete with a distant one for a book by a professor who teaches a course just across campus.

To fund their growing editorial independence and survive the financial pro-blems that many universities themselves now face in a period of stable enrollment and Federal cutbacks in education, university presses have had to become more financially inde-pendent. Some still receive subsidies from their parent institutions, but many must com-pletely fund their own operations. The larger presses may even earn a surplus, which they use to fund future books. . .and thus preserve their nonprofit status. Later we shall look at some of the problems university press people face as a result of today's financial realities.

As with all book publishers -- commercial or nonprofit, large or small -- university presses employ people in the four main areas of publishing: editorial, production, marketing, and finance. Let's look at the key jobs in each area and see how they differ (if they do) from similar jobs in commercial houses. We will also discuss the usual entry-level positions in each department.

THE EDITORIAL DEPARTMENT

The sponsoring editor

The publishing process begins when a university press finds an author with a publishable manuscript and signs a contract with him or her to publish it. The task of finding authors and signing book contracts is the responsibility of the sponsoring editor.

Sponsoring editors are usually assigned by academic discipline. In the larger university presses, an editor may work with authors in a single discipline; in smaller presses, the editor may well be responsible for several.

This method of assigning books and authors already suggests an important difference between sponsoring editors in university presses and acquisition editors at commercial houses: The sponsoring editor will be seeking manuscripts almost exclusively from college professors.

There is keen competition for authors even in the "genteel" world of university presses. Most press editors, therefore, can't afford to wait for manuscripts to arrive in the morning mail, so they frequently travel to university campuses in search of publishable manuscripts. The editor may make some appointments in advance, but will probably leave time to see professors without appointments -- it's called "knocking on doors," and all good editors are skilled at finding out about a prospect's writing plans without wasting too much of either party's time.

Once a likely manuscript is found, the editor must decide if it merits publication. Most university press editors rely on expert academic reviewers to assess whether a manuscript is right for that press. The editor sends the reviewer the manuscript and a specific list of questions about it. The reviewer is generally paid an honorarium for his or her services.

If the reviewer thinks the manuscript worthy and recommends publication, the editor must then propose it to his superiors. Many university presses have a board of advisors -- senior professors at the press's university who meet periodically to consider new proposals -- whose imprimatur is needed on any book proposal before it goes to contract. They read the academic review the editor has commissioned for each book and will probably ask the editor about the book in the meeting. If they approve the proposal, the editor prepares the contract to send to the author.

The editor's job, seemingly done, actually begins in earnest when the author signs the contract. Reviewers frequently suggest revisions to strengthen the books they are sent: If a specific book is accepted by the board of advisors, they may have done so with the understanding that the author will incorporate the reviewer's suggestions. The editor will work with the author during this revision stage and may make his own constructive editorial suggestions as well.

Sometimes an editor will have only a portion of a manuscript to review but, because of competition from other presses for especially promising books from well-known professors, will have to make a decision on the basis of such a fragment. If the academic reviewer of the partial manuscript likes it and if the board of advisors approves it, the editor will probably be even more involved in the final development of such a manuscript than he would in the case of a complete manuscript submission.

Do sponsoring editors in university presses usually have degrees in the subject areas in which they work? How can someone who is responsible for finding publishable mathematics manuscripts do the job without being trained in math? There is no simple answer to either question. Many university press editors do have degrees in their assigned subjects, but many others do not. Even editors specializing in highly technical subjects may have liberal arts degrees. Some press directors feel, however, that a sure instinct for good authors and manuscripts is more important (and more necessary in almost all cases) than a degree in a given subject. A good editor soon learns the best schools in the assigned discipline, who are the important researchers, who are the reliable reviewers. By putting all this knowledge to work, an editor can succeed despite the lack of a relevant degree.

But for those seeking their first job as a sponsoring editor at a university press, having a degree in an appropriate subject area will probably be considered a plus. Some presses will hire people directly into a sponsoring editorial job without previous publishing experience. Others will hire the person at a lower level -- as an editorial assistant to a sponsoring editor, perhaps, or as a manuscript editor -- and then promote faster if the person does well.

The other publishing position that probably offers the best training for someone aspiring to a job as a sponsoring editor is that of sales representative for a college textbook publisher. Their work takes them to college campuses daily, and they have to learn about disciplines and curricula, even do some scouting for manuscripts for their companies. As we've seen, this kind of work is the basis for the work of a sponsoring editor.

When the sponsoring editor is satisfied that a manuscript under contract is sufficiently developed to be published, it is sent to the manuscript editor, whose functions we will discuss next.

The manuscript editor

Even the most meticulous academic author is likely to misspell words and commit grammatical miscues. It is the job of the manuscript editor -- sometimes called the copy editor -- to catch the misspellings, grammatical errors, and myriad other mistakes that invariably creep into even the best-prepared manuscripts. It is also fair to say that some academic authors need more than a little "light editing." In these cases, the manuscript editor may edit the work quite heavily, even rewrite portions that require it.

Besides such copy editing chores, the manuscript editor may also mark the manuscript for composition, which involves indicating the different elements on the manuscript -- chapter titles, subheads in the text, illustrations, etc. -- so that the compositor will set them correctly (in accordance with the design provided by the designer).

It is essential that the author see the edited manuscript before it is set in type, because it is always possible that inaccuracies were introduced in the editing phase. This is an especially important requirement for highly technical books where the substitution of a seemingly-synonymous word can drastically alter the author's meaning in the specialized language of that discipline.

Though authors may occasionally grumble about the "intrusions" of the manuscript editor, most are glad that their manuscripts passed through the hands of such a professional before they were printed and released for the world to read.

People often ask the same question of manuscript editors at university presses that they ask of sponsoring editors: Do you need a specific degree to work on specific books? It is less likely that a manuscript editor has a relevant degree. Most work on manuscripts that cover a range of disciplines.

Manuscript editors will frequently tend to specialize in a related group of disciplines, however -- the physical sciences, humanities, or social sciences, for example. No matter which disciplines an editor works in, there is the pleasure of lifelong learning such work affords one. For the manuscript editor at a university press (in contrast to copy editors for the more well-known commercial publishers), a college education literally never ends.

The best training for the job of manuscript editor is to begin as an <u>editorial assistant</u>. This entry-level job involves learning how proofs flow between the compositor, the press, and the author, and keeping records of the flow of proofs, illustrations, and the other editorial elements that make up the finished book. Eventually editorial assistants begin to work on manuscripts and learn the editing skills necessary to move up.

When a manuscript has been edited, marked, and approved by the author, the manuscript editor sends it to the Production department.

THE PRODUCTION PROCESS

Production people work with outside suppliers -- paper manufacturers, printers, and binders -- to turn a manuscript into a finished book. The production function is nearly identical in a university press or commercial house -- university press books can be as simple or complex as commercial books and require the same kind of skill to produce them well -- so production jobs, therefore, are probably more like the same positions in a commercial house than any university press jobs.

Because so many university press books are important scholarly works expected to have lasting value, the production people pay special attention to the materials used in their books, especially the paper on which they're printed. Paper that contains acid from its original pulp will turn yellow and brittle over time. To be sure that their books will last, university press production people buy acid-free paper; many are beginning to indicate that specific books are on acid-free paper by printing a special symbol on the copyright page for quick reference by librarians.

The principle entry-level job in the Production department -- the same as the commercial houses -- is <u>production assistant</u>. It is the training ground that will enable you to acquire specific knowledge of the kinds of books that a given university press is doing and the skills needed to produce them.

Increasingly, candidates for production jobs are arriving with degrees from some of the fine colleges and universities that have programs in printing and production. This kind of degree is a definite advantage for those who are seeking production jobs in the larger university presses.

While the editors and production people have been preparing the manuscript and transforming it into final book form, the Marketing department staff has also been busy.

THE MARKETING DEPARTMENT

University press books are special: They require specialized marketing. As a general rule, they don't sell through the average bookstore in the same numbers as books from commercial houses. They *do* sell through college bookstores and through specialty bookstores in larger cities. But the major markets for university press books are libraries, institutions, and the world of academia -- markets best reached through mail promotion, not via bookstores.

As a result of this necessary market focus, university presses usually have large Advertising and Promotion departments but may have no salaried sales force at all. (This is not true of *all* university presses. Some presses band together and "share" a salesperson. Others use commissioned sales representatives -- who are paid for what they sell but otherwise cost the press nothing. Still others make arrangements with one of the large, commercial publishers. In this case, the commercial house's sales force "takes on" the books published by the university press and presents them to booksellers during their regular visits.)

To produce the many different mailing pieces directed at libraries and individual academics, most university presses need <u>advertising copywriters</u>, <u>graphic designers</u>, and <u>advertising managers</u> (who must know what mailing lists to buy for which kinds of books). Many of these same people will produce the advertisements that appear in scholarly journals and, in many cases, in the quality intellectual journals and magazines that may be utilized if a book is believed to have a broader audience.

Smaller university presses may use freelance people to produce the mailing pieces rather than incur the cost of a full-time staff. The larger presses, on the other hand, may have specific people on staff to perform each specialized task.

A few of the larger presses do have their own sales forces. These sales representatives call on bookstores and sell the new and backlist titles much as their counterparts at the commercial houses do. The principal difference between their roles is that the press representative will tend to call on the larger and better bookstores in major cities -- as well as the larger university bookstores -- where university press books have their greatest appeal.

The usual entry-level jobs in the Marketing department are <u>copywriter</u> and <u>sales representative</u>. For obvious reasons, there are more copywriter jobs open at any given time than sales jobs. Neither usually requires experience -- though it can help getting into one of the larger presses -- but both require a college degree.

THE FINANCIAL/ACCOUNTING DEPARTMENT

Most university presses have a Financial department or, at least, one person who is responsible for financial accounting and reporting. With the advent of computer billing and accounting, this person may also be responsible for the data processing functions. Any such position in the Financial department will almost always require a degree in accounting or finance.

THE PLEASURES OF A UNIVERSITY PRESS

Even given all of the mobility that exists between publishing houses, I still find one phenomenon most interesting: More people seem to move from commercial publishing to university presses than vice versa. While there's no empirical evidence to confirm this, I think it likely that once someone has experienced life at a university press, it's simply too difficult to return to the rigors of commercial publishing.

There is something quite satisfying about working for an organization that is, first and foremost, committed to publishing books of unquestioned quality. The discussion in one of our editorial meetings is likely to sound something like this: "I know this book will not be a bestseller, but it is an important book, so we should find a way of publishing it anyway."

Working for a university press will also keep you in touch with the academic world and, as I mentioned before, can constitute a kind of continuing college education. College professors are, as a general rule, stimulating authors whose books are a source of immense pride to those of us who work in the field.

But it should also be pointed out that the world of university presses is not all quiet browsing through scholarly manuscripts and afternoon teas with professors.

THE PROBLEMS OF UNIVERSITY PRESSES

University presses are chronically underfunded by their associated universities -- if they are funded at all. They must find and publish the best scholarly works with too-modest budgets for people, books and marketing. As a result, university press people usually consider themselves overworked and underpaid. While this may be a complaint of those in commercial houses too, industry statistics show that university press people are generally paid less than those at commercial houses doing the same kinds of jobs.

There is also intense competition between presses for the best scholarly works -- this can drive up the cost of signing a given book, further straining the press's financial resources. In addition to the higher advances against royalties that might be necessary to sign-up an important new book, a press may have to commit to elaborate (and expensive) production and/or marketing efforts to insure the book's success. Working within the tight budget limitations which are the rule, rather than the exception, most presses must continually balance the desirability of any book against its cost. . .just like the commercial houses.

Despite these problems, university presses continue to attract some of the best people in the world of publishing. There is no reason to suppose that they will not go on doing so as long as they exist. And certainly a lot of us who hope that they do.

* * *

In his present position at Oxford University Press -- one of the oldest university presses in the world -- Mr. Addison is responsible for the Bible editorial program and for books on economics and business.

Prior to joining Oxford in 1978, Mr. Addison worked in commercial publishing, mostly on college textbooks. He began his career with Holt, Rinehart & Winston as a college traveler, was promoted first to sponsoring editor, then to editor-in-chief of the basic books unit. He later joined Thomas Y. Crowell Company as general manager of the College Textbook department. He has also worked for John Wiley & Sons as an executive editor in their College department.

He has a B.A. from the University of California at Berkeley and an M.A. from New York University.

CHAPTER 4

The Special World of Scientific And Technical Publishing

By

Robert E. Ewing, Chairman Of The Board (Retired)
Van Nostrand Reinhold Company, Inc.

Before any attempt is made to comment on job/career opportunities in the area of scientific and technical publishing, let me try to define some terms for you. To begin with, you'll want to understand what subjects are normally considered within the scope of scientific and technical publishing. You may ask how it differs -- if, indeed, it does --from professional and reference publishing. Where, for instance, do books on business management fit?

As far as books are concerned, the term "scientific and technical" publishing is generally (though not universally) used to describe both a broad spectrum of subject matter and a diversified range of markets. Obviously, it covers all the traditional engineering disciplines -- civil, chemical, mechanical, electrical (and electronics), industrial, aeronautical, petroleum, etc., -- and the expected areas of science -- physics, chemistry, mathematics, and computers.

In the main (i.e., within most publishing houses), the term also includes any medical book publishing program -- particularly those aimed at medical (or nursing) practitioners. And in most publishing houses the business book program is part-and-parcel of the sci-tech assignment.

Isn't "professional and reference publishing" the same thing? Not exactly; or, rather, not always. It's true that in many quarters, and some publishing houses, the terms "scientific and technical" and "professional and reference" are synonymous and used interchangeably. In others, however, the professional and reference designation is reserved for such highly-specialized items as loose-leaf services, encyclopedic book sets, and the like -- material virtually always sold on some sort of subscription basis.

A TYPICAL SCI-TECH PUBLISHING HOUSE SETUP
. . .AND HOW TO GET IN

Entry-level job and career opportunities in this sci-tech area are not wildly different than those available in other types of book publishing houses (or specialties). There *are* variances, most of them a matter of emphasis.

A typical sci-tech house will be divided into the following departments: Editorial, Marketing, Production/Manufacturing, and Order and Accounting Services.

Editorial department

Scientific and technical publishing fundamentally begins with the <u>sponsoring (*aka* acquisition) editors</u>. It is their job to acquire usable manuscripts that can be turned into commercial (salable) properties. They do this in a number of ways: by maintaining numerous contacts in the fields, or subject disciplines, for which they hold editorial responsibility; by energetically keeping up with the literature in these fields -- particularly the magazines and journals in these areas; by regular attendance at trade shows and conventions.

Sponsoring editors also handle a substantial amount of what we call <u>over-the-transom book proposals</u>. These are ideas -- some submitted in outline form, some as complete manuscripts -- that arrive in the mail, totally unsolicited. Perhaps surprisingly, a certain percentage of these over-the-transom proposals end up as finished books. In this respect, sci-tech publishing varies significantly from general trade publishing, where unsolicited manuscripts are often returned without being opened. The use of literary agents, common in many other areas of book publishing, is a real rarity in sci-tech publishing.

Sponsoring editors, except in the very largest organizations, usually oversee a number of disciplines. A single editor, for example, might be responsible for civil engineering, building construction, mechanical engineering and, quite likely, architecture, too. He or she can hardly be expected to be knowledgeable enough to review and accept (or decline) a steady array of book proposals in all these disciplines. So sponsoring editors rely on a network of outside consultants and reviewers. The initial development and continued maintenance of these contacts is a key part of the sponsoring job.

After a manuscript has been accepted for publication, it is assigned to a <u>manuscript editor</u>, whose role is completely distinct from that of the acquisitions editor. He or she is primarily concerned with details: correct sentence structure, spelling, punctuation, consistent abbreviations, capitalization, etc. The manuscript editor is *not* a ghostwriter or rewriter, particularly in complex sci-tech areas, but *does* put the final touches on the author's work preparatory to its release to Production. Finally, the manuscript editor marks up the manuscript before it goes to the compositor for typesetting.

While both these jobs carry the title "editor," the above descriptions should clarify the distinct differences between the two functions. The sponsoring job normally calls for some previous publishing experience and is seldom considered an entry-level position. A college degree is not an absolute necessity, but is usually required. On the other hand, many sci-tech houses set up their own (often informal) training program for manuscript editing and recruit entry-level trainees to support their senior manuscript editors. A strong background in English is a prerequisite. A degree in the sciences or engineering will obviously be an enormous help. Finally, editorial departments -- no matter what their size -- normally require some amount of secretarial help and editorial assistance. This position will often be designated as "secretary/editorial assistant" and is, in many instances, considered an entry-level position.

Production (manufacturing) department

Following hard on the heels of the editing process, the Production (or Manufacturing) department takes over. It arranges for the manuscript pages to be turned into type and, eventually, for the book itself to be printed and bound. Some publishers have their own in-house composition capability but virtually none, sci-tech houses included, maintain their own printing and binding facilities. As a consequence, the Production department engages in a considerable amount of negotiating with outside suppliers -- purchasing paper, cloth, binding dies, illustrative material where appropriate, etc. Finally, the Production department decides which outside plant will be given the job of printing and binding.

This is a rapidly changing area of publishing. With computer composition and many "manuscripts" now on floppy disks rather than paper, the technology associated with producing books continues to explode. Production personnel, at the management level at least, require previous experience. There are, however, usually entry-level positions available in the manufacturing unit, either as clerk/typists or secretarial /assistants.

Marketing department

Given this broad range of subjects which may be published by the "typical" scientific/technical publisher, it should not come as a surprise that the marketplace they face is a complex arena. For most publishers, direct mail is the primary channel for marketing their products and, therefore, a key ingredient in their marketing plans.

In addition to this selling by mail order directly to the end user (usually an individual engineer, scientist or businessman), there exist several other outlets for sci-tech books. These can be divided into the following segments:

1. The dealer marketplace. . .

. . .including both retailers and wholesalers (or jobbers). (For all practical purposes, I have used these words "wholesaler" and "jobber" interchangeably throughout this chapter.) Most sci-tech publishers consider the retail market vital.

But the plain fact of the matter is that, important as this market may be, it is really quite small. There may be well over 15,000 retail bookstores in the United States, but the number of these that stock and display sci-tech books in quantities that could be considered even marginally significant is <u>less than 100!</u>

The other side of this marketing coin -- wholesalers -- are also few in number, but because of the key role they play in servicing the library outlet (which we shall discuss next), they exert a major influence in sci-tech book distribution.

2. The institutional (or library) marketplace...

. . .naturally assumes enormous importance to the sci-tech publisher. This is particularly true in terms of libraries housed in academia and those libraries maintained by major business corporations, research institutions, and the like. The big city public library systems will purchase some sci-tech material, as will the better and more affluent high school libraries, but below that level, the market for sci-tech material pretty much dries up.

3. The classroom

On an ever-increasing basis, sci-tech books in many fields are finding their way into classrooms, despite the fact that these specialized sci-tech books were written with the *practitioner*, *not* the student, in mind.

4. International sales

As you might expect, the scientific and technical publishing community has a massive stake in the international marketplace. English is now commonly acknowledged to be the international language for science and technology. Books of most of the other disciplines -- and particularly those in sciences such as chemistry, mathematics, physics, biology, and medicine -- can safely ignore boundaries of language or geography and do extremely well.

Even before the book itself is printed and delivered to the warehouse,the Marketing department has gone into action. Under the <u>director of marketing</u> (often a vice president), the sci-tech publisher will have a <u>promotion manager</u> and staff. There will undoubtedly be <u>copywriters</u>, <u>advertising artists</u>, plus an array of necessary clerical personnel. In some, but not all, sci-tech houses there will be <u>product managers</u>, a term almost unique to technical publishing, who coordinate, schedule and manage all aspects of marketing and promotion for a given product line. The product manager also tries to maintain a continuous flow of information to the company's other managers -- those responsible for library sales, bookstores, special sales, etc. It should be added here that while breaking into publishing as a "cub" copywriter in the promotion area is neither easy nor frequently done, it certainly *can* be done -- I began my career in publishing in just that fashion.

Another breakthrough area can be the <u>field sales staff.</u> Under the direction of a <u>field sales manager,</u> this unit calls on retailers and wholesalers stocking sci-tech titles, plus the reference departments at college and university bookstores. These sales forces are almost always comprised of a mix of "old hands" and (what the publisher hopes are) up-and-coming youngsters; the latter are frequently recruited fresh from college campuses.

The salesperson route is probably the ladder most widely used to: 1) make that important impression on management and 2) be given the opportunity to move into the home office. A college degree, while really not essential to perform the job itself, is nearly always required -- particularly when a salesperson's major responsibility is to sell and service college bookstores.

One word of caution: A substantial number of sci-tech publishers do not hire and run their own field sales unit, but rely instead on commission stringers -- independent businessmen who, in exchange for a percentage override in their assigned territories, pay their own expenses and make the requisite sales calls for a number of publishers. They (and a number of them are now women) usually represent a dozen or so product lines simultaneously.

Having earlier stressed the importance of the international scene to sci-tech houses, it stands to reason that opportunities are present in this area, though it is somewhat difficult to pinpoint them, since virtually every publishing house approaches the foreign market in what seems to be its own unique way. Some set up a foreign sales force with local personnel. Some establish full-blown foreign subsidiaries. Others use foreign warehousing and shipping facilities. Still others opt for joint ventures abroad. It is sufficient when job hunting to keep the critical importance of the international marketplace to the sci-tech community very much in mind.

Other departments/areas of opportunity

Like all companies, the sci-tech publisher needs to perform a wide range of services, both for internal record-keeping and for the orderly running of the business itself. Depending on the size of the operation, you are likely to see many, and in some cases, *all* of the following service units in place: Financial, Accounting, Data Processing, Credit, Billing, Collection, Warehouse, Shipping, and Customer Service.

A smaller publisher will combine a number of these "departments" under a single manager in a sort of "jack-of-all-trades" situation. But regardless of labels, on organization charts, all of these functions need to be performed before a sale is finally consumated.

The entry-level potential in these areas is excellent. With the exception of the data processing unit, all these groups have heavy personnel requirements and few of them demand prior experience for positions below management-level. While there are good opportunities here to break into publishing, the problem has been -- and to a large extent, still is -- being given the chance to move from these service areas into the marketing and editorial departments of the company. While this has been traditionally difficult, it is by no means impossible: Some of the industry's current leaders began their careers in this fashion.

* * *

  Mr. Ewing began his publishing career in 1947 when he joined McGraw Hill's Mail Sales Division as a copywriter. During the next 23 years he held a succession of positions at McGraw-Hill, including: asst. manager (Mail Sales Division), mail order manager (Mail Marketing Division), manager of McGraw-Hill Bookstores, director of marketing (Industrial and Business Book Division), general manager (Encyclopedia Division, Encyclopedia and Subscription Books Division, and Professional and Reference Books Division), and vice president.

  In 1970, he joined Van Nostrand Reinhold as president and CEO. He remained president until his election as chairman of the board in 1983. Mr. Ewing retired in June of 1985. Since that time he has remained active in the industry as a consultant to a number of important sci-tech publishing houses.

  He has been a lifelong participant in the Association of American Publishers and twice (1975-77 and 1984-85) served as chairman of the Professional and Scholarly Book Division.

CHAPTER 5

Book Clubs: An Unexpected(?) Area of Opportunity

By

Jessica Weber, President
Jessica Weber Design

(Until mid-1986, Ms. Weber was Executive Art Director of Book-Of-The-Month Club. This article, while revised for this second edition of the Book Publishing Career Directory, *is still written from the perspective of BOMC. -- Ed.)*

Book clubs, unlike publishers who do original books, are *solely* concerned with providing the means for people to buy books through the mail. This is known as <u>direct mail marketing</u> and it is what book clubs are all about, *not* publishing. (Publishers may have given us our existence, but we don't really *want* to be like them!)

At Book-of-the-Month-Club, we buy the rights (from a variety of publishing houses) to offer their soon-to-be-published books to our members at special, discounted prices. We then prepare flyers, little magazines and leaflets that are mailed to our members every three weeks or so. They let us know by return mail which books they want to buy, and we mail them the books. (Although I recently left BOMC to form my own design firm, I'm going to write in the present tense, as it I were still working there. I think it makes the chapter easier to read and understand.)

Direct mail is now one of the hottest fields to enter, and there are many jobs with book clubs open to entry-level students. In this chapter, I'm going to describe, in-depth, careers in art, and then later, other entry-level jobs available at book clubs.

A BOOK CLUB ART DEPARTMENT --
HOW IT WORKS, HOW TO GET IN

The Art department at Book-of-the-Month Club fulfills many functions. We design all of the literature that goes out to our members. We design book jackets for certain special books that we produce ourselves. We also design record jackets for our Record Division and our own direct mail recruiting -- When you get something in the mail asking you to join Book-of-the-Month Club, the mailing piece was probably designed by one of my art directors.

Entry-level opportunities

There are a lot of entry-level jobs in the Art department. We hire inexperienced staff to do strictly paste-up and mechanical work; after about a year, they will probably be promoted to doing layouts and design. Other entry-level jobs include junior designers and people who do nothing but photostat work.

In the case of Book-of-the-Month Club, because our staff is relatively small, there is a good chance that if you start out as a junior-level designer you'll be doing your very own designing very quickly. We like people to get involved in the total creation of what they're doing. Since our staff is quite small, we don't (and can't afford to) pigeonhole people.

What you'll be doing

As the "new kid" in the department, you will usually be assigned to work with one of the more senior people. You'll keep track of the various components involved in the particular project that your senior designer is working on. You'll probably be responsible for doing the mechanicals and, perhaps, even some of the design work for some or all of the project's pieces. You may spend a few hours hunting for photographs, doing picture research at the library or at a stock photo house, even assist at a photo shooting at a studio or on location. The art director may give you photographs to size for reproduction (which involves telling the photostat operator what size the photo should be to fit into the design). In many cases, you will help the senior art director choose colors for a particular brochure or promotion piece.

Career paths

After about a year, you will probably be promoted to junior designer. You will now be responsible for designing complete page spreads under the supervision of a senior designer.

After three years, if you have proven to be a gifted and hard-working designer, you should be promoted again (to senior designer or some such title); after five years, you should become a full-fledged art director. At this stage, the complete responsibility for the production of a brochure or magazine will be on your shoulders. It's a very exciting challenge, one that most designers strive for.

If, after just a year as a junior designer, you decide you want to change fields, there are many areas of opportunity open to you. You can work for a magazine, at a studio that produces annual reports or collateral material, or any number of other specialized areas. Starting an art career in an entry-level position at a book club provides such varied experience that you could probably switch over to advertising or editorial work without any problem.

How to prepare

How should you prepare for that first job in a book club's Art department? First, you <u>must</u> be a graduate of an art school. Second (and more important), you should have an exciting editorial portfolio, featuring design work that is conceptual in nature but in magazine or collateral (brochures and pamphlets) format. All of the designers on my staff went to art schools and specialized in editorial design.

We encourage candidates with an art school background to also have a college degree. We've found that a college education is simply invaluable in a job that primarily deals with words and thoughts. Not only do our designers design the printed page, they also read the copy that goes on them, so it helps to have a liberal arts background.

Based on my experience at Book-of-the-Month Club, I might also add that most of the designers love to read. Since we spend our days selling and marketing books to our members, it really helps to be interested in books -- the product that you're trying to sell.

Internships

We offer students Summer, Fall and Spring semester internships. Because we are located in New York City, there are many art schools with well-developed intern programs from which we glean interested students. Our interns generally work with us for a full year. And by the time they "graduate," they know <u>exactly</u> what it's like to work in a real Art department. They leave us with superior paste-up and mechanical skills; most learn new skills and methods and, by osmosis, become better designers.

If you're interested in working in a book club Art department, call the director of personnel or the head art director for internship information -- you might be surprised at who has a spot just for you. But don't expect to make a lot of money as an intern. Most of *our* students come to us *for free*. It's really a trade-off: We spend a great deal of time training them in exchange for their hands, hearts, and heads. It's an invaluable experience for all of us!

MOVING UP: HOW LONG TO STAY ON THAT FIRST JOB

A lot of "first-timers" wonder how long they should stay at a job before switching to another company in a search to "broaden their backgrounds." I personally stayed at my very first job, which was in publishing, for about a year and a half, and then jumped over to advertising. I was in advertising for a year, then jumped back to magazines. This time I stayed with one company for eight years.

I'm not sure my relatively stable career is a realistic indication of most people's situation. Most people, I think, start their careers. . .somewhere. . .and then jump around every two years or so until they find something that they really love. . .or that really loves them. I see nothing wrong with that kind of pattern -- I think it's good for beginners to get a lot of different experience.

You may find that you're "typecast" if you stay at one job for too <u>long</u> at the beginning of your career; you may even run into difficulties changing design directions later on. For example, if you've been an editorial designer for ten years, it's virtually impossible for you to suddenly cross over into the advertising field. This is particularly true in large cities where career tracks are very limiting and positions are very specialized. If you're lucky enough to live in a smaller city, this probably isn't so true; but in big cities it's the *rule*, not the exception. I would suggest to anyone just starting out not to lock themselves into a field unless they're absolutely,100% sure that they want to stay in it forever. And even that's hard.

Working for a book club can be especially rewarding if you love the printed page and are a real reader. Book clubs are those unique institutions where the written word is king and where there is great respect for writers and the printend word.

OTHER ENTRY-LEVEL OPPORTUNITIES IN BOOK CLUBS

In the Proof Reading/Editing department, there's a chance for you to start out as a <u>proof or copy reader</u> and work your way up to <u>editor.</u> Copywriting is an open field. Book club copywriters are a very special breed in that they have to write very short, concise copy to sell books. This is neither advertising nor editorial, it's <u>direct mail writing</u>. Because direct mail is so "hot" these days, there are other wonderful jobs available in this field. If you start out writing copy for a book club, it's very easy to switch over and get a job writing copy in the direct mail division of a major advertising agency. Advertising agencies are beginning to realize that direct mail (formally "junk mail" to many) has become a very big business, so many agencies are beginning their very own in-house direct mail divisions. Consequently, opportunities in this area are growing rapidly.

At Book-of-the-Month Club, we also have a group of professionals called <u>readers.</u> These men and women do nothing but read books all day long and then write critical reports on their merits (or the lack of them). Readers generally have a background in liter-ature. Most book clubs also have marketing departments, which are also excellent places to prospect for entry-level jobs.

Moving from such a position to an advertising agency is relatively easy to do.

DON'T JUDGE A BOOK BY ITS COVER!

When I graduated from Parsons School of Design and New York University and went out to "seek my fortune," I had never considered book clubs as a career possibility before. I had seen advertisements in newspapers urging people to *join* them, but it never

occurred to me that *working* for a book club could ever provide a career experience for me --
let alone the rich one I've had at Book-of-the-Month Club.

* * *

*Ms. Weber, formerly executive art director of Book-of-the-Month Club,
recently started her own company -- Jessica Weber Design -- of which she is president. In her
former position, Ms. Weber directed the design of Book-of-the-Month Club's five monthly
magazines and newsletters, record covers and collateral material for its Record Division, and
catalogs for its Merchandise Division.*

She was previously founding art director of the International Review of Food
& Wine *magazine. She redesigned the magazine when it was acquired by the American
Express Publishing Company and re-named* FOOD & WINE.

*Awards for her work have come from the New York Art Directors Club, the
Society of Illustrators, the Society of Publication Designers, and* Art Direction *magazine.*

*A graduate of Parsons School of Design and New York University, Ms.Weber
has been a faculty member of Parsons since 1980. She lectures frequently and has served on
numerous juries for visual art competitions. She is the President of the Visual
Communicators Education Fund of the Art Directors Club of New York and a member of
their Executive Board. She serves on the Advisory Board of the Medill School of
Journalism's Publication Program at Northwestern University in Evanston, IL, and is a
member of the Board of Directors of the Mercantile Library in New York.*

SECTION II

Opportunities
In
Editorial

CHAPTER 6

On Not Looking For A Job

By

Samuel S. Vaughan, Senior Vice President & Editor-Adult Trade Books
Random House, Inc.

Let's clear this up right away: I am crazy about this work. Luckily. Because it helps to be crazy.

The pay is poor at the bottom, middling in the middle, and almost no one gets rich at the top. The hours are nonsensical, roughly 9 - to - ridiculous, and the rewards and recognition are mostly hidden. Your work disappears into the work of others. Your ego must be subordinated to the ego of authors. Yet you must have and retain a sense of your own worth and character.

My advice to those of you faintly interested in book publishing: Go faint somewhere else. As one of my colleagues in another house remarked recently, we all get (far too many) calls from new people who think they "might" want to work in publishing. They seem to have no compunction about wasting an hour or two of our time while they try to make up their minds.

But if you (1) are crazy; (2) don't mind living vicariously off of others' fame; and (3) strongly desire to be underpaid and overworked. . .read on.

AN "OVERVIEW" OF TRADE BOOK PUBLISHING

"Trade" book publishing means the opposite of what "trade" means in magazine publishing. Trade *magazines* are for specialized audiences; most Trade *books* are for general audiences. Trade publishing is also sometimes called General Publishing.

Thus, a <u>trade or general editor</u> tends to be one who specializes in generalities. That is, I feel equipped to handle most fiction and "non-fiction" except books which require very considerable specialized knowledge. Some trade editors do have specialties: Judith Jones at Knopf and the ex-Dial editor Fran McCullough are known as cookbook specialists, in addition to their reputation for high-grade literary editing.

Five or six departments make up most publishing houses. They are: 1) editorial; 2) publicity and advertising; 3) sales and "marketing" (such terms vary in meaning but all are concerned with selling books); 4) art, design, and production (i.e., printing); 5) business and finance; and 6) rights selling.

Some houses are editorially-driven, to use the current expression. That is, editorial decisions -- the opinions of the editors -- come first. Other houses are marketing- or sales-driven; i.e., almost everything is decided first on the basis of its sales potential, as evaluated by the sales department. In a healthy house, I believe, both editorial voices and sales voices are respected. A house operated exclusively for or by its sales department could turn out to be purveyors of books as pure "merchandise;" a house operated exclusively by its editors could end up bankrupt.

HOW TO GO ABOUT GETTING INTO PUBLISHING

You go about. A great deal. Unless someone shoehorns you into a suddenly vacant desk with your name on it, you have to conduct a campaign.

To begin with, read. See the newspapers and trade magazines for any openings that are announced. Most aren't. They're filled from within or in a fast contact with the outside world. In a well-run, well-regulated world, a file of the best applicants would be regularly brought up-to-date and reached into the moment a chair became vacant. Nice idea, but not the way the world works. (Oh? You've noticed?) You have to apply and re-apply. Don't count on "The System."

Send a thoughtful resume and a short, polite, pointed cover letter to any of the editors in the publishing houses you want to try (see those listed in the back of this volume and in Literary Marketplace). Wait for them to respond, but don't wait *too* long. Tell them in the cover letter you'll follow up within two weeks -- and do so, with a phone call. You're trying to get an interview -- not a "job" -- at this point.

Try to make each interview lead to others, so that nothing is ever a dead end. After doing your best in the interview, ask whether the interviewer has one or two people you should see. Use these recommendations as a springboard for other interviews. Drop a lot of pebbles into the pond. Make rings.

Publishing houses come in all sizes and shapes, so although you may not be right for one job, you could be ideal for another. Try to get The Right Chair (though you may need to take whatever's available just to get inside).

I am convinced that anyone who is any good can get a starting job in publishing, if they take the time and make the effort to devise a strategy to hit the houses and get the interviews. . .and can stay alive, fed, and sheltered while working to break in.

THE IDEAL PUBLISHING CANDIDATE...

. . .Is a person who likes some of the books he or she's read, loves others, and has forgotten many. A person who wants to enrich the culture and at the same time enrich the company; who can manage the seemingly at-odds objectives of commerce and literature. A private person willing to go public. (At first I found the alternating, conflicting demands of the work -- working head down, in solitude, with words on paper -- at odds with the requirement to express to others, inside and outside the house, my feelings for a manuscript, my enthusiasms, my reservations, my convictions, to "sell." But I learned first to live with the contradictions, then to enjoy them.) Someone who has done something extra, not just a young person who spent time in school.

I look for extracurricular effort and/or enthusiasm. I am not looking for free-lance critics who want to tell me how imperfect most writing and most organizations are. Someone with energy, ideas, standards, follow-through, zest, flexibility. Attractive -- not pretty or handsome, but someone whose caring is evident, whose willingness to contribute, cooperate and understand is natural.

THE ENTRY-LEVEL JOBS IN TRADE EDITORIAL

Usually hitting a typewriter, answering the phone, and volunteering to read and report on book submissions and proposals. Much of your reading will be done on your own time -- on the bus or subway, at home.

Other entry-level "editorial" jobs might well occur in other parts of publishing -- selling books at retail or on the road for a publisher; in dogsbody jobs in art and design, or writing copy for advertising and publicity departments (though these departments offer fulfilling publishing positions above the dog's level); putting labels on books sent to reviewers; "cleaning" (bringing up to date) mailing lists, etc.

In other words, you don't have to begin in editorial to become an editor; if you work in other publishing departments, your chances of being a well-prepared editor are even better.

But don't work in other parts of publishing overlong (more than 2 to 5 years) or until you are making such decent money in the "other" job that you won't want to or can't sacrifice that job to move into editorial.

I was a young sales manager. When offered a chance to become an editor -- even a senior editor, as I was somewhat prematurely called then -- it was, in many eyes, considered a step backward.

Why did I do it? Because I was asked. And because I was a fairly good sales manager and wanted to be a first class editor.

43

THE MONEY. . .OR LACK OF IT

Starting salaries in trade editorial range from $12,000 - $15,000. You can expect, in most well-organized companies, regular raises of 5% to 7%; raises accompanying a promotion will be 10 - 15% or better. Advancement is rapid or glacial, depending on you, the "corporate culture" -- the tradition and temperament of the company -- how well the company is doing, and whether you switch jobs or companies. Long-term, loyal employment was once said to be the norm; publishing people now change jobs with the rabbit-like affinity of advertising agency people.

How long should you do scut work before getting a promotion? One year, two years, or five -- then you'll get promoted and still have some scut work to do. Every job is work, *real* work, in part. The lunches might be better, the books seem a little more selective (though they're not), but I still spent my first six years in publishing occasionally doing jobs I wasn't particularly crazy about.

Why? I wanted to learn publishing and had to make a living. I made some progress. Promotions came every two years, not always into what I wanted, but always representing a chance to move ahead. When I finally got where I wanted to be -- into Editorial -- I wasn't promoted again for ten years. But I had made it to the right place and, eventually, the promotions came.

The beginners I see today have a more urgent sense of time. Most will not go the distance. There is a decided difference between *being stuck* and *sticking it out*.

EDITORIAL JOB TITLES

They're grand, glorious, meaningful or meaningless. It all depends on the company.

You start as an editorial assistant or assistant to an editor. ("Secretaries" have disappeared. . .as some bosses will sadly say, "And how!")

The next step is to assistant editor, then associate editor, then maybe editor or senior editor, then executive or managing editor (managing is usually more administrative than straight editing), then associate publisher, editor-in-chief, president, publisher, or some combination.

YOUR TYPICAL DAY WILL BE --

Atypical.

But it usually starts with coffee, getting your own and maybe someone else's -- for your boss or the kid at the next desk or the first guest who has an appointment with your boss. You'll get good at getting coffee. And at opening the mail and trying to do something with it -- sorting it for your boss's convenience, routing some of it elsewhere. Answering the phone. And the phone and the phone. Calls from agents, other bosses, the mailroom with misaddressed mail you've just re-routed. Your Mother. People trying to sell stocks.

Also, typing, filing, fetching, kvetching, chatting with the woman or man waiting with you for the Xerox machine to be fixed. Much talk.

Talking to your typewriter or word processor and to yourself. Some of us major in muttering.

Making lunch reservations for your boss. Calling the deli for yourself. Finding ways to tell your editor that anyone who (A) likes this manuscript or (B) does *not* like this manuscript is seriously brain deficient and wholly lacking in any kind of taste. . .except bad.

Dealing with a rich supply of questions from others in the firm and those friendly creatures called authors: What's the pub date of the new book by Gina Lolla-Ballonga? How do you *spell* LollaBallonga -- with one or two e's? Where is my contract? My check? Why is my book out of stock? Don't you people know what you're doing? Can I take you to dinner? (or) How about you taking *me* to dinner?

So you squeeze in a few personal calls (most firms limit them to no more than fifteen a day) and sweat out your landlord or the arrival of the TV or telephone installer. But each day *will* be different.

IS COLLEGE NECESSARY?

Avoiding the larger societal implications of that question, you should know that most people in publishing have a college education. No, let's put it this way: Most of us have been to some college, somewhere. Our education continues -- or, for some of us, begins -- when we get into book publishing. That's one of our main pleasures and rewards: You can't stop learning. Authors, editors, sales reps, other publishers, the books, magazines, news-papers, newsletters, radio and TV shows you scan constantly: All will teach you something. Maybe they'll teach you that there's too much communication and too little knowledge. Too much "news," too few trustworthy facts. Too many "features," not enough substance. Too many opinions, too little wisdom.

But you'll learn and re-learn to respect books, one of the oldest of the media.

And as soon as you figure you have learned enough, you'll put in for early retirement.

GRADUATE DEGREES?

Sometimes useful. It helps to know a good deal about something, but by and large you will not receive extra compensation for graduate degrees in the liberal arts. M.B.A.s, yes, of course, but we are not speaking here of the illiberal arts. One of the best trade editors, Lawrence Ashmead of Harper & Row, has a graduate degree in geology. He never edits books in geology.

IS ENGLISH NECESSARY? "I *LOVE* BOOKS!"

Fluency with the language -- there are still some cities where English is the language of choice -- is helpful, maybe essential. All of us have to write: letters, press releases, book jacket copy, catalogue copy, author biographies, memos. And it's nice to be able to do so and have them become intelligible when read from left to right. Still, publishing is *not* necessarily a place for writers -- that is, those who want to be Writers above all else -- but it *is* a place for people who can express themselves.

And if you love books, that's nice. Because that love will be severely tested.

The first thing you sell in a job is your time. Then your skills, talents or brains. And the first thing you sacrifice in publishing is time to read on your own, to read what you *want* to read. We are all *supposed* to read what other authors are writing, other houses publishing. The hard truth is that many of us become semi-literate, spending nearly all our reading time on the books we are engaged in helping to publish.

So there is some "sacrifice" involved. The solution is to try to find books to publish , to "work on," that you want to read in the first place (the first market test for us is in our own hearts and minds) and like even on re-reading. I am currently engaged in re-reading and editing novels by writers as splendid and diverse as William F. Buckley, Jr., Wallace Stegner, Winston Graham, Hannah Green, and Bud Shrake. I don't mind *that* work a bit.

SO STOP LOOKING FOR A JOB.

If you want to "look in" on us, look first within yourself: for signs of a vocation, a calling, a compulsion, a commitment. This lunacy might or might not pay as well as selling insurance, bonds, or your body. But ours is an unfailingly interesting line of work -- grand or goofy or glorious at various times. And it's not for everybody.

But if you're beginning to believe it could be for you, welcome.

* * *

Before he accepted his current position at Random House in March, 1986, Mr. Vaughan spent his book publishing career at Doubleday & Company. He started there as an assistant selling "rights" and became advertising manager at 24; sales manager at 26; senior editor at 28; and, eventually, president, publisher and editor-in-chief over the next decades.

He was the the first chairman of the Education for Publishing Committee of the Association of American Publishers and was chairman of its General Books Council. Mr. Vaughan is a frequent lecturer at universities, did the Bowker Memorial Lecture, has written three books for children, two for adults, and extensively about publishing.

He went to Penn State and has four "ex-children" (all grown) who went to Brandeis, Berkeley, Coe, Lawrence, and Penn State.

Mr. Vaughan and the editors of this volume wish to express their special thanks to Ms. Angela Himsel and Mr. Jeff Cohen, two assistants at Random House who, according to Sam, "helped bring this manuscript closer to English and made sure I wasn't completely out of touch with *their* concepts of editorial reality."

CHAPTER 7

Editorial Opportunities in College Publishing

By

John S.L. Holland, Managing Editor
The Dushkin Publishing Group, Inc.

College textbook publishing differs markedly from general trade book publishing -- in its emphases, its atmosphere, its organization, its concerns, and, perhaps most important for anyone considering entering the field, in its job descriptions. Is textbook publishing a: glamorous as trade publishing? The answer depends on what *you* call glamorous. If you have an intellectual bent, if you think it sounds exciting to work with professors, scholars, and specialists in a range of academic fields, if you enjoy the challenge of exploring new subjects, then college publishing may be for you. This chapter describes the responsibilities of the various positions found in most college textbook publishing houses.

COLLEGE ACQUISITION EDITOR

A <u>college acquisition editor</u> (salary $20,000 - $50,000) is usually selected from a textbook publisher's sales force, since the position requires a sense of how a book will sell. Selling books to professors is the best way to obtain this feel for the marketplace. (The campus bookstore manager, who actually purchases the books, does so only after a professor has decided to adopt a particular text for a class). In addition, a person with textbook sales experience already knows a number of professors, in whose ranks the acquisition editor finds authors.

As an acquisition editor, you solicit manuscripts -- from college professors -- read them, send them to other professors to review, suggest changes and reorganizations, and submit proposals to an editorial board. For some manuscripts, you will work closely with a <u>developmental editor</u> (see the next job description). You will probably concentrate on one or more disciplines -- for example, history and art, English and geography, the social sciences, computer sciences. The subjects of the books you solicit are largely determined by the editor-in-chief, who may ask you to find an author for, say, a new introductory sociology book or a new volume in an existing history series. You will also be expected to discover or commission new books on your own initiative and to evaluate unsolicited manuscripts that are submitted to the publisher.

Once one of your books has been accepted for publication, you will help an author fulfill various obligations, such as obtaining permission for using material from other sources and providing roughly- drawn artwork. You will make sure that what the author has contracted for is submitted on time. You will arrange for the preparation of study guides, instructors' manuals, and any other ancillary material. You will present the book to the sales force at sales meetings and consult with the Promotion department about advertising and promoting the book. Your success as an acquisition editor depends on the success of your books and, often, on how well you have communicated with a developmental editor.

COLLEGE DEVELOPMENTAL EDITOR

A college developmental editor (salary $20,000 - $40,000) does just what the position title suggests -- He or she "develops" a manuscript from its first, sometimes rough, stage until it is ready for final polishing by the copy editor. The managing editor usually gives a developmental editor a manuscript, reviews written by specialists in the field, and instructions on how to proceed: "You are responsible for checking the contents of each chapter to ensure that the proper topics are covered, making suggestions to the author about deleting or adding topics, enhancing the author's style where necessary or desirable, and correcting mistakes in grammar, syntax, and so on. You may have to reorganize material to achieve logic and clarity. You should see to it that the writing and exposition are at a suitable level for the intended audience. Try not to disturb the rhythm or the 'voice' of the writing."

These instructions leave a lot to the discretion and professional opinion of the editor. To make the necessary decisions, to rewrite whole sections or chapters -- let alone discover and maintain an author's "rhythm" -- require experience and breadth of knowledge. Thus being an inveterate reader is a key requirement for this job.

Developmental editors usually specialize in particular disciplines. They may have specialist knowledge to begin with or develop expertise on the job. But they *have* to know their fields. For example, they must be able to spot whether a psychology text meant for freshmen lacks crucial information on cognitive perspective.

As a developmental editor, you must be able to work closely and amicably with authors. You may have to obtain additional reviews after a manuscript has been rewrit-ten or reorganized. You will be responsible for ensuring that permissions for reprinting material have been obtained. You will help the author draw up an index or give a profes-sional indexer instructions.

Developmental editors are usually promoted from the ranks of college manu-script editors.

COLLEGE MANUSCRIPT EDITOR

A college manuscript editor (salary $17,000 - $35,000) edits in much the same way as a developmental editor, but is not usually expected to do heavy rewriting or restructuring or to commission reviews. Like a developmental editor, a manuscript editor is concerned with the writing style and the presentation of ideas. Both look out for -- and repair -- such faults as wordiness, jargon, awkward constructions, infelicities of style, and obscure or ambiguous wording. They may work with an art editor (see job description that follows) and designer to develop an art program (photos, drawings, graphs, maps). They see to it that "breathing spaces" (headings and subheads) help students absorb a large amount of information. They make sure that summaries *really* summarize and that end-of-chapter or workbook questions are actually answered in the text. In short, they act as surrogates for the student who will be learning from the text.

Probably the best preparation for becoming a manuscript editor is to have been a college copy editor.

COLLEGE COPY EDITOR

A college copy editor (salary $12,000 - $22,000) may be the *only* editor to review a manuscript or the second reader (after another editor). As a copy editor, you must spot and correct errors in spelling, punctuation, grammar, syntax, and usage. You must know your dictionaries and standard reference works and be able to use library services efficiently and check facts quickly. You are familiar with the Modern Language Association and the American Psychological Association documentation styles and know when to use them. You can proofread, using proofreading symbols; typemark a manuscript for typesetters to follow; compile a table of contents and other "front matter;" and copy edit an index.

Most copy editors are probably recent college graduates, and many have started in publishing as assistants or secretaries. Anyone applying for such a position should be familiar with the bibles of copy editors: The Chicago Manual of Style, 13th ed. (Chicago: U of Chicago P, 1982); The MLA Style Manual (New York: MLA, 1985); Words into Type, 3rd ed. (Englewood Cliffs: Prentice, 1974). Other books on a copy editor's reading list are:

Cook, Clare Kehrwald. The MLA's Line by Line: How to Edit Your Own Writing. Boston: Houghton, 1985.

Coser, Lewis A., Charles Kadushin, and Walter W. Powell, Books: The Culture and Commerce of Publishing. New York: Basic, 1982.

Follett, Wilson. Modern American Usage: A Guide New York: Hill, 1966.

While the descriptions and responsibilities of these four basic editorial positions are probably common to any college department or publisher, the specific titles may vary. Ask the interviewer to describe the duties of your job, since what I have called a manuscript editor may be called a copy editor at another house, and vice versa.

COLLEGE ART EDITOR

A final editorial position -- <u>college art editor</u> (salary $12,000- $30,000) -- is somewhat of a misnomer, since it combines editorial and graphic duties. This person selects illustrations to match the ideas and subjects discussed in a manuscript. The illustrations may be photographs, charts, graphs, maps, cartoons, or fine art reproductions. So an art editor must be imaginative, well-read, and knowledgeable about collections of graphic materials available for commercial use.

The art editor obtains permissions and negotiates fees, and is sometimes pressed into writing captions and credit lines. The person in this position must deal tactfully with authors and be willing to pursue their often vague leads. The art editor may have to travel to secure needed illustrations.

The art editor keys the illustrations to a text, sizes and crops illustrations, and often, under the supervision of an editor and designer, makes a dummy of the book, with blueprint illustrations in place to guide the printer. A good background in fine arts, applied arts or photography would be helpful in securing this position.

* * *

Born, raised, and educated in the United Kingdom, John S.L. Holland worked in publishing in London and Sydney before coming to the United States in the 1960s. For 16 years he was a member of the College department of Harcourt Brace Jovanovich, Inc., in New York and San Diego. Currently he is managing editor of the Dushkin Publishing Group, Inc., in Guilford, Connecticut.

CHAPTER 8

Editorial Opportunities In Elhi Publishing

By

Robert B. Stewart, Vice President/Editor-In-Chief
Prentice-Hall, Inc. - Ed. Book Division
A Division of the Educational Group of Simon & Schuster, Inc.

Your undergraduate degree is recent vintage, and you have been "out of school" for two to four years, right? That practice teaching and summer camp counseling you did as a college student have paid off in your current job -- teaching school. There are pluses and minuses to that, and recently you've begun to sort them out. The administrative hassles you could do without, and the lunch duty, and that occasional unruly kid you just can't reach.

On the other hand, you like the touch-and-go in the classroom as your students pick up on the activities you have devised for that lesson in phoenemes or biomes, or square roots, or Kipling's imperialism. You have found the curriculum planning assignments more a fillip than a chore, and you look forward to the camaraderie of some like-minded colleagues. Although you've considered graduate school, you realize you just aren't ready to make the leap yet.

Have we got an idea for you? Yes, indeed. You're an ideal candidate for entering the highly-specialized field of elhi ('elementary/high school") educational publishing, whether you've been teaching third or tenth graders, and wherever you've been teaching in the U.S.A.

THE QUALIFICATIONS YOU THINK YOU NEED. . .AND DON'T

Do you have to be an English major? No, although it helps if you have at least a minor in the subject or, even better, a double major with another subject specialty.

Do you need newspaper/yearbook/literary magazine experience? No. The bookmaking aspects you'll learn on-the-job. But if you have done "literary work," by all means highlight it on your resume. If you enjoy using the written word as an effective means of communicating facts and concepts, you already have a key prerequisite for an editorial position.

Do you have to know how to type? No. Some of the top editors in the business are still original hunt-and-peck typists -- and pretty speedy, too. But, like most things in life, the more skillfully you can prepare your work -- neatly, quickly -- the better. So typing helps.

THE JOB APPROACH

Elhi publishers are continuously on the lookout for people like yourself, with subject area knowledge that's up-to-date, with a flair for organizing lessons and class activities, and with the savvy that can come only from managing a classroom. But you need to put all this on paper in a resume, for you won't be hired on good looks, good grades, or "personality" alone!

Check out the listings in the Job Opportunities Databank in the back of this Career Directory and the additional information available in Literary Market Place (LMP), which should be at your local library. Locate the elhi publishers in the geographic areas that you believe are feasible for you. New York City (and environs in New Jersey and Connecticut) has some of the biggest elhi publishers. But so do Boston and Chicago. And there are outposts elsewhere in Pennsylvania, Florida, Oklahoma, Texas, and California. Take your pick.

More important than geography, however, is the scope of the publishing operation and the business focus of the company. If you are teaching in the elementary area, certain publishers will appeal to you. (And you are probably already familiar with their products.) The same for high school. This is not to say that the field is split into two parts. It is not. There are a sizable number of K-12 (kindergarten through 12th grade) publishers. After all, the education market services a lot of K-12 kids (some 45 million), as well as their teachers and administrators.

A cover letter and standard resume are your "job passport." Compose your cover letter carefully. It's the first clue for the interviewer as to your facility with the language. Do not be too brief, but don't "oversell" either. One page will do nicely.

You can follow up with letters of reference, if requested, or samples of school materials you've devised. Expect a personal interview -- it would be most unusual for a job offer to arrive from a publisher in the mail.

If all goes well at the interview, you may be given a test assignment. Here's a typical "test" which you would be expected to complete on your own for a specific deadline. The example is from the social studies area, but tests from other subject areas would be similar:

1. Analyze and evaluate the two attached 8th grade American history chapters. Comment on chapter structure, special features, writing style/

reading level, visual program, and questioning strategy. Choose the better of the two and justify your choice.

2. Write a classroom activity for an 8th grade American history text, using the cartoon herein. Assume the cartoon accompanies text material about the subject at hand.

3. Choose a topic from one of the two journalistic pieces attached. Write a high interest feature (one manuscript page) for an 8th grade American history text.

4. Reorganize and edit the attached special feature on Peter Zenger by reducing the material to one or 1 1/2 manuscript pages and simplifying the content for a junior high audience, 7th - 8th grade reading level.

The test will provide your potential employer with a lot of good evidence of your budding writing/editing skills: how well you show an understanding of the needs and abilities of your target audience; how you apply your audience awareness in shaping material for exposition and for further interpretation; what you choose to highlight and to play down; and so forth. You will be judged also on the insight and judgment you display in your analysis of the various elements that come together to make an effective pedagogical tool.

THE ELHI PUBLISHING SCENE

The test is also of particular interest for what it reveals about the elhi publishing scene:

It is highly competitive and becoming more so as publishers scramble for market shares in a decade of gradually decreasing enrollments (an upturn in elementary schools is foreseen for the early 1990s).

Subject matter is determined by curriculum requirements, and it is safe to say that the U.S. has a "consensus curriculum" in that many states share the same educational goals and attempt to meet similar standards. If one could simultaneously visit an 8th grade American history class in Sioux Falls, South Dakota, another in Baton Rouge, Louisiana, and still another in Portland, Maine, one would find the same topic under discussion, the same overall historical storyline, and the same cast of historical personages. Therefore, to maintain a "competitive edge," your textbook must exhibit top quality work, editorial ingenuity, and extra-special visual/verbal appeal. You have to keep one jump ahead of the competition!

An elhi editor has to be flexible and talented, both as an editor of others' work but also as a writer/critic of his or her own material. Your subject expertise and pedagogical bent will stand you in good stead here, as you are already a good judge of what will attract a student's attention and hold it firmly as the necessary facts, opinions and ideas are expressed clearly and succinctly.

Sensitivity to readability is a "must" for an elhi editor, who should be familiar with both the strengths and weaknesses of the major reading formulas (Dale-Chall, Fry, Flesch), such measurements as the Cloze test, and how to make reading level compatible with the vocabulary and concept load of the subject being taught.

Sensitivity to controversial issues in the subject discipline, an ability to deal with conflicting viewpoints sensibly and resolutely, being alert to language and ideas appropriate to introduce into the classroom as well as relevant to the age and interest level of the students.

ELHI EDITING DIFFERS FROM TRADE AND COLLEGE EDITING

The test has even a further dimension of interest because it points up directly or by implication how elhi textbook editing differs from general Trade practices, even from editing college level textbooks.

First of all, elhi textbooks are designed to be revised -- the initial time, dollar and talent investment is high -- and a publisher wishes to undertake a project that will seize a market segment and expand it over time. The textbook will be kept current and valuable through repeated revision. (This is true also, though to a more limited degree, in college publishing, where the initial investment can be much more modest. It's not true of Trade publishing, except for reference works. No one, for example, expects John Updike to update his latest novel. If successful, it will be reprinted as is, repeatedly. A sequel may even be prepared. But no one would suggest a revised edition.)

The elhi editor plays a more central role in the development of the work than the editor in general Trade or even in college publishing. Curriculum requirements, market research needs, up-to-date subject matter research must all be brought together to form a book outline -- even a detailed table of contents, in some cases -- before authors are even chosen. (All this "backgrounding" isn't essential for the creation of an imaginative work, as Updike could testify. Nor would it be appropriate for the college professor-author with his specialized knowledge for advanced grade-level students, survey courses excepted.)

After choice of authors, the elhi editor must assign the writing workload (most elhi texts involve multiple authorship) and then follow up repeatedly on the progress made by the authors, staff and production editors, artists and designers. In short, the elhi editor must act like a general -- decisively, seriously, fairly.

The elhi editor also functions as a prime coordinator between the textbook and the auxiliary materials -- some for the teacher, some for students -- that may accompany it. A teacher's guide to the text material is a must. In the past few years, these guides have become complex and elaborate teaching aids, actually day-to-day, step-by-step formulas for presenting the subject matter. Test items are also essential so that the teacher can evaluate student performance. Students are provided with workbooks in many subjects, with lab manuals in the sciences, and with games, activities and many other learning aids.

So the elhi editor -- the general at the head of the troops -- must function to keep the creative group moving ahead on many fronts. (All of this points up another significant difference from Trade and college editing. In the latter, supplements are more limited in scope -- expectations are higher for instructors to choose and/or create their own backup materials. In the former, Mr. Updike would most certainly register surprise or even dismay at the prospect of supplying backup supplementary material for publication with his works.)

After the program is published, the elhi editor still plays an important role in the sales/marketing efforts that launch the textbook and its many auxiliaries into the marketplace. The editor will be called upon to describe the materials to the sales representatives -- the special strengths of the program in content coverage, readability, pedagogy, and so on. Subsequently the editor may be involved in special presentations to customers -- at state textbook adoption committees; at district, state, or national teachers' conventions; at local school district adoption proceedings, etc. Maybe this is not the glamor-ous life -- author-editor lunches at well-known restaurants, TV talk shows, nationwide promotion tours -- afforded some general Trade editors. But it's stimulating and productive for the elhi editor, who can then add the results of this experience "in the field" to subject matter knowledge and prior teaching experience in order to improve revisions of existing textbooks and the development of future programs.

Not to be overlooked is the salary differential for elhi editors and those in general Trade. According to the AAP (Association of American Publishers), which conducts an annual compensation survey, staff editor jobs in educational publishing generally pay better than comparable level jobs in general Trade. For beginning editors up through senior editors, the differential is from 12% to 18% of annual compensation. In elhi editorial management, the differential can be even greater, which is basically a reflection of the size of an enterprise. In summary, the K-12 educational publishers of basal series and programs for required curriculum courses are major publishing houses with sizable in-house staffs. By contrast, the general Trade publishing scene has many more small "independents" than giants, and salary offerings are by necessity more modest.

TYPICAL ELHI CAREER PATHS

Publishing companies differ in the manner in which the editorial hierarchy is established and maintained. There are also differences in terminology for job titles, rates of advancement, and compensation. But the following career ladder is probably typical of both a medium-size company (annual sales of $40 million) and a large one (sales topping $80-$100 million).

Assistant editor -- the entry-level position. With your qualifications and a successful interview and test assignment behind you, you could expect to begin your first job as an assistant to the other editors already assigned to the project team. You would be responsible for needed subject matter research and expected to be available for administrative tasks and minor writing/editing assignments. You might find yourself preparing and monitoring work flow charts, which is the swiftest way to become oriented to the complexities of an entire project's many parts and tasks. You could also be called upon to correlate the outline or table of contents of the project-in-progress with state or district curriculum guidelines.

Of course, you can expect to plunge into the editing/writing/rewriting matrix of the project alongside your fellow editors. You will find your energies divided between work done on your own and work done with others. But the results of both kinds of work will be shared with the group, so that within a few days on the job, you will begin to feel that you are an integral part of the project team.

If you have shown yourself capable and willing to assume greater responsibility, one to two years as an assistant editor should lead to the next step upward. As an associate editor, you will be responsible for preparing one or more auxiliary components for the project, as well as sharing responsibility with your colleagues for project assignments as needed. Because the auxiliary will be your "baby," you will be involved in all the aspects of bookmaking to which you've been exposed -- art, production, manufacturing. As the key editor for the auxiliary component, you will be accountable for readability, sensitivity issues, and the coordination of materials with subject specialists and teacher reviewers.

Scope of responsibility increases as your experience adds up. You can look ahead, if all goes well, to project editor status, in which the student text -- the chief revenue item -- becomes your "baby."

At senior editor level, a number of textbooks or a series, developed grade-level by grade-level, would become your province.

The executive editor is in charge of the entire product line and is thus responsible for allocating all the talent, time and dollar resources properly to maintain an ever-growing, profitable product line.

Are there other related jobs in educational publishing for which you might qualify? A good question and a resounding "yes" to answer it. You may find a growing interest in preparing space advertising, promotional brochures, or other sales support materials. Speak to the Advertising department. Or a desire to undertake market research may catch your fancy. See the director of marketing. Or a hankering for direct field contact on an everyday basis could lead you into the sales rep or sales consultant category. See the sales manager. In summary, opportunities within the company will become visible to you in the normal course of events. The outcome depends on your motivation and skills potential, coupled with the needs and future plans of the publishing company.

THE GOOD, THE BAD, AND THE NOT-SO-PRETTY

"All does not go well in the best of all possible worlds all of the time," as even the somewhat dense but good-natured Candide was able to advise his overly-sanguine tutor, Dr. Pangloss, by the end of Voltaire's classic novel. You should be prepared for very tough deadlines -- tougher than those faced in general Trade or college publishing. Of the 50 states, some 22 confine textbook purchases to a list of approved books. And the rules for submission can be rigid and non-negotiable. In many cases, when textbook adoptions cover a three to four year time span, if a state deadline is missed, the publisher cannot submit an entry again for sale in the state until the next adoption date. You will quickly learn the state adoption priorities and internalize them.

The teamwork necessary for successful project development may not be your bag. Consensus is necessary to maintain a working homeostasis, so you may have to forego some of your favorite notions or private ambitions. This is a truism in business, speaking broadly, but is mentioned here because the nature of elhi editorial work demands ego flexibility and cooperative group endeavor.

The positive benefits of project teamwork more often than not outweigh the negatives. This has been demonstrated over and over again by the great number of project groups with members who stick together willingly through good times and bad to achieve the team goal: successful completion of an educational program of which the group can be proud. Healthy peer relationships based on mutual professional respect have been shown to be, year after year, one of the most satisfying aspects of an editorship in elhi publishing.

* * *

"Teaching, writing and editing come together functionally in my current job," declares the author, *"and I'm hard put to think of a time in my worklife when these three roles didn't blend well."*

Since he attained his current position in 1977, Mr. Stewart has been responsible for managing product development -- editorial, art and production -- in all content areas for which his division offered textbooks.

"These days the teaching is mostly coaching while the writing is pretty much 'business prose,'" he admits, *"but the editing takes place every day in different subject areas and on many different levels with many different talents. Editing is truly the heart of the job."*

"I came to publishing after teaching college. My first assignment was gargantuan -- editing a best-selling, two-volume college text entitled Civilization Past and Present *at Scott, Foresman & Co. It rivalled H.G. Wells'* Outline of History *in size and majesty. I was probably able to succeed solely through naivete and ambition -- an unbeatable combination in youth."*

A high school version of Civilization *climaxed seven years at Scott, Foresman, followed by another seven years at Holt, Rinehart & Winston. He then decided to freelance, soon finding himself "working both sides of the street as well as all the intersections --*

59

authoring a humanities program, doing filmstrips, writing, ghostwriting, troubleshooting, editing, and more editing. All this led ultimately to editor-in-chiefship."

Stewart is an adjunct professor in New York University's summer publishing program and has been active on the education-for-publishing and research committees of the Association of American Publishers. Originally a Midwesterner and a graduate of the University of Chicago, he has spent most of his professional life on the East Coast "in that civilized enclave known as educational publishing."

CHAPTER 9

Planting Inflammatory Ideas In The Garden Of Delight: Reflections On Editing Children's Books

By

Ann Beneduce, Editorial Director (Retired)
Philomel Books
A Division of the Putnam Publishing Group

One of the unspoken hazards of being a children's book editor is the head-patting syndrome. This occurs in social situations, such as a dinner party, when you respond to someone's well-meaning inquiry as to what it is you "do." A momentary silence descends, while everyone feverishly searches his or her brain for a suitable comment. Then one person helpfully says, "Oh, I just love Dr. Seuss!" "What a fun job!" cries another. Like the character Treehorn, you feel yourself shrinking to the size of a two-year-old, while cringing from these verbal pats on the head from the grown-ups with whom you have been allowed to mingle.

IT'S NOT A GAME FOR CHILDREN!

But editing children's books is not really a game for children. It is a serious, multifaceted, demanding profession. Neither is it any more "fun" than any other kind of editing, though it is in some ways more rewarding. Still, the adult reaction to children's books -- the sense that the world of children's literature is a cloistered garden of delight -- is a response to which attention must be paid. For it is this sense of joy and wonder and, yes, even fun that one tries, as a children's book editor, to find and foster in the works one will publish for young readers.

School workbooks and textbooks are in a specialized class apart, and we are not concerned here with these. But the children's trade book is created for the young person's voluntary, recreational reading. It is meant to be read for pleasure. This pleasure may be derived from literature of various kinds and at various age and interest levels. There are fairy tales and fantasies, realistic novels and stories, books of riddles, games, and jokes, poetry, both light and serious, and beautiful picture books. Informational books offer pleasures of a different sort. "How to" books may provide tips on sharpening one's skills at baseball or building a home computer. Other books deepen a child's understanding of nature, politics, or history. There are even picture books to teach toddlers how to count to ten, or to tell time.

Throughout the wide range of subjects and styles, the challenge is consistent: Every children's book published has to have that special joy-producing ingredient that will make it stimulating to the growing aesthetic and intellectual capacities of young readers.

WHAT ARE "CHILDREN'S BOOKS?"

The term "children's books" covers a broad area. Children as an audience range from newborn infants to sophisticated high school seniors, and their interests and reading skills vary widely. Even the tiniest infants benefit from -- indeed, *need* -- verbal and visual stimulation. For them there are cloth or board books to play with, chew on, take into the bathtub, or sleep with, as well as picture books and stories for parents to read aloud and share with them.

Then come more complex picture books and "easy readers" for the six-, seven-, and eight-year-olds, who are just beginning to read independently.

Next come the eight-to-elevens, the so-called middle-aged children. This group wants more grown-up-looking books, still fairly simple to read but offering a broad spectrum of subjects in both informational books and in fiction, which at this age level includes romance, adventure, fantasy, science fiction, and realistic novels about children like themselves.

The category that once was named "teenage books" is now read by this pre-teenaged audience, while the actual teenagers read what are called "Young Adult" (YA) books. Young adult fiction is becoming more and more similar in subject matter to adult books, with the difference that the protagonists are still in their teens.

AND THE DIFFICULT TASK 0F EDITING THEM

Editing books for such a diverse readership is a protean task. Some editors find they prefer to specialize in one or another of the categories or age levels. Editing picture books, for instance, calls for a different sensibility and training from that required for doing young adult science books. Most Children's Book departments are big enough to have several editors, and to allow each of them a degree of specialization. The editor-in-chief, however, needs some expertise in all these areas, and in a small company may indeed handle the entire range. The diversity of skills and interests demanded to edit and produce such a variety of books is insurance against on-the-job boredom!

The basic technique of editing children's books is similar to that of editing any kind of books, and there is much valuable guidance to this in other parts of this volume. Every editor must work within a reasonable budget to produce a certain number of books of a particular character and quality for a specific range of readership, and to promote and market them in such a way that they will bring a financial profit to both the author and the publisher. This is an oversimplification, of course. Selecting the manuscripts and projects, negotiating contracts, working with authors and artists to help them bring the project to its best form (involving substantive editing, line-by-line editing, copy editing, lay psychoanalysis, nagging, and hand-holding), supervising the format, design, and actual production, overseeing the advertising, promotion, publicity, and sales, keeping track of royalties and subsidiary and foreign rights sales, checking on inventory and fulfillment of orders -- all these are also part of any editor's job.

THE AUDIENCE -- WHY OUR JOB IS SO DIFFERENT

The most obvious difference between the work of the children's book and the adult book editor is in the audience. The reading skills and interests of children vary much more widely than do those of adults. But the principal factor that distinguishes the work of the children's book editor is his or her special responsibility to the intended reader. Children are sensitive readers. Their attitudes are still in a formative stage. This means that editors have a duty, in addition to maintaining high standards of quality in a novel or a factual book, to consider its effect on the child's mind, personality, and character and on his or her developing interests.

Such things as avoiding racial stereotypes and sexism are also serious concerns of the children's book editor. This is, again, because the child's mind is open and vulnerable. Adult books containing these biases are published all the time, and are read by people with matching prejudices, for the most part, or by persons with well-informed views who can evaluate these negative opinions and deal with them. Children, however, are most likely to accept what is written in a book as true, and, therefore, such books can be harmful to them. It is the editor's job to guard them from misinformation.

For the same reason -- because the child *believes* in the reliability of the printed page -- factual books for children are generally much more carefully vetted than similar books for adults. Most editors have them double-checked by outside experts in the field concerned -- mathematics, ornithology, history, or whatever it may be -- to avoid passing on inaccurate information to young readers.

Reading skill and vocabulary vary at each age level, and the children's book editor must be sure that these factors have been taken into consideration by the writer. Some authors find it very difficult to adjust their writing to the age level of their prospective young readers. Children are just as intelligent as their elders, of course, but they have not lived as long, so they have not yet acquired the range of information or the complexity of language needed to understand a text written for adults.

However, it is very important not to let an author "write down" to them, or patronize them. There is almost nothing a young reader cannot understand if it is carefully and clearly set forth. If a new word is used, it should be defined. If something is mentioned that the child is unlikely to have learned previously, a sentence or two can be added to fill in the background. Short sentences are more easily read than long ones. And short words are more direct and easier to understand than long, Latinate locutions. On the other hand, if a long word is exactly the right word, it should be used, and its meaning made clear. To use a vocabulary restricted to words on school-graded lists would be a mistake, as there would be then no opportunity for a child to expand his or her language skills. Editors must be sensitive to the differences in reading levels, and make sure that the books they publish really communicate with their intended readers.

PREPARING FOR A CAREER AS A CHILDREN'S BOOK EDITOR

I am often asked what training would be useful to someone thinking of entering the field. Some things would apply equally well to someone planning to go into other areas of editing -- training in literature and the arts, and some time spent in one of the many good publishing courses and workshops available now. For editing children's books I would add some training in child psychology and developmental psychology. The essential factor is a real interest in children, a deep and urgent curiosity about all fields of learning, and a wish to convey the joy of learning and discovery, as well as an appreciation of the arts and literature, to young people.

Another question frequently asked is why most children's book editors are women. There are two reasons for this, I think. One is that all things concerned with children have been traditionally considered the special province of women, as part of their nurturing role. Fifty years ago, when children's book publishing was in its infancy in this country, women were naturally considered to be the people who would know know best what was suitable to foster its growth and development.

But there is another reason. The male editors and publishers who dominated the field of adult books felt that there was something less serious about children's books, something intellectually inferior, and they were not really interested in the field. Since they made it difficult for women to enter the adult realm of publishing, which men felt was their "turf," women who wanted to move upward into responsible positions in publishing had to enter through the back door and move up where they were permitted to do so -- in children's books, cookbooks, mystery stories, crossword puzzle books, and the like.

This was certainly true even when I began to work in publishing. Now that Children's Book departments earn as much as or more than their Adult Book counterparts in many publishing houses, success has removed the stigma from the category, and male editors are much more numerous in Children's Book departments than was formerly the case. (And the situation in Adult Book departments has also changed quite drastically over the years, so that there are now many women in the upper echelons of editing and publishing of adult books, a reflection of the change in society and values as a whole.)

THE UNIQUE WORLD AND PROBLEMS OF CHILDREN'S BOOKS

Children are eager to explore their world and their futures: They are seeking their own identities and possibilities. Books allow them to "try on" various kinds of personalities and lifestyles. If we expect them to change our world for the better, we must not infect them with adult fears or disillusionment; we must instead offer them insight and inspiration. In our children lies the whole potential of the human race. Children's book editors, like all who deal with the aesthetic and intellectual development of children, must take seriously the responsibility for giving them books that contain the ideas and motivation they need to fulfill their aspirations -- and our own.

Since children's books are written by adults, there is often a tendency on the part of the authors to use their stories to foist their own adult preoccupations on children. Fortunately, most writers of children's books have something of real value to share with their young readers. Their books, in all their variety, celebrate such things as humor, beauty, fantasy, truth, courage, friendship, and creativity. Others, however, may be fearful, angry, or disillusioned. Every editor has received, and rejected, hundreds of variations of the story of the lion who escapes from the zoo, only to discover its newfound freedom to be so frightening that it hastens back to the safety of its cage. However cleverly disguised, their message is clear: Don't try to be independent; settle for security, no matter how confining.

Some cases, however, are less clear-cut. A well-known artist once brought me a brilliantly innovative picture book in which the very small reader was supposed to search through ingeniously die-cut pages for a hidden surprise, at the same time learning such concepts as above, below, through, behind, etc., as well as shapes: round, square, triangular, and so on. But the prize at the end turned out to be a pirate's chest filled with jewels and coins. Beautiful and clever as the book was, we were dismayed. Would a toddler really be thrilled to find a box full of coins?

Are children that young already money-oriented? Or was this just a transference of the artist's own secret wish? And is a pirate's cache of stolen loot really a suitable thing to offer *anyone* as a reward? These were the questions we raised to the artist. Fortunately, he is a man deeply concerned with the effect of his books on small children, and he understood at once. Within a few days he had solved the problem perfectly. In his revised version, the child reader searched through the die-cut pages for a birthday gift that had been hidden by his parents. The present awaiting him at the end of the book was an adorable puppy -- a totally appealing gift on just the right emotional level for a small child.

One of the unique pleasures of being a children's book editor is working with such artists. There are many wonderful artists to be found today who are creating sensitive and innovative picture books, the kind that really encourage a child's creativity. Good illustrations can stretch the imaginations of children and expand their visual vocabularies. Books like those by the Japanese artist Mitsumasa Anno -- his alphabet books, his counting books, his wordless but very articulate journey books -- these open new worlds. Maurice Sendak opens different doors: His pictures reveal our inner world of dreams and emotions, a world familiar to children and adults alike. These are but two of the many brilliant artists on the picture book scene today. Working with artists and illustrators is not usually a part of adult book editing, but it is one of the joys of editing books for children.

Of course, while keeping in mind the best interests of the child who is the ultimate consumer, the editor cannot ignore the financial aspect of publishing. To do so would be unfair to one's employer, and also to the author and the reader. One must have a sense of the marketplace: The market is the barometer of the consumer's real concerns. However, in the case of children's books, producing books with an eye solely to financial return cannot really be called editing; it is just product processing. And these products -- these listlessly manufactured nonbooks -- can harm young readers either actively or, more subtly, through boredom.

Edith Hamilton has said that the mark of an educated person is his or her ability to be set on fire by an idea. Books for children should be "inflammatory" in this sense. Anything less robs children of the powerful magic of a dynamic involvement with the right book at the right time -- a significant experience every literate adult can remember.

* * *

Ann Beneduce began her publishing career in 1957. She has been a children's book editor since 1960, when she joined the J. B. Lippincott Co. From 1960 to 1980 she held top editorial posts in the children's book field at World Publishing Company, T. Y. Crowell, and Williams Collins Publishers (the American subsidiary). From 1980 to her retirement in 1986, she was editorial director of Philomel Books, her own imprint and a division of the Putnam Publishing Group.

SECTION III

Opportunities
In
Marketing
&
Sales

CHAPTER 10

Marketing And Selling Trade Books

By

Michael T. Pratt, VP-Marketing and Sales
Random House, Inc.

It is hard for me to imagine more rewarding careers in book publishing than those associated with marketing and sales. The people who perform in these areas, after all, are the ones who convince booksellers to make new books available to book readers; further, as you'll see in the chapters that follow, they create consumer demand for books through advertising, promotion and publicity. The men and women in marketing and sales, then, provide the final step in the long and complex process in publishing books.

Sales and marketing people in a consumer goods company like Procter & Gamble might "introduce" up to a dozen or so new products each year. In book publishing, the number of new books "launched" each year ranges from 250 for a medium-sized company to 500, 1,000, or more for the largest trade book publishers. The range is exciting and diverse, and includes fiction, general non-fiction, cookbooks, diet books, biographies and autobiographies, inspiration, history, finance and economics, and books of important current interest, such as environmental and political issues. Children's books are equally far-ranging, offering a world of words and pictures as diverse as a child's imagination.

Trade book publishers often describe themselves as being in the education and entertainment business. Recently, many of them have begun experimenting in non-book areas, most notably with video and audio cassettes. Now, we still offer readers advice on "how to" prepare a festive dinner or change the spark plugs in their car, but we also *show* them those same techniques on a television screen. And children can now watch <u>The Velveteen Rabbit</u> illustrated on their television screen while Meryl Streep, instead of Mom or Dad, narrates the story.

Audio cassettes are beginning to play a significant role in trade publishing. More and more people are choosing to listen to self-help, self-improvement and foreign language audio cassettes, as well as best-selling fiction and non-fiction books on tape.

Trade publishing is no longer just trade book publishing. And the career opportunities are growing as fast as the business is changing.

THE TASK OF MARKETING -- CREATE THE DEMAND

Someone has to convince booksellers that a publisher's new books (or video and audio cassettes) deserve a place on their shelves, a chance to find a life. This task -- to "create the demand" -- falls to each company's marketing people. And it involves far more than just "selling books" to the bookseller.

For example, the book's jacket (or cover) will be graphically designed to catch browsers' eyes. Posters and other in-store merchandising aids -- such as displays which hold several copies of a book in a featured spot on a table, counter, or primary floor area -- may also be utilized. Marketing people will design these displays to reflect the theme and the benefits of the books. Other creative devices -- mobiles, shelf danglers, slit cards, etc. -- may be devised in an ongoing process to attract the most attention to each book.

Generally, a marketing manager will work with the sales manager (and often the publisher as well) to determine which books need, or will most benefit from, special marketing attention. They will be responsible for creating a budget for the marketing plan, which may include author tours, advertising, and in-store merchandising aids. They must also consider how (or *if*) booksellers will respond to particular marketing devices. . .buying more copies than they otherwise would is one desirable response.

THE DEMAND FOR MARKETING AND SALES PEOPLE

Successful publishing requires the orchestrated and coordinated efforts of many people in a variety of different but inter- related jobs, and the marketing and sales staffs are certainly key to any such effort. These are also career fields which offer a number of exciting and rewarding opportunities.

Among the skilled professionals necessary in any book publisher's marketing department are <u>designers</u> and <u>copywriters</u>. They bring their separate talents to bear on creating attention-grabbing graphics and benefit-laden headlines. The natural background skills for entry-level positions in these areas are courses in design and journalism.

A <u>sales representative</u> is generally assigned to a specific geographic area (or "sales territory,") which will vary depending on the size of the publishing house and the number of sales representatives employed.

Typically, a publishing house will have 15-25 sales representatives. You can imagine that sales people assigned to a metropolitan area such as New York City, Los Angeles, or Chicago will have lots of customers in their "home base" and will, therefore, have less overnight, out-of-town territory. The same is true of especially "bookish" cities like Boston, San Francisco, and Washington, D.C. On the other hand, sales representatives in Cleveland, Kansas City, Atlanta, etc., will spend more nights in motels in order to cover the assigned accounts in their larger geographic territories.

The most common compensation is salary plus bonus. Most book publishers offer sales trainees a beginning salary in the $15,000 - $19,000 range, depending on the size and demands of the sales territory and the amount of related experience of the sales candidate. The bonus may be paid semi-annually or annually and is often based on sales performance in relation to established goals; in addition, it may often include other criteria, such as submitting weekly call reports and other administrative assignments on a timely basis. Bonuses may range from a few thousand to several thousand dollars annually.

An accomplished and enthusiastic representative will probably earn in excess of $20,000 annually in salary after three to five years of experience. A good sales manager or marketing manager would probably earn in excess of $50,000 and may exceed $75,000 or more, depending on the size of the company and the range of responsibilities and experience of the individual.

HOW TO PUT YOURSELF A STEP AHEAD OF THE OTHER SALES CANDIDATES

The skills needed to become a sales representative are a sales aptitude and an interest in books. Some people find selling easy and natural. Others must develop such "natural" sales skills through some sort of training program, either at school or on-the-job. A liberal arts background, with a major in literature, communications, or business, is common among many successful salespeople I know. I think such "broad-based" training is probably best.

A summer or after-school job stocking book shelves or working as a cashier in a bookstore will generally be considered an advantage when you begin looking for a trade sales position. So would any previous sales experience. I've heard sales managers say they will teach a trainee how to sell, or help them learn to appreciate books, but they don't want to have to do *both*. So while either reading experience or sales experience is helpful, if you have both, and your communication skills are good, you should be in demand.

Sales managers admit they are at a loss to determine which candidates are psychologically fit for the job of sales representative. Selling books requires a degree of initiative and motivation that many people lack. Consider the salesperson living in Cincinnati, whose territory may include Ohio, West Virginia, and Kentucky. His boss may be a regional sales manager living in Chicago, or a New York-based sales manager. Selling books requires having the motivation to work on your own, without immediate supervision and without the on-hand support system that you will find in other fields. If you are not highly motivated and independent, forget it; if you *are* highly motivated and *enjoy* independence, you'll probably find this an exciting field.

WHAT YOU'LL BE DOING AS A TRADE BOOK SALES REPRESENTATIVE

Your "typical" day as a new sales representative will vary with the nature of the publishing house, but the following is not uncommon: You will prepare for each bookstore appointment by reviewing your list of new book titles, considering which ones do and do not have sales potential for that bookstore's market. You will also think of merchandising ideas that might help you sell those books into the store and help the bookseller sell them to his or her customers. (You'll study the author information, for example, to determine if there is a particular local tie-in you can exploit to generate interest.)

Once in the store, you'll review your new list of titles with your customer, making recommendations on titles and quantities. After you have secured your new book order, you will inventory the books already carried by that store to determine those that have sold out and need to be reordered. Most books are sold on a returnable basis, so you will also pull off the shelves any books which the bookseller has been unable to sell. Those will be shipped back to your company by the bookseller, usually for full credit. While more and more bookstores are beginning to use computers to keep track of inventory needs, the majority still do not, and the sales representatives need to assist their customers with this.

All of this may take two or three hours, or all day, depending on the length of your list and the size of the store. And every appointment -- every bookstore -- offers new and different experiences. Your next stop may be a similar kind of store in the same city, but with a different clientele, or one in another city whose customers are looking for a completely different selection of books.

And each time you finish an appointment, you have an opportunity to evaluate your efforts. Former sales representatives often tell me what they miss most about selling is the instant gratification, knowing *immediately* whether they accomplished their goals, each and every day. So many jobs do not offer this. In most non-sales positions, employees may wait for an annual, or perhaps semi-annual review, to see how they "measure up". The sales experience allows you to get immediate "feedback," feel good about yourself and your efforts, and identify areas for self-improvement. . .every day.

A CAREER ITSELF...AND GREAT TRAINING FOR MOVING UP

Many salespeople find selling an exciting and professional career; others view it as a first step in their career path. Where can it lead? In my view, the opportunities are virtually unlimited. A natural progression would include positions as a regional sales supervisor, assistant sales manager, national sales manager, vice president of sales, etc.

No job in publishing offers a knowledge base like that of the sales representative. Those jobs closest to consumers and booksellers -- our customers --will *always* offer a continuing education of enormous value to a publisher. Wouldn't marketing decisions be enhanced if they came from someone with sales experience? Who else would know more about what would and would not entice booksellers and consumers? What graphic design or "look" in a book jacket would likely be more successful? The sales representatives see them all -- the books and ideas of all publishers, every day, on the shelves of their booksellers' stores. No one else in the company has that opportunity.

An intelligent publishing house looks at its brightest sales representatives as consultants. A career in marketing is a natural enough extension from sales, and I would not discount the possibility of becoming an editor, a publisher, or even president of the company. If you are bright, motivated, and determined, sales experience will serve you well in whatever career path you choose in publishing.

* * *

Michael Pratt's career in the book publishing industry spans more than 20 years and followed a three-year stint in retailing. His first two years were spent with Westminster Press, where he sold religious and children's books in seven Midwestern states. This was followed by two years as a sales representative for Harper & Row Publishers, Inc.

In 1969, he began his career at Random House, where he is now the senior marketing executive. His positions there have included: sales representative; assistant sales manager; national field sales manager; national sales manager; director of trade marketing and sales; division vice president, trade marketing and sales; and corporate vice president, marketing and sales.

Mr. Pratt is a Midwestener who grew up in Troy and Ashland, Ohio. His undergraduate liberal arts education was undertaken at Muskingum College, Ashland College and Temple University. He has taken various graduate courses and seminars from the American Management Association and the Wharton School of the University of Pennsylvania. He is included in Who's Who in America.

CHAPTER 11

Launching A Sales Career In College Textbook Publishing

By

Donald W. Burden, Senior Marketing Manager
McGraw-Hill Book Company

Professors anxiously awaiting your visit? This is probably a not-unwelcome switch from what you experienced as a student. And it will happen if you join the ranks as a successful field sales representative for a college textbook publishing house.

A career in college textbook publishing offers you a unique opportunity to cement a new relationship with those professors charged with the educational development of our valued student population. As a professional representative of an educational publisher, you'll be welcomed by professors who want to explore the contents of books that support their classroom and laboratory teaching.

COLLEGE PUBLISHING -- A LOT MORE THAN "JUST" TEXTBOOKS

Today, textbook publishing is a major segment of the communication industry. The demand for knowledge is ever-increasing. The impact of today's technology challenges everyone to keep abreast of these changes as it impacts their career -- their earning power and earning potential. Whether it be the Latest surgical technique in a specialized field of medicine, a recently unearthed archaeological find, or a new management or economic theory, the need remains for a medium to detail this information to a knowledge-seeking market. A major resource for distributing this information is the textbook.

But college publishing, which many of you may still think of as "only" textbooks, now includes a vast assortment of materials needed to master a subject or develop skills for a specific professional career. The major college publishing houses publish not only textbooks but a wide assortment of other supplementary print materials -- lab manuals for biology, chemistry, and physics; drill and practice audio tapes for foreign languages and music appreciation; software disks and documentation for engineering problems and calculations; practice working papers for accounting; and many more.

HOW COLLEGE PUBLISHING HOUSES ARE ORGANIZED

A textbook publishing company is generally divided into three departments: Editorial, EDP (Editing, Design and Production, <u>not</u> electronic data processing), and Marketing. A closer look at the inner workings of these departments will identify some of the career opportunities available to you. (*While the first of these is exhaustively covered by John Holland in his chapter on College Publishing Editorial Opportunities, we thought you might find this "view" of the editorial function from a marketing perspective instructive -- Ed.*)

The Editorial department

The Editorial department is directly charged with developing the content of textbooks and supplements. The key player or orchestrator of these functions is the <u>editor</u>, who rates top billing at the publishing house. It is the editor who is the product developer and product champion, the one who continually seeks writers within the academic community who can synthesize the subject matter into a publishable manuscript. The editor needs to be sensitive to current trends in teaching, the leading academics (authors) molding the subject matter, and the competitive books either published or under development at other publishing houses. An editor assists authors in molding the content, size, and publishing plan or schedule for each textbook and its supplements. Key to an editor's success is developing a book that will ultimately sell into the marketplace.

The EDP department

The EDP department, working in close concert with editors, is charged with preparing the manuscript for printing. It is this segment of the publishing partnership that is responsible for the line-by-line editing of the manuscript and designing it to insure that a sound educational design has been provided to compliment the material. Finally, the production team oversees the actual printing and binding of the textual material.

Enter the Marketing department

Traditionally, it is within the Marketing department that most individuals begin their careers in textbook publishing. Except for those individuals within the EDP department, whose backgrounds are a composite of highly-trained technical expertise, the clearcut entry-Level position into textbook publishing is as a <u>field sales representative.</u> This is the training ground, the arena in which you Learn about the environment that supports profitable publishing ventures.

YOUR JOB AS A COLLEGE FIELD SALES REPRESENTATIVE

A sales representative for a college textbook publisher is assigned a territory consisting of several colleges and universities. The boundaries of a territory will vary from one publishing house to another, generally depending on the number of books the publisher produces.

The basic job responsibilities of the sales representative are to contact college and university professors, administrators, and bookstore buyers and managers to sell and promote the publisher's List of books and supplements. Key to this basic objective is the need to explore and define markets for new books and products that need to be developed to maintain a publisher's growth commitment for the future. Reporting market trends and competitive information about books and authors is crucial to a sales representative's success. Identifying a professor as a potential author, encouraging and molding the professor to prepare a marketable manuscript, and eventually obtaining a contract for publication are other tasks commonly expected of a successful field representative.

Training

A new sales employee at a college textbook house can expect to participate in a structured training program in which he or she will Learn the basic framework of the college curriculum, detailed product knowledge (including key components of each book), territorial management, and selling techniques. Throughout the first months as a sales representative, additional guidance and support is provided by a <u>field sales manager</u>. Working in close harmony, selling books and expanding upon the individual talents and desires of each sales representative, the field manager coaches each member of his or her sales team in the skills needed for sales success and/or eventual promotion to a position in field management, marketing/product management, or editorial management. (Some individuals ultimately elect *not* to pursue a promotion, choosing instead to remain sales representatives. After a few years of learning the skills and the sales territory, the sales rep position can become quite lucrative, so promotion does not necessarily mean "greater" success. In general, the choices among these career paths will be determined in your second or third year as a field sales representative.)

Compensation

A highly motivated, successful college textbook sales representative is adequately compensated, depending upon his or her level of experience. Recent college graduates with Limited prior work experience customarily start at a salary ranging from $18,000 - $22,500. New employees with extensive prior experience -- often competitive publishing sales experience -- command salaries of $25,000+, with the "+" depending upon past performance. With each promotion, salary increases generally range between 12 & 18 percent. In addition to this annual base salary, sales reps usually participate in some sort of commission, bonus, or incentive payment program. These programs are frequently supplemented by special sales campaigns throughout the year. To support your efforts to maximize sales and fulfill the basic requirements of the job, most publishers also provide expense monies and a company car plan.

WHAT YOU NEED TO GET HIRED AND SUCCEED

A successful college textbook sales representative possesses highly refined communication and organizational skills. Since verbal and written skills are key components of the job, demonstrable proficiency in these skills is crucial for a student seeking a sales career in college textbook publishing.

Intellectual curiosity, flexibility, and an entrepreneurial spirit are common traits among the most successful college textbook sales representatives.

Traveling is a big part of the job, so be ready to do so -- Reluctance to spend time on the road away from your home base will make it difficult to get that first job. If you secure a job knowing that you are reluctant to travel, this will eventually impact negatively upon your career in publishing.

The bulk of college sales representatives are hired from the vast pool of college graduates with (at least) a bachelor's degree in the arts, sciences, humanities, or business. While those of you with engineering or nursing degrees may still be hired, the bulk of successful publishing personalities do not evolve from these more specialized areas. While publishers welcome applications from successful M.B.A. candidates, this specialized degree is not crucial to employment; neither is it a guarantee of a successful publishing career. Some teaching or sales experience is generally looked upon favorably during the interviewing process.

Introductions to a publishing firm often evolve from faculty members, many of whom are authors for one house or another. These knowledgeable individuals are familiar with the publishing industry and the personalities who lend character to it. So their recommendations are valued and will usually lead to an interview and, if you possess the credentials and desire we like to see, eventual employment. A direct inquiry through the Marketing department of the publishing house is always encouraged. Few, if any, summer intern programs are currently available.

CAREER OPPORTUNITIES -- EXPANDING AND INCREASING

For those sales representatives seeking a publishing career that encompasses more than a sales territory, the most frequently-trod career paths will lead first to marketing manager, sponsoring editor, or field manager positions. Both the marketing manager and sponsoring editor positions require relocation to the publisher's home office. On the other hand, the field manager will generally be located in a major metropolitan area that allows him or her easiest access to the group of sales representatives under his or her supervision.

Successful performance in these positions can result in increased responsibilities and promotion to <u>director of marketing services, editor-in-chief</u> or <u>regional manager</u>. From there, the common career path -- short of the ultimate vice president position -- will lead to <u>publisher</u> or <u>director of marketing</u>. Promotion from an editorial career track to a high level of responsibility in the marketing operation, and vice versa, are quite commonplace in most college publishing firms.

As the need for knowledge increases, the career opportunities for salespeople in college publishing will also increase. Books will remain a viable source of knowledge, but the art and science of book publishing will further expand beyond the confines of the printed textbook to include the dissemination of knowledge through electronic media.

Regardless of how knowledge is distributed, talents will be required and people gainfully employed to collect the information, mold it into comprehensible formats, and market it successfully and profitably.

And whatever new technologies impact the communications business, the fundamentals of publishing you will learn and practice as a college textbook sales representative will give you the basic sales skills and publishing knowledge that will insure you a rewarding career.

* * *

Mr. Burden has spent his entire publishing career with McGraw-Hill, starting as a college text sales representative in Southern California in 1963. In 1967 he was promoted to general manager of customer relations for McGraw Hill's Western Distribution Center in California. In 1974, he became district sales manager, responsible for nine Midwestern states.

He became a sponsoring editor in 1976 and was promoted to executive editor in 1979 before returning to the marketing area in his current position four years later.

Mr. Burden is an active member of the Association of American Publishers' Marketing Committee and the National Association of College Stores.

CHAPTER 12

Marketing And Sales Opportunities In Elhi Textbook Publishing

By

Fred Schilling, Director of Marketing
D. C. Heath and Company

Sales and marketing professionals in the elhi textbook industry are most often former classroom teachers and/or school administrators. In many instances, these educators have had highly successful teaching careers and, by serving on textbook selection committees, become known to textbook representatives and consultants as curriculum leaders.

Marketing and sales positions in the elhi industry provide excellent opportunities to apply one's professional educational experiences to a variety of instructional settings. School personnel look to the publishers, consultants and sales representatives for the instructional materials and textbooks they need to help them implement their school districts' curriculum objectives. Perhaps the most rewarding aspect of a marketing-sales career in elhi publishing is the collegial relationship that one is able to establish with the leading educators in one's sales territory.

THE ELHI INDUSTRY

In 1986, it is estimated that sales of elhi textbooks will exceed $1.5 billion. Language arts is the single largest segment of the elementary textbook market, accounting for over 50% of all expenditures; math textbooks run second, with 20% of the sales. The secondary textbook market remains slightly smaller than the elementary segment, with vocational education leading sales with 30% of the market, followed by math and science at 17% and 16%, respectively. The most rapidly growing area in secondary sales continues to reflect the renewed emphasis on modern languages.

Today's market environment requires professionals representing publishers to become more aware and sensitive to the divergent needs of their customers. More and more textbooks and other instructional materials are measured against curriculum frameworks and courses of study developed by local school districts or state departments of education.

It is essential that elhi marketers be able to clearly demonstrate how their instructional materials complement these local or state criteria. Additionally, they must communicate emerging education trends back to the publisher to assure that product development is responsive and adapts to the shifts in the elhi marketplace.

FUNCTIONAL STRUCTURING OF ELHI PUBLISHING HOUSES

Most elhi publishing houses are departmentalized according to function: editorial (which includes art and production); general administration (including manufacturing, distribution, human relations, finance and inventory control); and marketing/sales. Opportunities in editorial, manufacturing, and production have been discussed in detail elsewhere in this publication. Staffing of general administration positions often requires different skills and educational credentials, such as an M.B.A., accounting degree, or expertise in industrial relations.

Most often general managers have been promoted through a series of increasingly responsible marketing and sales or editorial positions. While this article focuses attention on the opportunities in marketing and sales, it is important to understand that a successful career in elhi publishing requires an intimate familiarity with the interdependencies, need for effective communication, and interface between the various functions.

THE SCHOOL MARKETING & SALES STRUCTURE

Since the early 1980s, a number of acquisitions and mergers have led to a significant amount of consolidation in school publishing. This has enabled many of the larger publishers to group their business activities according to areas of specialization, creating operating divisions such as elementary, secondary, and a supplemental print and software group. This type of organization allows publishers to become more focused and responsive to the needs of specific elhi market segments. Regardless of whether the publisher specializes in a specific market segment or publishes for grades K-12, the marketing and sales structure remains similar.

Director of marketing and/or national sales manager.

This position carries the authority and responsibility for directing field and other sales of text products; developing and executing advertising and promotion of these products (including space advertising, direct mail advertising, trade show and other marketing-related exhibits, sales staff selection, and the definition of function and training for the sales staff); market planning and budgeting; cost control and profit generation; field service, including teacher training; and participating in product development or revision. If the publisher has created a national sales manager's position, it is this person who assumes authority and responsibility for the sales functions. Depending on the organization of the publisher, the national sales manager usually reports to the director of marketing. If the national sales manager and director of marketing divide responsibilities, then they would both probably report to the general manager.

MARKETING ORGANIZATION

<u>Product manager</u> positions are often filled by the most successful sales representatives, educational consultants, line sales managers, or, sometimes, by editors seeking to broaden their publishing background. Product managers report to the director of marketing.

The product manager develops an action-oriented marketing plan that carefully details all activities associated with the promotion and maintenance of the product line. While developing and executing this plan, he or she interfaces with the advertising and promotion department to develop both print and non-print sales support materials; works with the exhibit manager to plan convention and trade show activities to help gain national attention for the product line; interacts with the executive editor during the developmental stage to be certain authors and editors are sensitive to the needs of classroom teachers and other educators; coordinates market research activities to test the features, advantages, and benefits of the product; provides forecasts and print quantities to inventory control; and acts as the home office liaison to the field sales force. Each product manager should be a true "product champion" and must be the most knowledgeable person in the company regarding his or her product line.

<u>Advertising and promotion manager</u>

The advertising and promotion manager most often reports to the director of marketing. In school publishing, the exhibit manager, advertising and promotion copywriters, creative director, public relations and communications functions are all usually found in this department. This is one of the few areas in the national marketing office where entry-level positions are sometimes filled with recent college graduates who lack teaching experience. Degrees in communication, journalism, advertising and marketing are helpful to the job candidate interested in this area of publishing. For a good, detailed explanation of this area -- and the appropriate jobs -- see Diane Kuppler's article in this volume.

SALES ORGANIZATION

Most school publishers have organized their field sales and consultant staffs into four to six geographic sales regions, supported by regional offices. These offices are supervised by a <u>regional sales manager</u> or <u>regional general manager</u> who is in charge of the first line sales managers, educational consultants, regional marketing staff, secretarial and clerical support. Many companies operate their regional offices as profit centers, and the general manager operates his or her region as a microcosm of the national office.

First line sales manager

The first line sales manager is responsible for meeting the sales goal assigned to him or her by the regional manager, while staying within the expense budget. He or she provides field supervision and training for sales representatives and, in some companies, for educational consultants. He or she may also schedule sales-service and sales-support personnel. The sales managers design and implement sales plans, recruit and hire field personnel, and help to train, plan and organize the activities of their subordinates. Sales managers are most often selected from the ranks of the most promising sales representatives or consultants. Organizational skills and proven leadership ability are traits associated with this position.

Sales representative or educational representative

This is considered to be an entry-level position for school publishing. (Despite the fact that "entry-level position" implies a place merely to *start* one's career, many men and women who have entered school publishing have found sales to be a worthy, lifelong professional career and remain sales representatives until retirement.) The sales representative is usually a former classroom teacher or administrator. Duties include presenting products and services to potential and existing accounts, actively selling products to meet sales goals, servicing the complete product line in a designated territory, and providing inservice training to customer schools.

To accomplish these goals, the representative must learn as much as possible about his company's product line and the curriculum needs of the territory's customers. . .and how to match the two. He or she will attend local, state, regional and even national exhibits and provide for inservice training of teachers using his company's products. Careful records of everything he or she does must be maintained -- these are forwarded to the regional or national office on a regular basis.

During a typical week, a sales representative will call by appointment on school administrators to determine if any of his or her products match areas where the school or school district is adopting new textbooks or other instructional materials. Depending on the size of the representative's territory, it will sometimes be necessary to travel overnight, as many as two or three times each week. It is not uncommon for representatives to be called upon to entertain key customers at dinner, lunch, or other social activities.

Consultants

If the principal responsibility of the sales representative is to "sell the product," it might be said that the consultants' job is to "keep the product sold." School districts rely heavily on the publisher to provide inservice training and staff development activities to assure that their products are used properly. Consultants are most often product specialists who have gained a reputation for expertise in a certain discipline such as reading, mathematics, or modern languages. They are usually former supervisors, department heads, or classroom teachers who have demonstrated effective teaching techniques in a specific subject area.

The consultant introduces products and methodology to key educators to generate sales, provides inservice training to customers, and reports market conditions, trends, and customer needs to management. Duties and responsibilities include organizing and conducting training workshops, visiting classrooms and demonstrating teaching techniques, training sales representatives in product knowledge, giving professional talks, attending exhibits, and providing service to customers who have purchased the publisher's products. Consultants are often selected to fill sales management, product management, and sometimes editorial positions. In most companies the consultant reports to the regional or line manager. Travel is often quite extensive and requires overnight trips two to four nights a week during the school year.

QUALIFICATIONS AND SUCCESS FACTORS

From the preceding discussion it should be evident that candidates must have a minimum of a bachelor's degree, although advanced degrees are preferred, especially for consultant positions. Teaching experience is clearly an advantage, especially for field sales and consulting positions. Salaries are competitive with the teaching profession and supplemented with a company car and bonus or commission incentive program.

Ideal candidates for entry-level field positions must have excellent verbal and written communication skills. They must be highly organized, possess the ability to prioritize tasks, maintain a balance between long-term and short-range goals while performing a variety of tasks simultaneously, enjoy working with people in both business and social settings, and be willing to travel extensively and work independently with a minimum of direct supervision.

* * *

Mr. Schilling began his career as a secondary teacher. He joined Holt, Rinehart & Winston's School Division in 1969 as a sales representative in the midwest region. In 1976 he was appointed to a division sales management position in California and, from 1979 to 1981, held positions as director of marketing services and director of sales administration in New York.

In 1981 Mr. Schilling joined Open Court Publishing Company as vice president of marketing and sales. Since 1985 he has served as director of marketing for D. C. Heath and Company in Lexington, Massachusetts. He has been active in the AAP School Division, serving on a variety of state action committees.

CHAPTER 13

Rights Aren't So "Subsidiary" Any More!

By

Josephine Fagan, Director of Subsidiary Rights
Crown Publishers, Inc.

Subsidiary Rights is an aspect of book publishing that has become increasingly important over the last decade or so. Twenty years ago, subsidiary rights *were* subsidiary to bookstore sales. Now it's possible to make *more* money from the sale of a book's subsidiary rights than from sales of the book! These rights can be crucial to the success of a book, a publishing list, even a company. Nevertheless, most people outside of publishing are not familiar with the concept of subsidiary rights or their importance to a publisher's health. So let's begin with a broad definition and then get on to specifics.

SUBSIDIARY RIGHTS -- WHAT THEY'RE ALL ABOUT

Subsidiary rights involves selling your book -- in part or in whole-- to third parties who will then resell it to their customers. The most common and often-sold rights are <u>serial rights,</u> <u>book club rights</u> and <u>paperback rights</u>.

Serial rights

Serial rights are book excerpts of varying lengths that are sold to another print medium -- usually magazines, newspapers or newspaper syndicates (who then sell to local newspapers across the country). These rights are broken down into two categories -- *first* and *second* serial rights.

<u>First serial rights</u> are excerpts that appear shortly before the actual publication of the book. They serve as "teasers" to the public and often help generate interest in the book that results in bookstore sales.

For example, several years ago my company published a first novel by a relatively unknown author. It was a "women's" novel that featured a glamorous heroine who is smart, beautiful, successful, etc., and who overcomes great personal trials to live, in the end, happily ever after. I'm sure you are familiar with the genre. Serial rights were sold to *Cosmopolitan* magazine, which we believed the perfect vehicle. At least partially as a result of that sale, the book went on to become a major hardcover best-seller.

More recently we published a college men's guide to women's colleges. First serial rights were sold to *Playboy*. Again, the perfect vehicle. The book went on to respectable trade sales.

First serial rights generally command higher fees (these can range up to tens of thousands of dollars depending on the book, the author's reputation, the magazine's or newspaper's circulation, etc.) because they provide the magazine or newspaper with a kind of exclusive scoop.

Second serial rights are excerpts that appear *after* the book's publication, sometimes *considerably* after. This type of excerpt provides a continuing source of income for the publisher and has significant publicity value in keeping a book in the public's consciousness. It is not terribly unusual to be able to sell second serial excerpts to a book that is several years old.

Book club rights

Book club rights involve selling the whole book to a club that will, in turn, sell it to their members through the mail at a discounted price. *(See Jessica Weber's discussion of direct mail marketing and book clubs in chapter 5- - Ed.)* There are many book clubs, ranging from large, general interest clubs to those targeting audiences with very specific areas of interest.

The two major general interest clubs are Book-of-the-Month Club and the Literary Guild of America. Whichever of these two clubs buys the book will receive exclusive book club rights from the publisher, print its own edition and then market it to its members through the mail. You've probably seen the advertisements these clubs run in major publications to solicit new membership. Generally speaking, these clubs have thirteen or fourteen "cycles" per year when they send a bulletin to their members with the top new selections ("Main Selections"), a few other new books ("Alternates"), and a recap of their back list (books they have previously offered as mains or alternates but are continuing to sell). The book club pays the publisher an advance against royalties (which can range from about $3000 to hundreds of thousands of dollars). This is paid to the publisher up front and then applied to the royalties which the contract specifies they are to receive. This income is generally shared 50/50 between the publisher and the author. On occasion, both Book-of-the-Month-Club and the Literary Guild will be interested in the same title (a happenstance that causes Sub Rights directors and everybody else at the publisher's offices paroxysms of joy). In that case, an auction develops. The two clubs bid against each other until one drops out. The book is sold to the highest bidder.

And the bidding can reach unexpected highs. I recall one instance where the opening bid on a first novel by an unknown author was $5,000. After three days of bidding, it was ultimately sold for $75,000. Often, however, because of their different memberships and images, only one will be interested in licensing rights. This provides the rights seller with little leverage to force the advance money up.

The smaller specialty clubs (professional, science, history, nostalgia, etc.) operate in basically the same way, paying an advance against royalties and selling books to their members through the mail at discounted prices.

Paperback rights

Paperback rights -- the largest income potential (once in a while, *millions of dollars*) for the hardcover publisher and author, the most "glamorous" subsidiary right and the one with the highest frustration potential for the person selling them.

Paperback reprint rights are license agreements between the hardcover publisher and a paperback publisher who agrees to publish a paperback edition approximately one year after a book's initial hardcover publication. There are two kinds of paperbacks: Trade paperbacks are usually done in the same size and format as the hardcover edition and are sold primarily through the same outlet -- bookstores. Mass market paperbacks are produced in rack-size (approximately 4" x 7") and are sold in numerous outlets in addition to bookstores -- drugstores, airports, magazine stands, etc.). Because mass market paperbacks can be gotten into the market place in major quantities, paperback publishers will pay higher advances for these rights. In any event, the hardcover publisher is paid an advance and royalties that are shared with the author (a percentage basis stipulated in the author's contract).

The paperback auction

You may have heard or read about the paperback auction, which occurs when the hardcover publisher has a "hot" property -- usually a book that has done very well in hardcover, is written by an author with a large following, or is the type of book that will perform well in paperback.

There are two kinds of auctions. One is an open auction, where no paperback publisher has established a minimum guaranteed bid (called a *"floor"*). The book is submitted simultaneously to several paperback publishers, a date is set for bidding, it is sold to the highest bidder on a "last-person-out" basis, and the hard-cover publisher and author sit back and count the money.

In the other case, a book is either shown to one paperback publisher first or one of the publishers who receives a simultaneous submission establishes the "floor" bid. The auction begins at that point (say, $50,000), instead of at zero. The floor holder usually has the privilege of topping the highest bid received at the end of the auction by 10%.

The paperback auction can truly be the glamorous part of the rights seller's job. If the timing is right and everything comes together, there is a great deal of excitement and a lot of money to be made. But as in all other aspects of life, timing is critical. Should the book be sold early? Should the hardcover publisher wait and take a chance that the book will "break-out" in hardcover? Should it be auctioned at all or should it be sold to one interested party?

My company recently published a book that promised to be very, very hot, even though the author's name was not a household word. There was a lot of excited "talk" about it in the industry. We decided to sell the paperback rights early (more than two months before we published the hardcover edition) in an open auction. The results were very gratifying: The paperback rights were sold for more than $500,000.

In another instance, we published what could be called a "pop-psych" book. Initially it didn't look like a "mega"-book. We couldn't get a reprinter to pay even $25,000 for the rights. Then, for a variety of reasons, the book clicked in hardcover and became a nationwide best-seller. Reprint rights were then auctioned for more than $600,000. We also recently sold the reprint rights to a novel for $100,000 on a negotiated sale basis -- no auction at all. As you can see, the variables and potential scenarios are almost limitless.

Unfortunately, not all books are immediately snapped up for paperback publication. There are many, many instances of hard-won, modest sales where the rights seller must cajole, convince, bombard and really *sell*, in the truest sense of the word. And there are many unfortunate instances where no amount of cajoling, convincing or bombarding works. At times, its like being a desk-bound Willy Loman.

The same auction fever -- or difficulty -- also applies to serial and book club rights. There can be high levels of frustration and rejection, but also major rewards and satisfactions in selling rights.

These three rights are the basic ones, the real "bread and butter" of most publishers' and authors' rights sales income. But subsidiary rights can take many other forms.

The other rights we sell

Some of the more obvious are film and/or TV rights, large type editions or books on tape for the visually impaired, condensation rights, and hardcover reprint rights (where a specialty publisher will do a small hardcover printing of an out-of-print title). Publishers now even deal with other industries. Many now work with the toy industry, licensing three-dimensional character rights to a character from one of their books and cross-marketing it in both industries.

As technology continues to change, the list of rights sold continues to grow. We now have audio and video cassette rights, even the potential to sell a book to a software manufacturer. Who knows where it will end?

But as the field continues to expand, it is more important than ever that the rights seller be aware of developments in the rights business. Who is buying what and for how much? Is there a book similar to one of yours that has recently been sold? Who is looking for a certain type of book to fill a gap in his publishing program? Is there a new market out there that others are tapping and you're not? The better informed you are, the more likely you'll be successful.

90

THE SUBSIDIARY RIGHTS DEPARTMENT...AND YOUR PLACE IN IT

Now that we have defined the basic subsidiary rights, we can discuss how the department itself works and what your role in an entry-level position might be.

In small publishing houses, all of the rights may be sold by one or, at most, two individuals. Most large trade publishers -- those producing over 300 new titles a year -- have several people in the Rights department. The <u>director</u> oversees the entire operation and handles the actual selling of major titles. There may also be a <u>manager</u>, the second in command, with primary responsibilities for selling as well as some administrative duties. Other members of the department will also be selling and negotiating.

Often, under the supervision of the director or manager, one person will specialize in serial and film rights, another in book club and/or paperback rights, another in selling rights to the publisher's juvenile books, etc. And each person often has more than one area of expertise.

As is always the case in sales, it is important, even critical, to have a good professional relationship with one's customers. In publishing this means several phone conversations a week, frequent lunches, etc. When you are dealing with an almost infinite number of magazines and newspapers, many potential book clubs, and at least 15 viable paperback customers, it's absolutely necessary to specialize to some degree, particularly if you are selling more than 300 titles a year! If you spread yourself too thin, both books and customers are bound to be ignored. In some houses, foreign rights and domestic rights are handled in the same department, which requires even *greater* specialization. Some publishers assign titles -- One person sells *all* the rights to his assigned titles. My own experience has been working with assigned *rights* -- We have one person handling serial and film rights, another handling book club and paperback rights. Each person then has the time to develop good relationships with a finite number of people instead of a scatter-shot approach.

In most cases, each salesperson will either have his own assistant or share one with another member of the department. <u>These assistant positions are the entry-level spots</u>. The salary you can expect probably varies widely from company to company, but a safe guess is a starting salary in the low-to-mid-teens ($11,000 to perhaps $16,000).

The selling of rights is a high volume business. Each book is submitted in manuscript form to potential customers. If no sale is made or if new customers emerge, the book is resubmitted in bound galley form and then again in bound book form. So a publisher with 300 titles may need to handle up to 900 submissions a year to perhaps 100 potential customers. Reviews, press material and any other pertinent information and details are also submitted. The bottom line: voluminous correspondence which needs to be typed, filed, and recorded. This is the "donkey" work of the department and it is performed by the assistants. There is also a large amount of telephone contact, from inquiries to follow-up calls and troubleshooting (yes, there is often trouble). The assistant can and should be able to field and handle many, if not most, of these calls.

The work may sound tedious and heavily clerical, but it is really the best way to learn this aspect of the business. An intelligent, ambitious assistant can take a great load of work from the rights seller, really become familiar with the ins and outs of laying the groundwork for a sale and negotiating a deal and become familiar with the customers. It's the best preparation I can think of for an eventual career as a rights seller.

Since subsidiary rights is now an integral part of the marketing plan of any book, there is much contact with and feedback from almost every other department in the company -- editorial, trade sales, publicity, promotion, advertising, production, art, etc. Each of these departments can provide the rights seller with invaluable information and selling tools necessary to his or her job.

So the rights seller (and the assistant), already visible in the publishing industry, also become highly visible within their own house. It never hurts to be recognized, particularly if you want to move up to the next level.

MOVING IN AND MOVING UP

It is very hard to predict a time frame for career advancement from an entry-level job in subsidiary rights. So much really depends on the individual company's policies. Do they groom and promote from within? Do they go outside for middle-level talent? Is it locked in at the top? Is the company's list growing at a rate that will require them to add staff? These are just some of the variables. Where you will be a year from now depends as much on *these* factors as on your own interest level, ambition and performance.

If you are good at your job, lucky enough to work for a company that promotes from within and with individuals who are willing to delegate authority and responsibility, after a year or so you should be able to start doing some submissions of your own, perhaps even some deal-making.

But there aren't *that* many top spots to go after. Publishing is really a very small industry, so subsidiary rights is a small piece of a small pie. And there is only *one* top rights person in each house. However, many of the skills you'll pick up working in rights are applicable to other areas of publishing -- particularly the "feel" one can develop for a salable book. Lately, several subsidiary rights directors have been named president, publisher and associate publisher of major firms and are now running companies and buying properties instead of just selling them.

THE SUCCESSFUL "RIGHTS SELLING' CANDIDATE

What qualities make for a good subsidiary rights candidate? You must enjoy people and be outgoing and enthusiastic. You will, after all, be trying to convince someone else to buy your product. You will need patience, not only because it may take a while for your career to progress, but because you may find yourself working on a sale for several months before you get positive results. You will rarely enjoy instant gratification. You also must love to read. To sell a book effectively you must have read it. Having read it, you might come up with an angle or a handle no one else has thought of. Be interested, be alert and try to be innovative in your approach. Your customers may not buy one particular book but they'll remember you when you take the next book to them. Subsidiary rights is not all glamour, million dollar auctions, lunches and pizzazz. If you examine the careers of the major rights people, you will find that a lot of hard work, energy and persistence built their careers. That and *luck* -- it never hurts to be in the right place at the right time -- are the keys to subsidiary rights success.

Publishing is really an apprentice industry; so is the area of subsidiary rights. No one graduates from college and immediately starts selling rights. It takes time to familiarize yourself with the company, the list, the routines, the procedures, the customers.

But as Yogi Berra said, "You can observe a lot just by watchin'." And from the watchin' comes the doin'.

* * *

Ms. Fagan was promoted to director of subsidiary rights for Crown, which includes Clarkson N. Potter, Inc. and Harmony Books, in 1985. She had been manager of subsidiary rights for six years and prior to that was manager of copyrights and permissions. Ms. Fagan began her publishing career at Doubleday & Co., first in the Contracts department, later in the Adult Trade Editorial department.

SECTION IV

Opportunities
In
Advertising
&
Publicity

CHAPTER 14

Advertising -- The Inspiration
And The Aspiration

By

Diane A. Kuppler, Director-Advertising & Promotion
College Division, Prentice-Hall, Inc.
Simon & Schuster Higher Education Group

What's the difference between joining a book publisher's Advertising department and going to work for an advertising agency?

Essentially the differences are minimal. At an ad agency, you might work on a range of products, from soup to nuts, while at a book publisher your product group -- books -- will remain the same. But the fundamental elements of advertising are identical wherever you are: to produce advertising that gets results.

One major difference, however, is that publishers more often hire individuals with little or no practical experience, whereas ad agencies generally prefer to hire individuals with proven ability (read, experience). So the Advertising department of a book publisher is an ideal place for most aspiring copywriters and designers to get their start.

The setup of individual Advertising departments, both within and among publishing houses, varies greatly, depending not only on the size of the house, but also on the size of the various publishing divisions. For example, a publisher's College Textbook Division might be much more profitable and thus larger than its Elhi (Elementary/High School) Division. A publisher with a large, successful college text product line might also have a large, in-house college advertising support staff. This is by no means a rule of thumb. Some publishers with productive divisions might have small advertising staffs that rely heavily on the services of outside freelance support.

So if you plan on pursuing a career in book publishing advertising, do some research: Identify each publisher's areas of specialization or particular strength (i.e., college texts, elhi texts, professional/trade or mass market books, etc.) to ascertain which area you feel best suited for and to gain a better idea of the areas where your greatest chances for opportunity lie.

WHAT DOES THE ADVERTISING DEPARTMENT DO?

Typical advertising functions in the publishing industry generally fall into one or both of the following categories:

A. <u>To produce promotional advertising that generates qualified sales leads</u> (that are then followed up with a sales call by the publisher's sales representative or an examination copy of the book being promoted). . .Or

B. <u>To produce advertising that generates either single or multiple order sales.</u> This kind of advertising assumes no follow-up sales call; the ad must make the sale by itself.

The publishing divisions most likely to produce the first type of advertising would be those involved with educational markets -- college textbooks, elhi texts, and other educational/developmental kinds of learning materials.

Naturally, the audience for these products are educators -- your own college, high school, or elementary teachers, for example. The types of promotional/advertising pieces that educators in these markets would be exposed to might include any of the following:

* Informational brochures
* Flyers
* Booklets with photos, artwork, or reproductions of sample pages from the text
* Catalogs
* Sales letters
* Educational wall posters, calendars, etc.
* Advertising in educational journals
* And any other related sales support literature

These pieces are usually informational in both tone and approach. The copy may or may not tend toward "hard-sell." However, the decision to "adopt" the text (a term publishers use to describe a school's or individual instructor's decision to order ten or more copies of a text for class use) is rarely made on the basis of the ad piece alone. Before an instructor will commit to using a new text in the classroom, he or she must first see it and thoroughly examine its content, tone, level, and approach. So the purpose of any ad for the educational market is primarily to inform. The way you inform, of course, can range from the very straightforward to the very creative.

The audience receiving the second kind of advertising might be the professional business person, persons involved in specific trades, or individuals with specific hobbies (i.e., photography, woodworking, flower arranging, personal computers, etc.), and, of course, the general public.

The types of advertising used to promote books to these audiences might include:

*Direct mail/direct response packages (including any or all of the following: 2-, 4-, 6-, or 8-page sales letter, detailed brochure, premium offer, or card)
*Brochures
*Flyers
*Catalogs
*Space advertising (ads in newspapers, magazines, etc.)
*Point-of-purchase displays or promotion
*And any other type of promotional, attention-getting tools.

This type of advertising is also informational, but it is primarily attempting to elicit an immediate response: the purchase of the book by an individual.

These are just two of the most basic ways that books are promoted and advertised. There are many, many other options available and many areas where techniques used to promote books are "traded" from publishing division to publishing division.

ADVERTISING'S RELATIONSHIP TO OTHER DEPARTMENTS

Since advertising is so closely related to the marketing function, it is almost always included somewhere under the overall umbrella of a publisher's Marketing department. In fact, these two departments are integral to each other: Advertising depends on Marketing to supply the order to advertise, identify the target audience, and supply them with the information they need to accomplish the task. Marketing depends on Advertising to produce the vehicle(s) that will effectively inform the appropriate audience(s) that a new product is available and generate either sales leads or actual sales.

The degree to which the Marketing department dictates the form, format, and content of advertising pieces varies greatly from publisher to publisher, and even from division to division. Some Advertising departments have more freedom than others in planning and budgeting advertising. However, most are given a general advertising budget that is determined by the director of marketing and controlled by the advertising honcho.

Aside from the Marketing department, the Ad department will usually work closely with a number of other departments in a given division. Within the College Division, for example, the College Ad department would have considerable contact with the acquisition editors (who contract the books), the production editors (who transform the typewritten manuscripts into bound books), the Art department (where the book's pages are laid out and designed), and the authors themselves.

The advertising staff would also have contact with various outside vendors -- printers, typesetters, illustrators, photographers, and other suppliers.

There may also be opportunities to travel to conventions, sales meetings, and trade shows, where advertising people can actually meet and talk to their audience.

OPPORTUNITIES IN THE ADVERTISING DEPARTMENT

The typical Advertising department may include any or all of the following job titles, depending on its size, its needs, and the number of new books it publishes each year:

Advertising director/advertising manager/promotion manager

These three titles are basically synonymous, varying in usage usually according to the size of the actual department (i.e., advertising director usually connotes a rather large department with several sub-levels, whereas advertising manager might connote a smaller department). Regardless of the particular title variation used, the individual in this position is in charge of the general operation and management of the department, responsible for maintaining the advertising budget and ensuring that department goals are met. This person must be knowledgeable in all phases of advertising, creative, and print production.

Asst. ad director/asst. ad manager/asst. promotion manager

Again, these titles are basically synonymous, varying only according to department size. The person serving in this capacity is usually considered as a backup to the head of the department and is responsible for department production and operations, general training and development, involvement in special projects, troubleshooting, and setting standards.

Naturally, neither of these two top positions is considered entry-level, but they are indeed positions to which an individual can aspire. Salary ranges, depending on department size and degree of responsibility, will range anywhere from $25,000 to $50,000 or more.

Copy chief

Responsible for setting and maintaining the quality of copy, planning and organizing the work, writer training and development; may become involved in some budgeting and may also maintain a freelance support network.

Art director

In charge of the daily operations of the design staff. Sets creative standards, performs budgeting duties, trains and develops staff, and may maintain a freelance support network.

These two positions usually require a strong familiarity with the publisher's product line and at least several years of practical and proven experience. They are also, of course, positions to which new copywriters or designers can aspire. Salaries range between $18,000 and $40,000.

Copy supervisor

Responsible for maintenance and approval of the workload of a small group of copywriters, whose writing responsibilities may or may not be specialized (e.g., technical writing, business book writing, etc.).

Design supervisor

Responsible for maintenance and approval of the workload of a small group of designers. May be involved in budgeting.

These positions usually require proven ability, a solid grasp of the fundamentals, and an ability to work well with people. They are growth positions with salaries ranging from $18,000 to $30,000.

Copywriter (entry-, intermediate- or senior-level)

Responsible for researching and writing advertising copy, which involves concept development and contact with a designer or art director, marketing manager, editor, and/or author.

Designer (entry-, intermediate- or senior-level)

Responsible for creating the layout and design for the advertising copy, which involves conceptual collaboration with the writer or copy chief, marketing manager, editor, and/or author.

These are the two most likely entry-level positions with considerable opportunity for advancement and growth. Starting salaries can range between $14,900 to $17,000 for entry-level, $16,000 to $21,000 for intermediate-level, and $18,000 to $27,000 for senior-level copywriters and designers.

Advertising space/journal writer

Responsible for researching and writing copy for space or journal ads; may involve concept development and journal research to target the best market.

Production assistant

Acts as a support person to the design staff and performs many design/production related duties.

Mechanical artist

Responsible for taking the elements of the designer's "dummy" (a rendering of what the printed piece will look like) and pasting them into position for the printer to photograph.

These three positions may be entry-level, but usually require some practical skill or knowledge. Salaries can range from $13,000 to $17,000, depending on skill.

Many Advertising departments may also have several miscellaneous support positions such as:

*Budget coordinator/controller -- budget tracking and department bookkeeping.

*Traffic controller/production manager -- responsible for keeping track of the workflow in and out of the department.

*Sales support group manager -- responsible for producing sales support material to be used by the marketing or field staff personnel.

*Freelance coordinator -- responsible for keeping track of freelance work in and out of the department.

Once again, the range of responsibilities, accountabilities, and duties can vary significantly from division to division and publisher to publisher. When you are in an actual interview situation, ask as many questions as you can think of to get a good feel for the department and the opportunities you will be afforded.

HOW IS AN AD PIECE CREATED? THE COPY/DESIGN COLLABORATION

As most copywriters and designers would agree, there is no "typical day" -- anything *can*, and usually *does*, happen! So to give you a better idea of what is involved in both the copy and design functions -- the two most likely opportunities for an entry-level position -- let's look at the step-by-step creation of a single ad for a new book.

A directive to produce the ad comes from Marketing. A copywriter and designer are assigned. The process begins with their joint pursuit of the single, most important selling idea and/or concept that should be used to promote the book.

Since an ad's mail (or drop) date is scheduled as close as possible to the book's availability date, the copywriter usually has to write about a book months before it is even printed. He or she must dig out the most important facts about the book and its marketing strategy by talking to the marketing people, calling the author, reading the book's preface, reviewing its table of contents, reading through a questionnaire form completed by the author, and, in many cases, (especially when the ad is intended to generate single copy sales) by actually looking at the typewritten pages.

After reviewing this material, the copywriter fleshes out the concepts and key selling ideas and creates benefit-oriented copy that will create attention, interest, desire, and the hoped-for action (to generate either sales leads or actual sales).

In much the same way that a copywriter communicates on a verbal level, the designer must convey the key ideas through visual devices, such as choice of typeface, color, use of artwork (photos, illustrations, examples), folds, use of white space, size, and visual tone.

Once the ad is written and designed, it is ready to be approved by whichever in-house or out-of-house persons a publisher's "approval policy process" dictates.

When the approvals are completed, the copy is returned to the designer to begin production. Now the pressure to meet the pre-determined drop date becomes even more intense. From this point on -- until the day the piece goes to the printer -- the copywriter/designer team will race the calendar to make sure that the ad mails on time.

The final, approved copy is sent to the typesetter and then proofread; mechanicals are built and then proofread; the ad is sent to the printer, who returns a "blueprint," which is proofread. (One mistake is too many.) And finally the finished, printed ad piece is delivered.

This whole process can take anywhere from days to weeks to months. What's more, during any phase of the writing, designing, or production of that single piece, the copywriter and designer might (and probably will) have several other projects in various stages of completion.

THE IDEAL ENTRY-LEVEL CANDIDATE HAS:

*Good organizational skills and the ability to handle a lot of volume and detail simultaneously.

*A genuine love of either writing or designing.

*A high energy level -- anything can and will happen during a normal work day.

*The ability to think on one's feet -- there are always times when you have to come up with a quick alternative or idea on the spot.

*A certain amount of poise and professionalism -- especially if you will be dealing with people outside of the company. Every person with whom you interact views you as a representative of the company you work for.

*The ability to take criticism constructively -- being creative is a highly personal process, but not everyone will love your ideas every time.

*The ability to manage stress and pressure -- Advertising makes some pretty tough demands at times.

*A sincere willingness to learn, explore, and try out new ideas.

*A responsible, mature attitude -- advertising always has deadlines that have to be met.

*Self-motivation, initiative and drive.

*The skills and desire to be a team player -- the business of advertising always involves people working together toward a common goal.

*Good communication skills -- you must be able to express your ideas clearly, regardless of whether they are verbal or visual.

*And last, but certainly not least in the publishing industry, a genuine love of books.

THE NECESSARY SKILLS AND APTITUDES

For a copywriting career:

1. B.A. or B.S. in any field, but preferably in advertising, communications, English, or journalism.

2. Any kind of writing experience -- short stories, articles for the campus or school newspaper, literary magazine, yearbook, etc.

3. Any kind of advertising experience, whether through class assignments, an internship, or freelance activities.

4. Good writing and organization skills.

5. Good grammar and punctuation skills.

6. Research skills -- the ability to pull out and organize the pertinent facts.

<u>For a design career:</u>

1. B.F.A. or B.A. in graphic design, communications design, or advertising design.

2. Practical production experience for the campus yearbook, newspaper, literary magazine, or any other publication.

3. Any part-time or freelance design experience.

4. Exposure to an agency or in-house Advertising department -- either through coursework or a design internship.

NOTE: Knowledge of mechanical preparation and/or exposure to type selection and type specification should be considered helpful (the former even desirable), but not necessary.

The ideal candidate applying for either position should have a neat, clean, and carefully organized portfolio of samples, which can include both class projects and self-initiated ideas.

A FINAL ADVERTISEMENT

The business of advertising is certainly challenging, never dull, sometimes frustrating, but *always* interesting and rewarding. It's a vocation that affords you virtually unlimited opportunity for creativity and self-expression in your work. The atmosphere is generally relaxed, but the energy level is high and the demands can be tough. In order to succeed you must be devoted to your craft and to constantly expanding and refining your skills. Ultimately, the successful copywriter evidences a good "design sense," and the successful designer has a good "copy sense." If you possess that, then the opportunities become even greater.

* * *

Ms. Kuppler began her career as an arts and entertainment critic for a local newspaper and a cable television station, for which she also hosted a half-hour program on community affairs.

After joining Prentice-Hall in 1976 as a copywriter (in those days copywriters also designed their own ads), she quickly moved up the ranks to special projects writer/designer, supervisor in charge of both copy and design development, copy chief, assistant director, and in 1984, to director of college advertising. In the Spring of 1986, Ms.

Kuppler's responsibilities expanded to include overseeing Prentice-Hall's Higher Education Group Publicity Department.

Presently, she manages a 50-person staff consisting of designers, writers, supervisors, publicists, and various support personnel. She is responsible for overseeing the production of some 900 individual pieces of advertising and promotion per year.

CHAPTER 15

When's The Last Time *You* Got Something For Free? Book Publishing Publicity/Public Relations

By

Julia Knickerbocker, VP/Associate Publisher/Director of Public Relations
Simon & Schuster, Inc.

I get people to do things for me for free. It's a great job, but, as you might imagine, a bit of a challenge!

THE PUBLICIST'S TASK -- ATTENTION!

The task facing every book publisher's Publicity or Public Relations department is to draw attention to the books their house is launching, either through book reviews, print interviews with the author (separate from the normal book review page or section) and/or radio and television appearances. Many books need some combination of all of the above.

And though it might sound hard, it still *sounds* a lot easier than it really *is*! Unlike advertising -- which is bought and paid for -- the articles, reviews, appearances, mentions, etc. that the Public Relations department generates are, strictly speaking, free. They don't cost us anything except hard work. Which might be welcome news to the accountants, but is why our jobs are so challenging-- when is the last time *you* got a total stranger to do something for you for *free*?

Public relations vs. advertising

It's not difficult to call up a magazine and pay them whatever they charge to run an ad promoting your book. It's somewhat more involved to call a magazine *editor* and convince him or her to interview an author or feature the book or author in an article. Or to convince a particular *reviewer* or review medium, who can only feature a handful of the tens of thousands of books that are manufactured each year, to include yours in an upcoming issue or column.

While it's easier to pick up the phone and place an ad, it's a trifle more expensive -- the cost of an average full page newspaper or consumer magazine ad these days is roughly $12,000. For <u>one</u> ad. For *that* kind of money, I can send an author to a dozen cities, get him onto 20 or 30 television shows, 30 to 40 radio shows, and probably generate an equal number of magazine and newspaper interviews and features. And I'd get the author far more exposure *that* way than the ad could ever *hope* to generate.

Despite the high (and going higher) cost of advertising, many companies, publishers included, use it extensively. Why? Because it is usually easy to discover whether or not a particular ad or series of ads has been successful. You can code each ad and trace every response, every sale it generates. Then you can total up the orders and see the kind of money made (or lost) as a result of each media placement.

How do you quantify the results of an author's appearance on the "Mornings At Nine" show in Des Moines, Iowa, or on the Style page of the *Oshkosh News*? Readers who go to a bookstore to buy a particular book don't usually tell the bookstore manager *why* they are buying it, let alone *where* they heard about it. And while you can trace the effect of such public relations efforts indirectly -- why *else* did sales double in Des Moines that week? -- you can rarely obtain the kind of solid, quantifiable sales figures that any businessman likes to be able to see and feel.

At the same time, no one can *buy* the kind of exposure a good publicist can generate for a book. While most of the largest and/or most progressive publishing houses now recognize the "power of publicity," I think Simon and Schuster is probably the most aggressive house in the industry in terms of publicity. S & S's top management views us, at least metaphorically, as the key component of their advertising effort. And, like the Advertising department, they expect us to achieve *real* results.

Luckily, although they sometimes seem to want a miracle a day, they do give us the books to do it with and the support staff to pull it off. The results we've achieved as a result of this corporate emphasis and support prove that they're right -- <u>a solid, professional publicity effort can absolutely change the life of book</u>

A PUBLIC RELATIONS SUCCESS STORY

One example: In 1985, we published <u>Less Than Zero</u>, a first novel by Brett Ellis. First novels are traditionally the most difficult books to promote (and sell); there's nothing to build on -- no previous books (let alone a previous bestseller), no reputation, no ready-made audience. As a result, the first novels that sell enough copies to even pay back the publisher's advance can probably be counted on one's fingers. . .well, maybe just the ones on the *left* hand.

And while Ellis' book was, in our opinion, a superior first effort that should attract a wide audience, if we had left it entirely to the vagaries of the review media, I frankly believe the book would have had an okay, if short, life.

We thought it deserved better, so we began to "hype" Ellis himself -- we created a promotional effort based on his youth and talent and marched him from one press interview to another. And, as so often happens when a book really *is* superior, the publicity effort started to build upon itself, to develop its own momentum -- an article in the *Village Voice*, which led to a more extensive one in the *Los Angeles Times*, which led to more and more print reviews and articles.

Finally, we had attracted so much attention for the book that we were able to get Brett invited onto the "Today "show, virtually an unheard-of feat for a first novelist. Then, using the tape of his "Today" show appearance, we convinced MTV to interview him, despite the fact that they had *never* featured an author before.

As a result of this full-bore effort, Less Than Zero sold 80,000 hardcover copies, a very impressive number for almost *any* book, let alone a first novel. I think it even made a couple of best-seller lists for a week or two. And a great deal of its success was purely because of the publicity effort we generated.

There's probably no book in existence that wouldn't sell more behind a professionally-mounted publicity effort. Of course, when your publishing house launches hundreds of books every year, as Simon & Schuster and just about every other major house does, you simply can't create a massive, concerted publicity drive for every single one. You don't have the time or the staff. So you have to pick out the ones that you think have the best shot.

Then again, some books don't *need* a big approach. Not every book lends itself to an author's tour, for example. . .though few *authors* would agree! Some are just purely review books, in which case we have to make sure the reviewers are aware of it and going to pay attention when it comes around.

The bottom line: You do as much as you can for each particular book and put your greatest effort (and time, our nemesis) into the books with the greatest potential.

TYPICAL PUBLIC RELATIONS DEPARTMENT SETUP

There are probably far fewer professionals in the Public Relations departments of most major houses than you would think. At Simon & Schuster, for example, I have a staff of 16. . .and we handle upwards of 400 titles a year.

We are officially part of the overall marketing effort -- I report, for example, to Simon & Schuster's marketing director. The other departments we tend to work most closely with are: Advertising (we provide them will reviews and quotes they'll want to feature in their ads); Sales Promotion (who will occasionally do glitzy press kits that cost a fortune; they are *not* for every book); and Sales (to make sure books are out there -- and in the right stores -- when our publicity efforts take off).

Our department is set up in a three-tiered structure. At the top -- the first tier -- are myself (underline: director of public relations), one underline: associate director and one underline: assistant director. Two underline: senior publicists are the second tier. The remaining members of the department -- assistant publicists and assistants to the publicists make up the third and final tier.

That's the corporate setup. From a practical, everyday standpoint, the department staffers are divided into four underline: publicity teams. The entire list of books is divided up among these four teams, though not haphazardly. Rather than simply apportioning them equally, I tend to assign them according to each individual staffer's affinity. If one of my publicists were particularly good at promoting cookbooks, for example, I would assign him or her *all* the cookbooks. Since it's a subject he or she cared about, he or she might well do a better job with those books. Others might be great at fiction or politically oriented. While I feel any professional should be a capable generalist, and my staff all are, some are particularly talented, knowledgeable or interested in specific areas. Taking advantage of such individual talents is not just good management, it may well make a difference in the publicity effort and, therefore, the success of a book.

underline: Publicity assistant is the entry-level position. You'll start out typing labels and releases, fielding phone calls for your boss (one of the publicists), and preparing bills (for authors' tours). When an author is out on tour, you'll be the one calling the newspapers, magazines, TV and radio stations the day before scheduled interviews to reconfirm the author's schedule. You may spend some time researching mailing lists that we may want to use to promote a specific book. (At S & S, we have 45 - 50 major consumer lists on our computer, but we occasionally need a whole new one -- e.g., people interested in dance (for a new ballet book), gardeners (for underline: The Vegetable In Your Life), etc.

After a little while -- 6 months or so -- you'll get a chance to arrange telephone interviews, maybe even make some television or radio bookings. For all this admittedly boring, "grunt" work, you will be paid the princely sum of $11,500 or so.

After a year (absolute minimum) or two (more likely), you'd be ready for promotion to underline: assistant to the publicist (salary -- $16,000 to $18,000). Here you will spend nearly all your time arranging bookings. A talented assistant can expect to be promoted to the next level -- underline: senior publicist (or, in some houses, just underline: publicist) -- in two to three years.

At Simon & Schuster, a senior publicist is the head of each of the four teams mentioned earlier. Each publicist or senior publicist (salary -- $22,000 to $35,000) has probably five years experience (or more) and works with senior management (myself, the associate and assistant directors) to conceive the overall public relations program for each book assigned to their team. This includes everything from which media should receive initial galleys to whether a full-blown author's tour is advisable (as opposed to just local promotion). Is a press release required with each submission or just a thoughtful letter? Should direct mail be used? If so, are there any special lists that the book may require? Can the author supply us with specific ideas, lists of contacts, etc.?

Those publicists who reach senior management level may earn anywhere from $35,000 to nearly $100,000. An assistant or associate public relations director at a larger house would probably be in the $35,000 to $40,000 range. A public relations director at a smaller house might make the same or a little more. And the directors at the largest houses will probably earn a minimum of about $50,000, up to a top of very near $100,000.

THE IDEAL CANDIDATE FOR A PUBLISHING PUBLICITY CAREER

While your individual major is not too important, you must have a college degree. (I seem to see a preponderance of English majors, but that's *their* preference, not mine.) What *I* want is someone for whom books are already an important part of their lives, someone who already reads book reviews because they care about books. That's why I frequently ask candidates what books they read for their own pleasure -- it's a quick way to find out if books are *really* important to them.

Experience in a book publishing company -- summers, part-time during the school year, whatever -- is important; it's a further sign to me that you want to get into book publishing publicity, *not* just find a public relations job anywhere. I therefore highly recommend internships. It's nice if you have attended one of the better-known publishing courses -- the NYU summer course, Denver, Radcliffe, etc. -- but isn't really essential if you evidence the right other credentials and attitude.

If you've done a lot of writing -- reviews for a local newspaper or magazine, features, etc. -- it's a very definite plus. And, of course, I'd like to see your best samples. A good publicist has to be able to communicate on all levels -- written, verbal, even visual -- so *any* evidence showing these skills will help you land that first job.

What should you be *like* to succeed in public relations at a book publishing house? First, you must have a very high energy level. Actually, given the high stress levels of the profession and the hours (long hours are the *rule*, not the exception), you need *inhuman* energy. Second, an ability to cope with infinite detail; it's one thing to book an author on a number of shows, but if you don't get the boring details right -- what time, where, etc. -- you won't survive. Third, you should have a near-infinite capacity to deal with frustration. You'll have to graciously accept an awful lot of "no's," be able to face and handle the rejection, persevere, and try another way.

ENTRY-LEVEL OPPORTUNITIES
...AND MOVING TO OTHER DEPARTMENTS

I don't believe entry-level public relations jobs at publishing houses are really at a premium. Many new employees are sure they want to be in book publishing but unsure of a particular department or specialization; so we get our share of entry-level people who start in our department and use it as a "stepping stone" to other jobs at Simon & Schuster. Sometimes a manager in some other department spies a particularly promising assistant publicist and initiates the transfer himself. (This is always done in a very straightforward way. If someone from another department wanted to "hire away" one of my staffers, they would tend to speak to me first. But it *does* happen, often to everyone's benefit.)

The result is that there tends to be a fair amount of turnover at the entry-level in our department. I suspect it's similar at other houses. Which means there are frequently openings for people who *do* actually want to get into book publishing publicity!

Moving to other departments in Simon & Schuster from a first job in the Public Relations department is not particularly difficult. Once you have a toehold here, you will find out about openings in other departments far more quickly than the general public and can move along to another area if you so desire and if the right opening exists. I don't know about policy or ease-of-transfer at other houses, but I suspect that if someone is really talented but wants a different job, the house would want to keep him or her in whatever capacity possible and would attempt to affect the necessary transfer.

WHY YOU SHOULD JOIN US!

Entry-level jobs in our field, as should be obvious from our previous discussion of job responsibilities for the assistants to the publicists, are far from glamorous. And not everyone can handle the hours, the pressure, the stress, or the rejection.

And it *can* be difficult and scary. When I first started, the thought of picking up a phone and talking to a total stranger was absolutely *terrifying*. And that was a major part of my job! I used to write out my first sentence so at least I'd *start* the conversation right.

You'll make mistakes, some of them horrifying. Twenty years ago, on my first job, I booked an author on two shows simultaneously -- one taped, one live. Logistically, that was fine, but unfortunately, the author wound up appearing on two shows on competing networks in the *same time slot*. Neither the producers, the author, or my boss were particularly overjoyed.

But I still get a "rush" from my job. Every time I think I'm totally burned out and can't do it, something wonderful happens. As I was working on this article, I think I finally managed to get the show "20/20" to do a piece on Roger Vadim, whose book we're publishing. I know that kind of publicity will make a difference. And I guess I'm happy because that means *I* made a difference.

Then there are the books that get me thinking in some crazy, creative directions, like the pop-up dinosaur book we recently published. It features a *pterosaur*, a flying reptile that became extinct millions of years ago (and the family name of a similar and more well-known flyer -- the *pterodactyl*). I learned that the Smithsonian Institute constructed a computer operated, 36-foot replica of a pterosaur that actually flies.

I don't know exactly how I'm going to do it, but watch the skies above New York City -- somehow, I'm going to get that model up there! And I'm not going to explain it, just wait until people see the book in stores and let them make the connection at the checkout line.

I guess I'm not really close to burnout -- not if I can keep thinking up promotions like *that*. But as much as I enjoy the whole range of public relations functions, I wouldn't want to do *any* of it in any other field, even though I know I'd be better paid. I just love books. I really do. And that's all I want to promote.

If *you* love books and really want to effect what happens to some you care about, come join us. You'll *love* it!

* * *

Ms. Knickerbocker has been with Simon & Schuster since 1981. She was previously director of publicity and public relations at William Morrow & Co., which followed a previous 3-plus year stint at S & S as co-director of publicity (the department was much smaller then). She was also director of public relations for Mason and Lipscomb, now difunct, and Avon Paperbacks.

Ms. Knickerbocker began her career as a receptionist/proofreader for a small house, M. Evans and Co. The company had never had a public relations director, a job which Ms. Knickerbocker created for herself after two years there. She quickly developed a high-profile reputation -- two of the books she promoted while on her first job were Body Language and Open Marriage.

She graduated from Radcliffe with a B.A. in English and is a member of the Woman's Media Group and the Publishers Publicity Association; she was also on the board of the latter group. She lectures on her specialty at Stanford University every summer as part of their well-known Publishing Course.

SECTION V

Opportunities
In
Design
&
Production

CHAPTER 16

A Diversity Of Artistic Challenges

By

Zlata Paces, Vice President/Design Director
MacMillan Publishing Company

Book publishing is not the homogeneous business many of you probably think it is. Rather, it's an industry that encompasses a great diversity of products that are, for the most part, produced in book form -- Trade books, reference books, children's (juvenile) books, professional books, general books, dictionaries, college books, school books, and more. While these may all be *books*, they differ radically in terms of design requirements (not to mention editorially, marketing-wise, etc.).

If you are interested in a career in book design, this is an important distinction, because while you will need to learn certain basic skills -- those necessary just to become a competent designer -- each of these specific book categories presents its own unique problems and a diversity of design challenges. Each of these challenges may well demand a variety of sophisticated design approaches. To see why this distinction is important, let's first look at the general or basic functions any book designer must fulfill.

THE FUNCTIONS OF A BOOK DESIGNER

The overriding concern of any book designer is an attempt to translate the overall (sometimes ephemeral) "concept" of a manuscript into a living, breathing, physical book. In order to achieve this objective, the book designer must responsibly carry out five more specific functions:

1. Decide on the size of the book (with the Production department).

2. Develop the overall look or style of the book.

3. Develop the typographic approach to the book.

4. If the book requires, choose illustrative materials -- photographs, illustrations, tables, technical drawings, maps, etc.

5. Technically prepare the book for release to the Production department.

While these functions are, in a general sense, endemic to the design of any book, certain aspects of the overall design will tend to be emphasized or de-emphasized according to the specific book category. A brief look at some of the major categories should help to explain the disparate tasks a designer may have to undertake on books within each:

Trade books (fiction and non-fiction):

Emphasis is on cover design -- trade book covers need to make an impact so the book, while on display among many other titles, will "jump off the shelf."

Additional emphasis on good type design, readable typeface, well-proportioned type area, pleasing unit or chapter handling.

Reference books

Sections within book must be well-defined to be easily recognizable; organization of material very important.

Dictionaries

Excellent layout and an interesting handling of spot art must be utilized to enhance the usually monotonous type requirements. (A good example of successful design -- the Random House Dictionary.)

College books

Like reference books, organization is very important. Type must be easy to read and categorize specific sections of the book.

Elhi (elementary/high school books)

Complicated by the variety of products -- pupils' books, workbooks, teachers' guides, etc., all with different objectives, all demanding varied design skills and ideas.

In general, layout is important -- each book must be understandable and easy to follow for both students and teachers. Type legibility is a high priority. Depending on the specific subject, the designer may have to handle a great amount of visual materials on each page.

Children's/juvenile

While a specific technical approach may apply, the overall concept of the book -- and the handling of the elements that will achieve it -- is usually a cooperative effort between the designer, illustrator, author and editor.

THE SETUP OF A TYPICAL ART DEPARTMENT

The Art department is a service department within any publishing operation, which means it must work together in close cooperation with both editorial and production to visually interpret and practically achieve the editorial concept of each book.

While titles will tend to vary from publisher to publisher, a typical Art department setup would include an <u>art director</u> on top, a small number of <u>senior designers</u> and many more <u>designers</u> (and, probably, some <u>"board" people</u> to handle paste-ups, mechanicals, etc.).

The art director is the department head, responsible for the total visual output of the Art department, as well as its budget, staff, and, perhaps most important, deadlines. Compensation may range from $30,000 to $55,000 (or more).

A senior designer will be responsible for all of the design functions necessary to produce whatever specific books have been assigned to him or her. Salary would range from $17,000 to perhaps $33,000.

These two positions are those to which you should aspire -- they are the professionals who have learned the necessary design and management skills necessary to supervise a number of ongoing projects and the staff who help produce them. (In some large houses, there may be some additional titles at this level of responsibility. The <u>associate director of design</u> (salary: $28,000 to $43,000) would work immediately under the art director. One or more <u>design managers</u> (salary $25,000 to $40,000) would supervise a number of senior designers and designers.

In many houses, the entry-level job is called just <u>designer</u>, though once again, titles will vary quite a bit. In any case, this position requires no experience, but does require a good layout sense and a basic knowledge and understanding of design. Compensation would range from $14,000 to $22,000.

If you are hired by a publisher, with whatever title that entry-level position carries, you will probably start out doing mechanicals. If you are especially capable, you might be given some simple paging job and/or some uncomplicated type-specing (specifying the typeface, sizing, etc.) jobs.

As we've already seen, a designer's specific functions may vary quite radically from book to book, depending upon the type of book he or she is working on. But forgetting those nuances for now, each book must go through a similar routine:

First, the manuscript should be read by the designer so he or she begins to understand the intent of the book. Discussion follows between the art director (with or without the designer) and the Editorial and Production departments to clarify and codify their coordinated visual approach to the book.

Second, the Art department develops the art budget for the book.

Third, the Art department (having received budget approval) develops a design approach and prepares sample pages to illustrate the overall design, type selection, relative positioning of heads, subheads, captions, etc.

Fourth, when this approach has been approved (possibly after more discussion and some revisions), the actual "book work" begins: The manuscript is marked up and sent to be typeset. When type is received the galleys are broken into pages (depending on the complexity of the book, this may be done directly at the typesetter's or in-house); dummies of the book are prepared, then adjusted after further input from editorial; and, finally, mechanicals are prepared. The book is ready to be released to the Production department.

There may also be a group within the Art department responsible for the photo/art research function. This group will be headed by a research supervisor (salary: $22,000 to $35,000); the entry-level position in this area is research assistant (salary: $14,500 to $27,000). Getting into this area would require a good eye and an intellectual knowledge of a variety of subjects, though a college degree is not necessary. A photographic background would be most helpful -- as beginning duties would entail searching for photos -- but a sense and knowledge of history is probably of paramount importance.

HOW TO BREAK INTO A PUBLISHER'S ART DEPARTMENT

A candidate looking for an entry-level design job should have a carefully-prepared, professional-quality portfolio, be self-assured (but not overly aggressive), have a pleasant personality that projects a sense of self-worth, and an interest in both the creative and practical aspects of a design career. If you are solely interested in working "on the board," an art school degree is sufficient. Otherwise, I recommend college.

Some publishing companies hire summer interns in their art departments. I suggest you utilize the internship information in the Job Opportunities Databank in the back of this Career Directory to search them out. Internships are scarce, but they offer an excellent chance to "get a feel" for the kind of everyday work you'll be asked to do in an entry-level design job.

The importance of the portfolio

Wherever you apply and whatever you eventually want to do in the field of design, a portfolio is an overriding necessity -- many jobs will be won or lost strictly on the basis of its professionalism (or the lack thereof). It should be neatly organized and contain the following elements:

1. A series of neatly-prepared finished layouts.

2. A series of rough layouts ("thinking" layouts, rough comps, maybe some tighter comps) for at least two or three of the finished layouts included -- this will show the art director the progress from concept to execution.

3. Xeroxes of some finished layouts with neatly marked type specifications.

4. A specification (type-spec) sheet.

5. Mechanicals -- some simple, one-color; some with overlays, color and break indication. These should be as finished and professional-looking as possible.

6. The dummy of a small book with art and type areas indicated. If you are interested in children's books, you should include a dummy of an entire book.

A book designer is very involved with a great amount of type; therefore, an in-depth knowledge of type is definitely an asset when applying for a position in book design.

Where you're headed

The layout, type and good design skills you will learn at your first job should enable you to function in any other field of design. It is up to you to recognize your talent and decide, after that initial year or two on the job, if there are other areas of design you may wish to pursue.

Moving (upward, hopefully!) to another publisher after a year or two (even three) at your first job is a good idea (unless you're very happy there and are being given increasing responsibilities). Such a move will normally allow you to take the skills you've learned and apply them in a different arena, perhaps to learn additional design methods or styles, or to work on a variety of different books.

Progress from an entry-level position to senior designer or even art director may take anywhere from three to seven years (or more). To become a senior designer you must, of course, have mastered all the basic design skills. But you also must be able to handle a number of projects simultaneously, possess the supervisory skills necessary to oversee junior-level designers, and the diplomatic skills to work effectively and efficiently with the Production and Editorial departments.

To become an art director -- the top of the ladder -- you must be capable of working under extreme and sometimes constant pressure, taking responsibility for your staff's work, controlling budgets, and estimating the financial aspects involved with each book or program, and, perhaps most important of all, delivering the products on time. You will need to acquire a complete working knowledge of production, printing processes, color judgment and estimating.

Talent will out

Make no mistake -- no matter what school you attend, how many and varied your pre-interview preparations, how much you spend on your portfolio case, _talent_ is really the prerequisite to any design job. Skills can be learned; talent must already exist. It's a hard, cold fact, but true.

But talent alone does not guarantee success, although talent combined with hard work and the determination to succeed _no matter what_ can overcome any seemingly-insurmountable obstacle. I started in this business with a great handicap -- I barely spoke English. It didn't stop me.

My first job was with a magazine. I was assigned to work on the "back of the book" layout, probably the least exciting or challenging design job of all. But I didn't see it that way -- to me, each new task was an invaluable learning experience. So I was very diligent and enthusiastically "attacked" every job assigned to me, no matter how basic.

In my hours away from work, I carefully studied all the leading magazines, especially their type design. I took issues of _Esquire, Ladies' Home Journal_, and many others and prepared my own type specifications for each of their feature articles. Why did I do all this? Just to improve my knowledge of type and to become more aware of type design.

As my current title and responsibilities attest, this hard work paid off. So if you have the talent, remember: It may be a prerequisite, but it will only get you in the door. What other "rooms" you're able to visit, how long your "tour" takes, and what "floor" you eventually wind up on is really up to your ambition and your own hard work. Take the chance -- it's worth it!

* * *

In her current position, Ms. Paces is responsible for creating over 200 books a year, including all phases of design -- covers, text, etc. -- and typography specification and purchasing. She received her B.A. from Hunter College. During her career, she has designed hundreds of magazines, promotion pieces and books, projects as diverse as the Girl Scout's Handbook and A History Of The American Nation.

She has been a judge in numerous Art Directors Club competitions and is a recipient of various awards from the Society of Illustrators, the Art Directors Club and other organizations. She currently teaches a course in book design at the Parsons School of Design.

CHAPTER 17

Production: We Make Things Happen!

By

Lyman O. Louis, VP-Manufacturing & Purchasing
CBS Educational & Professional Publishing
A Division of CBS Inc.

Judging by the backgrounds of those people currently in production functions in publishing, advertising or printing, most attribute their positions to serendipity. This is certainly true in the book publishing area. Whether they're involved in producing books, records, catalogs, transparencies, disk programs, or other educational material -- or all of the above! -- the backgrounds of the production managers I've known or worked with seem to be as varied as the areas of the country from which they come.

But common to all production managers is strong logistical ability, good mathematical skills, pride in developing tangible products, and an ability to grasp technical details. Communication skills -- written and verbal -- are essential.

EDUCATIONAL REQUIREMENTS AND TRAINING OPPORTUNITIES

The educational backgrounds vary from specific degrees in printing management, operations analysis, production or industrial management to the more design-oriented majors. But liberal arts students with degrees in social sciences may be found working next to biology majors or those technically-trained pros mentioned above. Despite the variance, there is one key to success -- a college degree.

Those graduates with degrees not specific to the production area frequently applied for or actually started out in other positions and later gravitated to production management to fulfill a desire to create -- or disseminate on a large scale -- art, ideas or products.

In many houses, preliminary, on-the-job training exists for students just out of college who impressed the interviewer with their communication skills, were involved in coursework that required a certain "comfort-level" with statistics and enjoyed keeping track of a lot of pieces going in different directions. . .simultaneously.

FUNCTIONS OF A PRODUCTION MANAGER

The specific functions which a production manager might perform would include the following: At an initial meeting, editors, marketing managers or others might present the seed of an idea for a new book, which will not become a reality for over a year; a college title for which several chapters already exist; or a trade book which is approaching reality, but with which production is not yet involved. At this stage, the production manager needs to determine costs and schedules. Where specifications (the essential ingredients of costs and schedules) do not exist. the production manager makes assumptions based on experience and further discussions with editors and marketing managers. Suppliers are called in to bid on the various facets of the job, from composition, film preparation, and separations, to printing, paper manufacturing, and binding.

Once the budgets have been approved, the final prices and vendors determined, and the specifications firmly established, the purchase orders are written. Then the production manager follows up to make sure all the many tasks and pieces are performed and received on time. Finally, the first copy of the book is delivered. And if the editors, designers and authors are pleased with the final result, the production manager holds a copy and enjoys that rare moment of satisfaction in a job well done.

The production function is complicated in that more than one job is going through at the same time. A given production manager might be responsible for from 20 to 50 jobs per year. But the Manufacturing department at my company, for example, which is responsible for the printing, paper, and binding for new books and reprints, handles 8,000 book titles per year. . .with only *four* operators. Even with all the pressure such high volume automatically brings to bear, the feeling of accomplishment is the same when a major title comes through, requiring special care or effort to bring it in on time.

My own job is proof enough that production is complicated and that a "typical" day really doesn't exist. I often meet with my staff first thing in the morning to check on particular problems of interest to all. This might be followed by an interview of a potential new employee or a review of the progress on a new computerized estimating system. Before lunch I might prepare a productivity report for senior management or check on a couple of jobs that had presented some unique challenges or problems the day before.

After lunch a vendor might present a new proposal for a piece of equipment his company may be considering and we would discuss its applicability to our future requirements. This might be followed by a meeting with a senior manager of the School Division regarding some problems which have surfaced in a new math program they are developing or an editor in the College Division about a new psychology text. And so the day goes. Often I travel to visit various suppliers or monitor a job on press.

Our Manufacturing department currently employs some 30 people involved in purchasing paper, printing, binding, media products (such as floppy disks or spirit masters), packaging, promotional materials (including catalogs and the like), and office equipment (from typewriters and desks to software and terminals.

124

THERE ARE SUBSTANTIAL ENTRY-LEVEL OPPORTUNITIES

While the production function in a printing or publishing facility is not a *conspicuous* employment opportunity, it is fulfilling and rewarding. . .and there *are* substantial opportunities for people with the right skills.

Entry-level positions are typically planning assistant, secretary, manufacturing assistant or estimating trainee. Depending on the level at which you start and your ability, promotions should occur in six months, two years and five years. After five years, most entry-level people have become full journeymen production managers; many are unit managers. After eight years, it would not be unusual to be a departmental manager and part of the management team.

The particular assignments for each of these job titles will vary depending on the needs of a department and your own particular ability. However, you might initially be involved in preparing purchase orders, setting up meetings with vendors, making travel arrangements, logging material in and out, and/or beginning to request bid proposals and analyze bids, as well as controlling various components of a simple job as they move through the system.

Starting salaries vary by size of company and geography. Depending on experience and major, a beginning salary might be from $14,000 up to $18,000 in the New York market. Three to five years out, $25,000 might be a reasonable objective, with departmental management earning $40,000 and up. Clearly this varies according to situation, ability, opportunity, etc., but these salaries are probably fair estimates for larger companies in the New York market. These companies also tend to have better benefit programs, including health programs, employee investment funds, company stores, educational assistance packages, and many other programs which improve the salary considerations.

Certainly at our company -- and many other houses -- there is adequate exposure and renumeration for night school or seminar courses to fill in technical gaps that might exist in an otherwise suitable entry-level candidate's knowledge. Again, a college degree is preferred for virtually every position in order to afford the individual a reasonable chance for promotion and career advancement. (While exceptions may sometimes be made, the climb up the career Ladder will definitely be more difficult for non-degreed individuals.)

If all of this sounds like the kind of career you've been looking for, come join us! Production is an exciting and fulfilling occupation if you have energy, enthusiasm and the strong desire to "make things happen."

* * *

In Mr. Louis' current position, he is responsible for the manufacture of some 3,000 book titles a year. A past president of the Seattle Club of Printing House Craftsmen, he was formerly an executive with the North Pacific Bank Note Company in Seattle. He is a member of the American Institute of Graphic Arts, and a member and former chairman of the Publishers Committee of the Advisory Commission on Text Book Specifications.

Mr. Louis holds a B.A. in general business from the University of Washington and a B.S. in printing management from Carnegie-Mellon. He has taught at the Burnley School of Professional Arts and the Association of the Graphic Arts.

Listed in <u>Who'sWho</u>, he is also chairman of the board of the Greater Westchester Youth Orchestra Association and a partner in Sugarbush Farms, which raises, trains, and leases show horses.

SECTION VI

The
Job
Search
Process

CHAPTER 18

Getting Started: Self-Evaluation And Career Objectives

Getting a job may be a one-step, couple of weeks, or months-long operation.

Starting, nurturing and developing a career (or even a series of careers) is a lifelong process.

What we'll be talking about in the four chapters that together form our Job Search Process are those basic steps to take, assumptions to make, things to think about if you want a job -- especially a first job in book publishing. But when these steps -- this process -- are applied and expanded over a lifetime, most if not all of them are the same procedures, carried out over and over again, that are necessary to develop a successful, lifelong, professional career.

This is a most important point. Because while actually getting a job may be the *last* step in your initial job search, it is just the *first* step in the search process that will become your career.

What does all this have to do with putting together a resume, writing a cover letter, heading off for interviews, and the other "traditional" steps necessary to get a job? Whether your college graduation is just around the corner or a far-distant memory, you will continuously need to focus, evaluate and re-evaluate your response to the ever-changing challenge of your future: Just what do you want to do with the rest of your life? (If your school days are already a distant memory, but you're considering a complete career change after years in the workforce, you face the same set of problems, questions and decisions. Whether you like it or not, you're all looking for that "entry-level opportunity.")

With the important dual concepts of "career" (not job) and "process" (not "four steps to a better resume") established, let's get back to basics -- just how *do* you go about getting that entry-level opportunity?

And remember, no matter what we or any other "experts" out there say or advise, it's your life and your career. Every decision, every mistake, every "good move" are yours to make. . .or avoid.

You're already one or two steps ahead of the competition -- you're sure (pretty sure?) you want to pursue a career in book publishing. By heeding the advice of the many professionals who have written chapters for this Career Directory -- and utilizing the extensive industry and publisher information we've included -- you're well on your way to fulfilling that dream. But there are some key decisions and time-consuming preparations to make if you want to transform that hopeful dream into a real, live publishing job.

Right now, the entire job market is open to you. Confused and intimidated? You have every right to be. But you *can* take control. There is no reason to end up in a dead end job, settle for anything less than you really want, or miss out on a job for which you're perfectly qualified -- if you take immediate charge of your own job search. Treat it like a military campaign. That means detailed research and analysis, good organization, dedication and, probably most important of all, perseverance.

The actual process of finding the right publishing house, the right career path, and, most importantly, the right first job, begins long before you start mailing out resumes to potential employers. The choices and decisions you make now are not irrevocable, but this first job will have a definite impact on the career options you leave yourself. To help you make some of the right decisions and choices along the way (and avoid some of the most notable traps and pitfalls), the following chapters will lead you through a series of organized steps. If the entire job search process we are recommending here is properly executed, it will undoubtedly help you land exactly the job you want.

If you're currently in high school and hope, after college, to land a job in a publishing house, then attending the right college, choosing the right major, and getting the summer work experience many publishers look for are all important steps. Read the section of this Career Directory that covers your job specialty -- many of the contributors have recommended colleges or vocational schools they favor.

If you're hoping to jump right into the book publishing industry without a college degree or other professional training, our best and only advice is -- don't do it. As you'll soon see in the detailed information included in the Job Opportunities Databank in section VII of this Career Directory, there are not *that* many job openings for students without a college degree. Those that do exist are generally clerical and will only rarely lead to promising careers.

THE CONCEPT OF A JOB SEARCH PROCESS

These are the key steps in the detailed job search process we will cover in this and the following three chapters:

1. *Evaluating yourself*: Know thyself. What skills and abilities can you offer a prospective employer? What do you enjoy doing? What are your strengths and weaknesses? What do you *want* to do?

2. *Establishing your career objectives*: Where do you want to be next year, three years, five years from now? What do you ultimately want to accomplish in your career and your life?

3. *Creating a publisher target list:* How to prepare a "Hit List" of potential employers -- researching them, matching their needs with your skills, and starting your job search assault. Preparing publisher information sheets and evaluating your chances.

4. *Networking for success:* Learning how to utilize every contact, every friend, every relative, and anyone else you can think of to break down the barriers facing any would-be publishing professional. How to organize your home office to keep track of your communications and stay on top of your job campaign.

5. *Preparing your resume:* How to encapsulize years of school and little actual work experience into a professional, selling resume. Learning when and how to use it.

6. *Preparing cover letters:* The many ordinary and the all-too-few extraordinary cover letters, the kind that land interviews and jobs.

7. *Interviewing:* How to make the interview process work for you -- from the first "hello" to the first day on the job.

8. *Fielding the offers:* Evaluating all the companies that are suddenly offering to hire you. Accepting and declining offers.

9. *School year and summer internships:* Applying the lessons you have learned to the even tougher task of finding an internship (especially a paying one) in a publishing house.

We won't try to kid you -- it *is* a lot of work. To do it right, you have to get started early, probably quite a bit earlier than you'd planned. Frankly, we recommend beginning this process one full year prior to the day you plan to start work. (Doing it right takes a lot of months, so although you may be able to do it more quickly, if doing so requires a lot of corner-cutting, why not allow yourself the time to do it completely and do it right? You can't lose, but you could win big -- exactly the job you want.)

So if you're in college, the end of your junior year is the right time to begin your research and preparations. That should give you enough time during summer vacation to set up your files and begin your library research.

Whether you're in college or graduate school, one item may need to be planned even earlier -- allowing enough free time in your schedule of classes for interview preparations and appointments. Waiting until your senior year to "make some time" is already too late. Searching for a full-time job is itself a full-time job! Though you're naturally restricted by your schedule, it's not difficult to plan ahead and prepare for your upcoming job search. Try to leave at least a couple of free mornings or afternoons a week. A day or even two without classes is even better.

Otherwise, you'll find yourself, crazed and distracted, trying to finish a one-hour interview in the ten-minute period between your 18th Century Literature lecture and your Creative Writing seminar. Not the best way to make a first impression and certainly not the way you want to approach an important meeting.

Ultimately, this process will lead to success, clinching the job you want and launching a successful and fulfilling career. While you can certainly get a job without going through the time-consuming process we're advocating (or by merely trying out the bits-and-pieces you think you need), the odds of it being the right job -- the best one for you -- would not induce *me* to bet the family farm.

Now, let's go through each of the steps of our job search process in detail.

THE SELF-EVALUATION PROCESS

Plato had it right: "Know thyself." Learning about who you are, what you want to be, what you *can* be, are critical first steps in the job search process and, unfortunately, the ones most often ignored by job seekers everywhere, especially students eager to leave the ivy behind and plunge into the "real world." But avoiding this crucial self-evaluation can hinder your progress and even damage some decent prospects.

Why? Because in order to land a job with a house at which you'll actually be happy, you need to be able to identify those publishers and/or job descriptions that best match your own skills, likes and strengths. The more you know about yourself, the more you'll bring to this process and the more accurate the "match-ups." You'll be able to structure your presentation (resume, cover letter, interviews) to stress your most marketable skills and talents (and, dare we say it, conveniently avoid your weaknesses?). Later, you'll be able to evaluate potential employers and job offers on the basis of your own needs and desires. This spells the difference between waking up in the morning ready to enthusiastically tackle a new day of challenges and shutting off the alarm in the hopes the day (and your job) will just disappear.

Identifying what motivates you

Let's start the evaluation process by attempting to identify, in the most general terms, what really motivates you. According to one theory, there are five primary motivations, one of which is the primary force driving each individual:

1. *Money*. The "Almighty Dollar" is "God;" everything else pales by comparison.

2. *Power*. While power-driven individuals can often become quite wealthy (if they have the talents to go with the drive), making money is really an afterthought. High-ranking government officials could command high multiples of their current salaries in private industry. Business tycoons worth billions still work 16-hour days. For them, power is its own reward.

3. *Fulfillment*. Many creative types -- future art directors and editors -- are driven by this need for creative accomplishment. Add future United Way

fund raisers and anyone whose credo is "feeling good about what they're doing."

4. *Affiliation*. Individuals who don't care where they work, how much they make, or how many bosses they have -- just as long as they like their work, the company environment, and, most important, the people they work with.

5. *Fame*. While it might eventually lead to fortune (and even to power), fame is its own reward for those who seek it. They shouldn't expect to lead a traditional, nine-to-five existence.

It's quite possible for two or even three of these factors to seem to be equally strong motivators -- we've met a few power-hungry, money grubbers who say they like people. But, if you examine yourself closely, we think you'll find that one and only one of these factors is the key to your personality.

What does it all mean? If you've truthfully and accurately assessed your personality -- your "style" -- you are already in a better position to choose the proper career path, and evaluate how well you will "fit in" at a particular house After all, if you're primarily Money-driven, you better reconsider accepting a job (or, worse yet, planning for a career) that won't. sooner or later (sooner, better) lead to the Big Bucks. If you're Power-driven, be sure that there is a clear-cut path to the top of the mountain. After all, that *is* where you intend to be in the not-too-distant future, isn't it? Etcetera.

Creating your self-evaluation form

If you found it difficult to characterize yourself in such general terms, let's try a more specific process. After you've completed this detailed evaluation, you should have no trouble identifying which of the five factors is your primary motivator.

Take a sheet of lined notebook paper. Set up eight columns across the top -- Strengths, Weaknesses, Skills, Hobbies, Courses, Experience, Likes, Dislikes.

Now, fill in each of these columns according to these guidelines:

Strengths: Describe personality traits you consider your strengths (and try to look at them as an employer would) -- e.g., persistence, organization, ambition, intelligence, logic, assertiveness, aggression, leadership, etc.

Weaknesses: The traits you consider glaring weaknesses -- e.g., impatience, conceit, etc. (And remember: Look at these as a potential employer would.. Don't assume that the personal traits you consider weaknesses will necessarily be considered negatives in the business world. You may be "easily bored," a trait that led to lousy grades early on because teachers couldn't keep you interested in the subjects they were teaching. Well, many entrepreneurs need ever-changing challenges. Strength or weakness?]

Skills: Any skill you have, whether you think it's marketable or not. Everything from basic business skills -- like typing, word processing and stenography -- to computer, accounting or teaching experience and foreign language literacy. Don't forget possibly obscure but marketable skills like "good telephone voice."

Hobbies: The things you enjoy doing that, more than likely, have no overt connection to career objectives. These should be distinct from the skills listed above, and may include activities such as reading, games, travel, sports and the like. While these may not be marketable in any general sense, they may well be useful in specific circumstances (If you love travel, you may be perfect for that editorial spot at the publishing house that specializes in producing travel books, atlases, etc. And your "hobbies" may just get it for you!)

Courses: All the general subject areas (history, literature, etc.) and/or specific courses you've taken which may be marketable (computer, business, marketing, economics, etc.), you really enjoyed, or both.

Experience: Just the specific functions you performed at any part-time (school year) or full-time (summer) jobs. Entries may include "General Office" (typing, filing, answering phones, etc.), "Sales," "Writing," "Research," etc.

Likes: List all your "likes," those important considerations that you haven't listed anywhere else yet. These might include the types of people you like to be with, the kind of environment you prefer (city, country, large places, small places, quiet, loud, fast-paced, slow-paced) and anything else which hasn't shown up somewhere on this form. However, try not to include entries which refer to specific jobs or companies. We'll list those on another form.

Dislikes: All the people, places and things you can easily live without.

Now assess the "marketability" of each item you've listed. (In other words, are some of your likes, skills or courses easier to match to a publishing job description, or do they have little to do with a specific job or publisher?) Mark highly marketable skills with an "H." Use "M" to characterize those skills which may be marketable in a particular set of circumstances, "L" for those with minimal potential application to any job. Some obvious examples: Typing, word processing and stenography are always marketable, so you'd mark them with an "H". Teaching, computer and accounting skills would also qualify as highly marketable. Similarly, if you listed high energy or perseverance as a strength, any advertising sales manager will find it a highly desirable trait. Speaking French, however, gets an "M." While not marketable in all job situations, it might well be a requirement for certain industries (e.g., importing and exporting) or jobs (working on the English translations of Proust and liaisoning with the French publisher's staff)).

Referring back to the same list, decide if you'd enjoy using your marketable skills or talents as part of your everyday job -- "Y" for yes, "N" for no. You may type 80 words a minute but truly despise typing (or worry that stressing it too much will land you on the permanent clerical staff). If so, mark typing with an "N." (Keep one thing in mind -- just because you dislike typing shouldn't mean you absolutely won't accept a job that requires it. Most do.)

Now, go over the entire form carefully. Look for inconsistencies. For example, if you did not list "persuasive" as one of your strengths, but were a smashing success during that summer sales job, revise your list of strengths accordingly. After you are satisfied that the form is as accurate as you can make it -- and gotten over the shock of some of your honest answers -- pass it along to a close friend or two. Ask *them* to check it for accuracy -- you'll not only uncover areas you may have fudged a bit, but learn a great deal about what the rest of the world thinks of you. After they've completed their assessment of the person you've committed to paper, put the form aside for the time being.

ESTABLISHING YOUR CAREER OBJECTIVE(S)

For better or worse, you now know something more of who and what you are. But we've yet to establish and evaluate another important area -- your overall needs, desires and goals. Where are you going? What do you want to accomplish? Go back to the definition of the Five Motivating Factors. Do you know which one you are yet? If so, that will help define some of the directions you will be charting in this next step. Many of these goals will have already been highlighted during your self-evaluation or grow naturally out of that process.

You'll use these initial entries to prepare your Five year Game Plan, a flexible but straightforward list of the things you want to do and accomplish, both personally and professionally, during that period.

If you're getting ready to graduate from college or graduate school, the next five years are the most critical period of your whole career. You need to make the initial transition from college to the workplace, establish yourself in a new and completely unfamiliar company environment, and begin to build the professional credentials necessary to achieve your career goals.

If that strikes you as a pretty tall order, well, it *is*. Unless you've narrowly prepared yourself for a specific profession, you're probably most *ill*-prepared for any real job. Instead, you've (hopefully) learned some basic principles -- research and analytical skills that are necessary for success at almost any level -- and, more or less, how to think. But that's all. You probably don't have the faintest clue about how the book publishing business (let alone a specific house or department) functions or any of the specific information necessary to perform even the lowliest task.

It's tough to face, but face it you must: No matter what your college, major or degree, all you represent right now is potential. How you package that potential and what you eventually make of it is completely up to you. And it's an unfortunate fact that many houses will take a professional with barely a year or two experience over *any* newcomer, no

135

matter how promising. Smaller publishers, especially, can rarely afford to hire someone who can't begin contributing immediately.

So you have to be prepared to take your comparatively modest skills and experience and package them in a way that will get you interviewed and hired. Quite a challenge.

Preparing your Five Year Game Plan

To help clarify your personal and career goals, let's create your Five year Game Plan. On a new sheet of paper, make three vertical columns and title them "1 year," "3 years" and "5 years." Under each heading, list your personal goals within that period. Be as general or specific as you'd like, although since you're just starting out, you may not know enough to be very specific. Don't worry. As you actually get out there and start your career, you'll quickly learn what you like, what you don't like and, hopefully, will keep and revise this form to reflect your growing list of objectives.

These objectives can be personal (get married, have your first child): material (house, car, plane, boat), general career-related (publish your first book, edit your first best-seller), very specifically job-related (earn a vice presidency, get that private office), or anything else that's important to you.

Attach this Game Plan to the Self-Evaluation Form. Together, they represent a clear picture of who you are now, who you want to be, and the interim steps you expect to take to achieve that transformation.

This is, of course, a highly simplified (and may well be a *too*-quick-and-easy) explanation of a most difficult step in any self-evaluation process. And there are a number of different ways to approach such a task. If you find yourself confused or unable to list such goals, you might want to check a few books in your local library that have more time to spend on the topic of "goal-oriented planning." Three that may help: 1) The ubiquitous What Color is Your Parachute, still the Bible of the job search field (though if you find it absurdly complicated, you're not alone): 2) After College: The Business of Getting Jobs by Jack Falvey, a far more readable (though somewhat controversial) overview of the job search process; and 3) (by the same author) What's Next? Career Strategies After 35, for you post-35ers our there.

None of these self-descriptive exercises are static, one-time-only events. Continue to update both forms as you proceed on your job hunt. This will enable you to consistently match industries, publishers, job descriptions, and even actual job offers to the "you" on that piece of paper. Keep track of your career progress as you begin that search, enter the market, and, finally, begin your career. Then see how closely your real progress matches the steps you charted. (You may well consider keeping something like a "goal chart" throughout your life -- it's one way to keep some control over a life and/or career that may soon seem anything but planned!)

As you delve more deeply into the career options available to you in this industry, you may well want to add more "functional" and "job specific" objectives to these forms.

YES, BUT IS BOOK PUBLISHING RIGHT FOR *YOU*?

Presuming you now have a much better idea of yourself and where you'd like to be -- job-, career- and life-wise in the forseeable future -- let's make sure some of your basic assumptions are right. We presume you purchased this Career Directory because you're considering a career in book publishing. Are you sure? Do you know enough about the industry to decide whether it's right for you? Probably not. Do you know enough about the two other major areas of publishing -- magazines and newspapers -- let alone the possibilities of getting involved in one of the peripheral areas, such as working with a literary agent? Doubtful. So start your research *now* -- learn as much about the magazine business as you now know about yourself.

Start with the Introduction and Section I. These six articles will give you an excellent overview of the book business, some very specialized (and growing) areas of the industry, and some things to consider about yourself and publishing. This will give you a relatively simplified, though very necessary, understanding of just what people who work in book publishing actually do.

Other sources you should consider consulting to learn more about this business are listed in the various Appendices.

In Appendix A, we've listed all the trade organizations associated with the book publishing industry. While educational information available from these associations is often limited (and, for the most part, already a part of this Career Directory), you should certainly consider writing each of the pertinent associations, letting them know you're interested in a career in publishing, and would appreciate whatever help and advice they're willing to impart. You'll find many sponsor seminars and conferences throughout the country, some of which you may be able to attend.

In Appendix B, we've listed the trade magazines dedicated to the highly specific interests of the book publishing and book selling communities. These magazines are generally not available at newsstands (unless you live in or near New York City), but you may be able to obtain back issues at your local library (most major libraries have extensive collections of such journals) or by writing to the magazines' circulation/subscription departments.

You may also try writing to the publishers and/or editors of these business publications. State in your cover letter what area of the business you're considering and ask them for whatever help and advice they can offer. But be specific. These are busy professionals and they do not have the time or the inclination to simply "tell me everything you can about book publishing."

If you can afford it now, we strongly suggest subscribing to *Publishers Weekly*, the major trade magazine for the book business -- plus whichever of the other magazines are applicable to the specialty you're considering. If you can't subscribe to all of them, make it a point to regularly read the copies that arrive at your local public or college library.

These publications may well provide the most imaginative and far-reaching information for your job search. Even a quick perusal of an issue or two will give you an excellent "feel" for the industry. After reading only a few articles, you'll already get a handle on what's happening in the field and some of publishing's peculiar and particular jargon. Later, more detailed study will aid you in your search for a specific job.

Authors of the articles themselves may well turn out to be important resources. If an article is directly related to your chosen specialty, why not call the author and ask some questions? You'd be amazed how willing many of these professionals will be to talk to you and answer your questions. They may even tell you about job openings at their companies! (But *do* use common sense -- authors will not *always* respond graciously to your invitation to "chat about the business." And don't be *too* aggressive here.)

Whether you've interned at a publishing house, majored in English, and/or written/edited every college newspaper and magazine in existence, you may still wish to attend one of the book publishing institutes at some of the major colleges across the U.S. We have listed the most well-known and well-respected of these in Appendix C. (Someone already in the industry who wants to learn more so they can move up or to another area of specialization, would probably find these courses extremely helpful, too.)

In other words, make sure you learn what really makes this business tick. Take some notes as you continue your research. What is the book business really like? Where are the geographical centers? What's the mix between large and small publishers,? What kind of house (or books or authors) do you think you'd like to work with? What are the pay scales like? Are there specific jobs that seem to pay a lot more to start or offer superior "down-the-line" potential? Is it a growth industry? Where's it heading? What areas of opportunities do the top people expect to see happening in the next decade? What specialties seem likely to be in demand? Finally, how well do you, as you defined yourself during your self-evaluation, really mesh with the industry? Does it sound like the kind of business you want to be involved in? Or does long-range career success require skills you don't have and/or don't particularly care to acquire?

Is the industry growing and changing in ways that interest you? Is there room for advancement and creativity in the position you believe you are most suited for? Can you work in publishing for a few years and achieve the professional stature necessary to start your own business? (Do you eventually *want* your own business?)

How much money do you want to earn your first year? Three years from now? Are your expectations realistic? Keep in mind, someone with little or no experience, right out of high school or college, shouldn't plan to earn $30,000 their first year. Given the realities of the business, there are a lot of professionals wishing they made that kind of salary after *five* years! If "Big Bucks" are your objective, the book publishing industry might not be for you.

You'll find such research to be a double-edged sword. In addition to helping you get a handle on whether the book business is really right for you, you'll slowly learn enough about particular specialties, publishers, the industry, etc., to actually sound like you know what you're talking about when you hit the pavement looking for your first job. And nothing is better than sounding like a pro. . .except being one.

Don't get us wrong. We're not trying to talk you out of a career in book publishing! But we do recommend studying the business until you can satisfactorily answer these questions. Only then will you know enough about the publishing industry to be sure it's where you want to be.

BOOKS ARE IT. NOW WHAT?

After all this research, we're going to assume you've reached that final decision -- you really *do* want a career in book publishing. It is with this vague certainty that all too many of you will race off, hunting for any publisher willing to give you a job. You'll manage to get interviews at a couple of houses and, smiling brightly, tell everyone you meet, "I want a career in publishing." The interviewers, unfortunately, will all ask the same awkward question -- "What *exactly* do you want to do at our house?" -- and that will be the end of that.

Once again, someone's been trying to make this search process easy and shorten it considerably. It doesn't work that way. It is simply not enough to narrow your job search to a specific industry. And so far, that's all you've done. You must now establish a specific career objective -- the job you want to start, the career you want to pursue. Just knowing that you "want to get into book publishing" doesn't mean anything to anybody. If that's all you can tell an interviewer, it demonstrates a lack of research into the industry itself and your failure to prepare any semblance of a five year plan. Do you want to start as an editorial assistant, hoping to work your way up the ladder to editor-in-chief, or catch on as a sales rep, with VP-sales your eventual goal? The two entry-level positions are completely different. They require different skills and educational backgrounds. And, of course, lead in completely different directions.

Interviewers will *not* welcome you with open arms if you're still vague about your career goals. If you've managed to get an "informative interview" with an executive whose company currently has no job openings, what is he supposed to do with your resume after you leave? Who should he send it to for future consideration? Since *you* don't seem to know exactly what you want to do, how's *he* going to figure it out? Worse, he'll probably resent your asking him to function as your personal career counselor.

The executives you're preparing to see will not be offering jobs in "publishing." They'll be looking for an assistant editor, designer, or promotion copywriter, among other entry-level job descriptions. It's *that* specific career objective they'll want to hear from you.

139

Remember, the more specific your career objective, the better your chances of finding a job. It's that simple and that important. Naturally, before you declare your objective to the world, check once again to make sure your specific job target matches the skills and interests you defined in your self-evaluation. Eventually, you may want to state such an objective on your resume and "To obtain an entry-level position as an assistant editor at a major Trade publishing house" is quite a bit better than "I want a career in publishing."

Do not consider this step final until you can summarize your job/career objective in a single, short, accurate sentence.

CHAPTER 19

Targeting Publishers And Networking For Success

If you've spent the time and effort going through the self-evaluation process in the previous chapter, you're now sure -- you *know* what you want to do. The next question: Where are you going to get a job doing it? There are thousands of book publishers, ranging in size from the biggest (Simon & Schuster, Random House, McGraw-Hill to the smallest (a plethora of "small press" publishers). Small or large? New York or Oshkosh? Just which of the publishers is the right one for you?

YOUR IDEAL PUBLISHER PROFILE

Let's establish some criteria to evaluate potential employers. This will enable you to identify your target companies, the places you'd really like to work. (This process, as we've pointed out, is not publishing-specific; the same steps, with perhaps some research resource variations, are applicable to any job, any company, any industry. But for this volume, we are now specifically concerned with jobs in the book business. If you are primarily interested in working for a newspaper, see the newest volume of our *Career Directory Series* -- the <u>Newspapers Career Directory</u>. And for you aspiring magazine editors, designers and advertising salespeople -- the second edition of our <u>Magazines Career Directory</u> is also available.)

Take another sheet of blank paper (yes, it's time for another list) and divide it into three vertical columns. Title it "Book Publisher -- Ideal Profile." Call the left-hand column "Musts," the middle column "Preferences," and the right-hand column "Nevers."

We've listed a series of questions below. After considering each question, decide whether a particular criteria *must* be met, whether you would simply *prefer* it or *never* would consider it at all. If there are other criteria you consider important, feel free to add them to the list below and mark them accordingly on your Profile.

1. What are your geographical preferences? (Possible answers: U.S., Canada, International, Anywhere). If you only want to work in the U.S., then "Work in United States" would be the entry in the "Must" column. "Work in Canada or Foreign Country" might be the first entry in your "Never" column. There would be no applicable entry for this question in the "Preference" column. If, however, you will consider working in two of the three, then your

"Must" column entry might read "Work in U.S. or Canada," your "Preference" entry -- if you preferred one over the other -- could read "Work in U.S.," and the "Never" column , "Work Overseas."

2. If you prefer to work in the U.S. or Canada, what area, state(s) or province(s)? If Overseas, what area or countries?

3. Do you prefer a large city, small city, town, or somewhere as far away from civilization as possible?

4. In regard to question 3, any specific preferences?

5. Do you prefer a warm or cold climate?

6. Do you prefer a large or small publishing company? Define your terms (by number of titles, in print, income, employees, offices, etc.).

7. Do you mind relocating right now? Do you want to work for a publisher with a reputation for *frequently* relocating top people?

8. Do you mind travelling frequently? What percent do you consider reasonable? (Make sure this matches the normal requirements of the job specialization you're considering.)

9. What salary would you *like* to receive (put in the "Preference" column)? What's the *lowest* salary you'll accept (in the "Must" column)?

10. Are there any benefits (such as an expense account, medical and/or dental insurance, company car, etc.) you must or would like to have?

11. Are you planning to attend graduate school at some point in the future and, if so, is a tuition reimbursement plan impotant to you?

12. Do you feel a formal training program necessary?

13. What kind of books (general Trade, scholarly, children's, elhi, college, medical, scientific/technical, etc.) would you prefer to work on?

14. Do you want to work only for a particular publisher? (If you're narrowing your search this much already, you better hope they publish a *lot* of books!)

It's important to keep revising this new form, just as you should continue to update your Self-Evaluation Form and Five Year Game Plan. After all, it contains the criteria by which you will judge every potential employer. It may even lead you to avoid interviewing at a specific company (if, for example, they're located in a state on your "never" list!). So be sure your "nevers" aren't frivolous. Likewise, make your "musts" and "preferences" at least semi-realistic. If your "must" salary for a position as an assistant editor is $30,000, you will wind up eliminating every house out there!

Armed with a complete list of such criteria, you're now ready to find all the publishers that match them.

CREATING YOUR COMMAND CHART

Here comes another chart, one we'll call your "Command Chart" or "Publisher Evaluation Chart." When completed, it will be the summary of all your research and contain all the information on the publishers you've initially targeted. As you start networking, sending out resumes and cover letters, and preparing for interviews, you will find yourself constantly updating and referring to this Chart.

Create one vertical column down the left side -- this is where you'll begin listing the companies you're considering. Then make as many columns across the top of the chart as you need to list all your "must" and "preference" criteria so you can "grade" the houses accordingly.

For example, using a list of possible entries on a hypothetical Publisher Profile, we would write in the following column headings and make an entry for each targeted house in the appropriate space (from those possible, noted in parentheses):

1. STATE: (List those you'll consider).

2. CITY: (Identify).

3. PUBLISHER SIZE: (Number of titles).

4. FORMAL TRAINING PROGRAM: (Check if "yes" and note important details -- who's in charge, number of new trainees hired each year, etc.).

5. BENEFITS: (Leave enough room to list all company-wide benefits. Circle those especially important to you).

6. TRAVEL: (Enter percentage anticipated).

7. SALARY: (You'll probably want to leave this blank until able to enter a specific salary offer, but may want to include anything you discover about that publisher's general pay scales, etc.).

Feel free to combine, add to, alter, and use this new chart in any way that makes sense to you. While you will probably set up individual files for the publishers high on your list (after "starring" the top ten or fifteen you like most), this Command Chart will remain an important form to refer back to.

TARGETING INDIVIDUAL PUBLISHERS

To begin creating your initial list of targeted publishers, start with the Job Opportunities Databank (Section VII. We've listed virtually every major publisher, most of which completed questionnaires we supplied, providing us (and you!) with a plethora of data concerning their overall operations, hiring practices, and other important information on entry-level job opportunities. This latter information includes key contacts (names), statistics on 1985-6 hiring of high school, college and graduate students, the number of entry-level people they expect to hire in 1987, along with complete job descriptions and requirements.

This section also includes lists of publishers offering salaried and non-salaried internships, or some of each, and those with formal training programs for "new hires." All of the detailed information in these two chapters was provided by the publishers themselves. To our knowledge, much of it is available only in this Career Directory.

We have attempted to include information on those major publishers that represent most of the entry-level jobs out there. But there are, of course, many other publishers of all sizes and shapes that you may also wish to research. In the next section, we will discuss some other reference books you can use to obtain more information on the publishers we've listed, as well as those we haven't.

OTHER REFERENCE TOOLS

In order to obtain some of the detailed information you need to completely fill in your Command Chart, you will probably need to do further research, either in the library or by meeting and chatting with people familiar with the publishing houses

As we've already mentioned, more than once, you should consider Literary Marketplace -- available from R. R. Bowker (205 East 42nd St., New York, NY 10017) -- the natural companion to this Career Directory. It lists all of the houses we've featured in Section VII (plus hundreds more) and offers a plethora of additional listings of companies and services allied with the book business. If a listing in chapter 23 instructs you to contact "department heads," for example, regarding employment opportunities, those names would most likely be included in the house's LMP entry. (If you are not interested in working in the U.S. or Canada and are searching for a job overseas, another Bowker publication -- International Literary Marketplace -- is an invaluable source. It lists more than 9,000 publishers in 160 countries. Check you library -- it costs $65.00.)

For more general research (pertinent to all publishers,), you might want to start with How To Find Information About Companies (Washington Researchers, 1985); the Encyclopedia of Business Information Sources (Gale Research, Book Tower, Detroit, MI 48226); and/or the Guide to American Directories (B. Klein Publications, P.O. Box 8503, Coral Springs, FL 33065), which lists directories for over 3,000 fields.

If you want to work for one of the associations which serves the book publishing/selling industry (or the fields with which it's most closely allied), we've listed all those in Appendix A. Other associations may be researched in the Encyclopedia of Associations (Gale Research Co.) or National Trade and Professional Associations of the United States (Columbia Books, Inc., 777 14th St., NW, Suite 236, Washington, DC 20005).

There are, in addition, some general corporate directories which may give you additional information on major publishers. (But do remember: Most publishers are not major, not publicly owned companies, and, therefore, not particularly forthcoming with information or listed in such all-inclusive reference books.) These volumes should all be available in the reference (and/or business) section of your local library:

*Dun and Bradstreet's family of corporate reference resources: the Million Dollar Directory (160,000 companies with a net worth of more than $500,000), Top 50,000 Companies (those with a minimum net worth of just under $2 million), and Business Rankings (details on the top 7,500 firms). A new volume from Dun's -- Reference Book of Corporate Managements/ America's Corporate Leaders -- provides detailed biographical data on the principal officers and directors of some 12,000-odd corporations. Who says you can't find out about the quirks and hobbies of the guy you're interviewing with? All of these volumes are available in most libraries or from Dun's Marketing Services (3 Century Drive, Parsippany, NJ 07054).

*Standard & Poor's Register of Corporations, Directors and Executives includes corporate listings for over 45,000 firms and 72,000 biographical listings. (Available from Standard and Poor's, 25 Broadway, New York, NY 10004.)

*Moody's Industrial Manual (Available from Moody's Investors Service, Inc., 99 Church St., New York, NY 10007.)

*Thomas's Register of American Manufacturing (Thomas Publishing Company, 1 Penn Plaza, New York, NY 10001.)

*Ward's Business Directory 1986, a three-volume reference work that includes listings of nearly 100,000 companies, the majority of them privately-held, and details that are usually most difficult to acquire about such firms (number of employees, annual sales, etc.). Published by Information Access Company.

Primary sources which should be utilized from now on to complete your research are The Wall Street Journal, Barron's, Dun's Business Month, Business Week, Forbes, Fortune and Inc. Naturally, the trade magazines which you've been studying (and to which you've already subscribed) like *Publishers Weekly*, offer a steady stream of information. Become as familiar as possible with the publishing companies, authors, jargon, topics covered, and the whole, evolving industry.

One last note on potential sources of leads. The Oxbridge Directory of Newsletters (available from Oxbridge Communications, 183 Madison Ave., Suite 1108, New York, NY 10016) lists thousands of newsletters in a plethora of industries and might well give you some ideas and names. And the Professional Exhibits Directory (Gale Research Co.) lists more than 2,000 trade shows and conventions. Such shows are excellent places to "run into" sales reps, editors, etc. and offer unexpected opportunities to learn about the business "from the horse's mouth."

NETWORKING FOR SUCCESS

You're now as prepared as any Boy or Girl Scout in history. You know not only the field you want to enter, but an exact job title, summarized in a concise career objective. You know whether you're heading for a general Trade house or a university press. And you have a complete preliminary list of firms, with detailed data on each, that reflects your own needs, wants and goals.

It's time to start *networking*, telling everybody you know and everybody *they* know exactly the kind of job you're looking for. Faster than you expect, you will begin to develop a network of friends, relatives, acquaintances and contacts. It is most likely that the skillful use of this network and *not* the more traditional approach to job hunting -- studying the want ads and sending out resumes to PO Box Numbers -- is going to be the key factor in landing the job you want.

Why? Because on any day of the week, the vast majority of available jobs, perhaps as high as 85% of all the jobs out there waiting to be filled, are not advertised anywhere. Many of those jobs that are advertised only remain in the classifieds for a day or two. After that, they're pulled and, for the next few weeks, various company personnel sift through resumes while the job is still sitting there, unfilled, just waiting for the right applicant to grab it!

There are some things to keep in mind while you prepare to crack what others have labled "the hidden job market." First and foremost, remember that there are *always* jobs out there. Nearly 20% of all the jobs in the United States (and probably many more in publishing, a notoriously fluid field) change hands every year, good years and bad. People retire, move on to another job or industry, get promoted. Companies expand. The result is near-constant movement in the job market, if only you know where to look.

Second, people in a company will generally know about a job opening weeks before the outside world gets a clue, certainly before (if) it shows up in a newspaper ad.

Third, just knowing that this hidden market exists is an asset a lot of your colleagues (hereafter, let's just consider them competitors) don't have.

Last, but by no means least, your industry and company research has already made you one of the most knowledgable graduates out there. This will undoubtedly work to your advantage.

Creating your network

In order to succeed, you must exploit any and every resource -- people who can help you get a job -- you have. Start with family, no matter how distant the relationship (especially if they work in publishing!), friends, acquaintances (no matter how shaky). You ought to be speaking to your professors, especially those who teach journalism (but don't exempt the advertising, marketing, public relations or English professors -- you don't know *who* they know). Write to the important trade journals and industry associations. Let them know what you're looking for and, especially, the kinds of preparations you've already completed and the specific publishers you'd like to work for. Ask them for a list of upcoming seminars or conferences you may be able to attend -- these are excellent sources of professional contacts.

Although we keep speaking in terms of "contacts" and "names," what you're really trying to do when you "network" is to make friends (or at least friendly acquaintances). After all, a friend is, almost by definition, someone who'll do you a favor when you need it. And, based on this concept, there is definitely a right way and a wrong way to network, a variance of attitude and style, perhaps, that separates successful people from less successful ones. The successful ones know full well that they are seeking a job, and, though intent on "using" whomever they meet in that search, are not obnoxious about it and don't emphasize the inherent manipulation involved.

This is a subtle point, but let me give you an example: Not long ago, someone I knew from a previous job called. She had been a friend, though not a close one, but when I moved on to another company, I had helped her take over my previous position. So I had some professional respect for her and thought a lot about her talents and abilities. Anyway, the phone rings. Here's the entire conversation from her end: "Hi. I'm networking and just wanted to know if you knew about any jobs." Over and out. Now considering that I hadn't heard from her in a couple of years, one would think it only polite to do a little chit-chatting before getting down to the (oh-so-obvious) business at hand. Not only did I suddenly not feel particularly happy to hear from her, but I was obviously being used and didn't like it. (The "I'm networking" statement is such an obviously lousy way to start any conversation that I won't even comment on it further.)

In other words: *you* know you're networking, *they* know you're networking. But have a little class, and remember that what you're really trying to do is make some friends. Friends help each other.

Telling everyone you know of your job hunt may lead to a series of informative interviews or conversations with publishing professionals. Such informal meetings

147

may well lead to more formal interviews for job openings at their own companies, either with them or their colleagues. At worst, if they work at one of your target publishers, they may be able to answer some important questions: Who's hiring entry-level people? Whom should you apply to? What's the interviewer like? Needless to say, someone who's actually worked at a particular publishing house can supply you with a lot of not-so-public and personal information you'll never find in the handout from Personnel.

Once you meet someone (or even talk with them on the phone), they are always potential sources of information and future contacts. Whether they've been helpful or not, don't be afraid to ask them for the names of three or four additional people, at their own or other companies, who might be in a position to help you out.

You're bound to get a lot of "no's" along the way, but that's just the Law of Averages at work. Don't take any rejection personally, and don't let a string of rejections stop you from asking for help from yet another new acquaintance. The more contacts you're able to make, the more people you have working, trying to find *you* a job! As any salesperson will tell you, the average prospect says "no!" five times before he buys. Expect a lot of "no's" to eventually lead to a lot of "yes's."

If you consider such networking to be nothing more than brazen hustling and a far too blatant approach, banish that feeling. You must be prepared to use these contacts in any way possible (keeping our previous "attitude discussion" in mind). They are your key to the right job, the right career and, if money motivates you, the Big Bucks. Fear must be considered an undesirable obstacle. Get rid of it.

Do keep in mind, however, that the request you make to each person should be both legitimate and thought-out. As we've stressed throughout this Career Directory, busy people do not have time for students who just want them "to tell me something about book publishing." But a sincere request for information, politely solicited, is answered more often than you think.

Just as important, don't avoid networking because of some misguided notion that "you need to do it on your own." What will *that* prove? Especially if you don't get the job you want! Networking isn't "taking advantage" of anyone -- no matter how many connections you have at a publishing company, no one is going to hire you if you're not qualified.

Expanding your network

Just because you're aware of and actively following up on the 85% of jobs that are unadvertised, there's no reason to completely ignore the 15% that do show up in a trade magazine or newspaper (like *The New York Times)*. Scour the Classified Ad sections of these publications as well.

If your school's career counseling office has a resume forwarding service or files of employers seeking qualified students, use them. This is a major source of entry-level jobs for many students.

Finally, you may consider registering with an employment agency or recruitment firm, though, frankly, we don't recommend the time or the effort. Most such companies are simply not interested in handling entry-level people (since they rarely are asked to find them). It is a buyer's market out there.

The best way to expand your network will inevitably turn out to be the way you got it started -- persistence, research, sales.

Organizing your home office

With so many other people working for you, you must carefully and completely organize your own personal employment office. If you've already started filing detailed company data in separate folders, you're already a step ahead.

We suggest preparing a separate folder for each person you're working with, along with a centralized phone list. Throughout your job search, be prepared to keep accurate and organized records every step of the way. Keep copies of your research notes, photocopy every letter you mail, and keep detailed notes of telephone conversations. <u>Always</u> send off a timely and polite thank-you note to those helping out. That simple gesture will demonstrate a degree of professionalism and good manners often overlooked by students.

If you can afford one, consider purchasing a telephone answering machine. An employer who may have seen and liked your resume -- one who's even willing to interview you -- will rarely call more than once to set up an appointment.

As you continue your networking and library research, you'll slowly learn more and more about the publishers you've targeted (and some you've missed). Add new ones to your "Command Chart" as you uncover them and continually update the information on all those you've listed. If you "starred" your "top ten" target companies, you'll want to at least have individual folders for them. You may also want to prepare a folder for any publisher at which you've interviewed, even if you're not interested in working there, just to make it easy to find the information. Above all, continue to phone and write everybody!

CHAPTER 20

Preparing Resumes And Cover Letters

Your resume is a one- or two-page summary of you -- your education, skills, employment experience and career objective(s). It is not a biography, but a "quick and dirty" way to identify and describe you to potential employers. Most importantly, its real purpose is to sell you to the publisher you want to work for. It must set you apart from all the other applicants (those competitors) out there. So, when you sit down to formulate your resume, remember you're trying to present the pertinent information in a format and manner that will convince an executive to grant you an interview, the prelude to any job offer.

In order to begin preparing your resume, you will need to assemble all the following information:

1. The names, addresses and telephone numbers of all your past employers.

2. The key personnel with whom you worked and a concise summary of the work you performed.

3. Any letters of recommendation from these employers.

4. Awards and honors you have received.

5. Clubs, honor societies and other activities (including any leadership positions held).

6. Marketable skills (typing, word processing, computer literacy, foreign languages, writing, sales, etc.).

7. Your grade point average (include it only *if* it's a B+ or better).

8. Your major field of study.

9. A concise career objective.

10. Hobbies and other interests.

Once you have this information in hand, you have a lot of options about what to include or leave out. In general, we suggest you always include the following data:

1. Your name, address and telephone number.
2. Pertinent work history
3. Pertinent educational history
4. Academic honors
5. Memberships in professional organizations.
6. Contributions to professional publications.

You have the option of including the following:

1. Your career objective
2. Personal data (marital status, etc.)
3. Hobbies
4. Feelings about travel and/or relocation
5. Military service history

And you should *never* include the following:

1. Why you left past jobs
2. Photographs or illustrations (of yourself or anything else!)
3. References
4. Past salaries or present salary objectives/requirements

Once you've decided what you want to include, there are two basic resume frameworks in which you can lay out the information.

CHRONOLOGICAL AND FUNCTIONAL RESUMES

The two standard resume formats are chronological, arranged by date (last job first), and functional, which emphasizes skills rather than the sequential history of your experiences. Generally, since students have yet to develop specific, highly employable skills or the experience to indicate proficiency in specific job functions, they should use the chronological format. A bit of sales, a touch of writing, and a smidgen of research will not impress anyone on a functional resume. The latter is useful, however, if you have a great deal of pertinent job expertise, since it emphasizes qualifications and abilities in terms of job titles and responsibilities. Dates are usually omitted (though we personally feel that leaving dates out altogether lessens the effectiveness of any resume. We'd find a way to include dates -- perhaps in a brief, chronological, job history section.) At the end of this chapter are examples of both.

(There are other kinds of resumes -- analytical, synoptic, "creative" approaches that defy easy classification. None of these are as efficient or easily understood and accepted as the two basic formats. And none of them are at all adaptable to an entry-level candidate. So stick with the chronological or, in exceptional cases, the functional.)

GUIDELINES FOR RESUME PREPARATION

Your resume should be limited to a single page if possible, two at most. It should be printed, not xeroxed, on 8 1/2" x 11" white, cream or ivory stock. The ink should be black or, at most, a royal blue. Don't scrimp on the paper quality -- use the best bond you can afford. And since printing 100 or even 200 copies will cost little more than 50, tend to overestimate your needs and opt for the highest quantity you think you may need.

When you're laying out the resume, try to leave a reasonable amount of "white space" -- generous margins all around and spacing between entries. A resume is not a complete biography and anything that is not, in some way, a qualification for the type of position you're seeking should be omitted.

Be brief. Use phraseology rather than complete sentences. Your resume is a summary of your talents, not an English Lit paper. Choose your words carefully and use "power words" whenever possible. "Organized" is more powerful than "put together;" "supervised" better than "oversaw;" "formulated" better than "thought up." Strong words like these can make the most mundane clerical work sound like a series of responsible, professional positions. And, of course, they will tend to make your resume stand out. Here's a "starter list" of words which you may want to use in your resume:

achieved	administered	advised	analyzed
applied	arranged	budgeted	calculated
classified	communicated	completed	computed
conceptualized	coordinated	critiqued	delegated
determined	developed	devised	directed
established	evaluated	executed	formulated
gathered	generated	guided	implemented
improved	initiated	instituted	instructed
introduced	invented	issued	launched
lectured	litigated	lobbied	managed
negotiated	operated	organized	overhauled
planned	prepared	presented	presided
programmed	promoted	recommended	researched
reviewed	revised	reorganized	regulated
selected	solved	scheduled	supervised
systematized	taught	tested	traced
trained	updated	utilized	wrote

An important suggestion: When you've completed writing and designing your resume, have a couple of close friends or family members proofread it for typographical errors *before* you send it to the printer. For some reason, the more you check it yourself, the less likely you'll catch the errors you missed the first time around. A fresh look from someone not as familiar with it will catch these glaring (and potentially embarrassing) errors before they're duplicated a couple of hundred times.

How to use your resume

Lastly, let's discuss how to use this marvelous resume you've put together. In general, always carry a supply of resumes with you so that you can give one to a prospective employer as you sit down to interview (or, if necessary, send it ahead to someone you're planning to meet with).

But don't just send resumes out to everyone and anyone you can find, just so you can chortle to friends about the "hundreds of resumes" you've managed to send through the post office. We've heard too many personnel directors lament the lack of "aggressiveness" in today's entry-level job candidates. "They're not hungry enough," these potential employers cry. Well, we don't think that's really true. The problem is that too many of you are spending far too much time doing too many *wrong* things, all the while congratulating yourselves on how "aggressive" you're being. Your job search is not a contest to see how many stamps you can waste. Getting resumes out to people is *not* the objective; identifying and contacting the right people at the houses you'd really like to work for and making sure they have the information they need (and that may or may not be a resume) to evaluate you as a potential new hire *is*.

The important thing to remember is that if you are utilizing the networking principle as efficiently and successfully as possible, the resume will become a mere addendum to the whole process. People will already be willing to see you; the resume will just give them an easy place to start the discussion. *Not*, as is too often the case these days, the piece of paper that personnel directors look over in search of reasons to eliminate you!

PREPARING COVER LETTERS

A cover letter should be included with each resume you send out. It may be addressed to a particular individual your networking has identified (or with whom you've already met or spoken) or sent in response to a newspaper ad (even those that refer you solely to post office boxes). Whatever the case, each cover letter should be personalized -- targeted to the individual company, executive and position. To our mind -- and most executives with whom we've talked seem to agree -- the cover letter tells them more about a candidate, and is, therefore, more important from your standpoint, than the resume.

Each cover letter should be error-free, neatly typed, and correctly formatted. Such a letter should probably never be handwritten. A handwritten note screams of informality, so don't use one unless that's the precise impression you're trying to convey.

154

Students, in particular, sometimes send out cover letters reminiscent of letters home from camp, complete with the requisite stains from lunch. That is both unprofessional (you *are* trying to impress them with your professionalism) and downright offensive to any potential employer. These letters should be business letters. If you are unfamiliar with the correct way to format such a letter -- and, sadly, far too many of you *are* -- study the examples we've included (and, if necessary, go to your local library and study the appropriate books in the business section).

Address each letter to the proper person at the publishing company (i.e., don't write to the editor-in-chief to find a job in field sales). If you intend to send out a series of "blind" cover letter/resume packages to a number of houses -- those where you're not sure of any job openings -- the personnel office is usually *not* the place to direct an unsolicited resume. When we surveyed the major book publishers to compile data for the new edition of this <u>Career Directory</u>, only a small minority of the respondents suggested contacting personnel first. Generally, the smaller the publishing company, the more often they counseled students to "go right to the top" -- the president or chief executive officer. The larger companies generally directed entry-level applicants to the appropriate department heads. (The rest either didn't list a particular preference or referred students to other specific executives, by name). The Job Opportunities Databank in Section VII of this Directory, which details the extensive data we received from publishers, lists the name and title of the specific individual each company recommended you initially contact.

Some newspaper or trade magazine ads will not include a contact name, but will instruct you to send your resume to a post office box. In this case (and this case only), "Dear Sir:" is an appropriate salutation. And if the ad lists a series of instructions ("write, don't call;" "send letter including salary requirements; send unreturnable copy sample;" etc.), follow them <u>exactly</u>. Don't call: don't ask for your sample back. Failing to follow precise instructions (they are there for a *reason*) could mean you already failed their "pre-screening interview." You'll have lost the job before you even started chasing it!

The correct format

First paragraph: State the reason for the letter, the specific job or type of work for which you're applying, and where (or from whom) you learned of the opening.

Second paragraph: Indicate why you're interested in their company and that particular position and, more important, what you have to offer them. Without repeating information from your resume verbatim, explain the appropriate academic or work experiences that specifically qualify you for the position.

Third paragraph: Refer him to the resume you've enclosed and add anything else you feel it's important he know about you.

Final paragraph: Indicate your desire to meet for a personal interview and your flexibility as to the place and time. Try to close the letter with a statement or question that will encourage him to take some action. Instead of "looking forward to hearing" from him, tell him when he should expect to hear from you. Otherwise, be prepared to *not* hear from him. Publishing executives get streams of letters, and can't *(don't)* answer most of them.

This is a very general approach to a "standard" cover letter. If you are particularly good at writing a strong sales "pitch," you're probably already used to writing such letters and need little help from us. But if you aren't adept at such letters, fitting your thoughts into the orderly paragraphs we've outlined should help you prepare more effective cover letters.

Try to personalize each one -- mention the company's name whenever and wherever you have the chance. Refer to some of their specific book titles or authors, trade advertisements, awards, or anything else your research has uncovered. Executives at the top publishing companies receive hundreds of applications, letters and unsolicited resumes from students and others looking for jobs. . .*weekly*. They can spot a "form letter" a mile away. Take this opportunity to show them that you are, in fact, serious about working at their company and that you've taken the time to learn something about them. And don't hesitate to demonstrate the fruits of your research in your letters.

Don't make a common mistake and simply recopy half your resume into the body of the cover letter. The letter offers you the opportunity to be a little creative, compensate for some glaring weakness or omission in your resume, and make a good, professional first impression. If the cover letter doesn't "sell" them, they may never even bother looking at the resume.

Two sample cover letters are reproduced at the end of this chapter (after some sample resumes). Cover Letter 1 might have been written in response to a small "want ad" in *Publishers Weekly,* one that didn't identify the publisher and directed all inquiries to a PO Box number. Letter 2 is one we'd write to the marketing director at a publisher one of our contacts told us might be hiring two or three new people for their Marketing/Sales Training Program.

SAMPLE RESUME 1: CHRONOLOGICAL (SIMPLE)

RESUME OF JIM BISHOP

ADDRESS

1 Main St.
Boston, MA 01234
(617)555-1111

PERSONAL

Born: May 30, 1956
Marital Status: Single
Height: 6'1"
Weight: 185

CAREER OBJECTIVE

A position as an assistant art director at a large, major publishing company.

EDUCATION

1982-1986: Providence College, B.A., Studio Art
1978-1982: O'Neill High School, Clifton, NJ
1981: Boston University, Art Workshop

EMPLOYMENT

1986-Present: General boardwork, L'Escape Artistes, Paramus, NJ

1985/6 School year: *The Beagle*. Art Director for the 12,000 circulation student newspaper.

Summers, 1982-1985: Kraft Lithographers. Mechanical, paste-up artist.

PROFESSIONAL MEMBERSHIPS

The Advertising Club of New York (Young Professionals Division)

BUSINESS SKILLS

Mechanical and paste-up skills: typespecing; typing (50 wpm), word processing, computer literate.

REFERENCES

Available Upon Request.

SAMPLE RESUME #2: FUNCTIONAL

JIM BEAM
76 Cortlandt St.,
New York, NY 10017
(212)555-1111

Career Objective: A position as a Trade book sales representative

SUMMARY

I am completing my degree in journalism, specializing in marketing, at University State. Last summer, I interned as an assistant account executive (with copywriting responsibilities) for a local advertising agency. I also have one year's experience selling advertising space (and supervising a staff of three salespeople) on my college newspaper. Both jobs have convinced me I will be successful in book sales.

EXPERIENCE

Summer, 1985 & 86: Intern, Kay Silver & Associates, Inc.
Summer, 1984 : Intern, Committee to Re-elect Kim Kerr

1985/86 school year:Ad Director, *The Daily Planet*
1986/87 school year:Salesman, Joe's University Book Store.

EDUCATION

B.A. Journalism (Marketing) University State - June, 1987
(summa cum laude).

PROFESSIONAL MEMBERSHIPS AND BUSINESS SKILLS

Member of the young Professionals Division of the Advertising Club of New York. Skills: Sales, media placement, typing (50 wpm), word processing, computer literate.

PERSONAL

Age: 21: Health: Excellent. Language Skills: Fluent (read/write/speak) in German and French.

References Available Upon Request

SAMPLE RESUME #3: CHRONOLOGICAL (DETAILED)

GILDA H. RADNER

HOME ADDRESS: SCHOOL ADDRESS:
80 Stemmons Freeway,   4240 Hill St.,
Dallas, TX 87540   Los Angeles, CA 90410
(214)788-0000   (213)001-0100

JOB
OBJECTIVE

A position offering challenge and responsibility in book publishing marketing research , advertising or promotion

EDUCATION

U.C.L.A.

1983-1987 Graduating in June, 1987, with a B.A. degree in Marketing. Deans List four years; Summa cum laude.

Fields of study include: marketing and advertising theory, research, business law, economics, mass communications, statistical analysis and research methodology.

Graduate courses in advertising theory and policies, consumer behavioral theory, sales management.

1979-1983 Greg Wright High School, Los Angeles, Calif. National Honor Society. Senior Class President. United Way Club Head Fund Raiser.

WORK
EXPERIENCE
(SUMMERS)

1986: JIM CANNON , INC., Los Angeles, Ca. Administrative assistant in Research Department. Trained in behavioral research techniques. Responsible for record keeping, expense reports, public relations, lab report dissemination,correspondence.

1984 & 1985: KISCHTRONICS, San Diego, Ca. Basic sales and management training at this major research and development facility. Duties included billing, inventory control, shipping and distribution, lab maintenance and delivery schedules.

COVER LETTER 1

May 6, 1987

Bill Killpatrick
422 W. 22nd St.,
New York, NY 10000
(212)888-1111

Post Office Box 1000
<u>Publishers Weekly</u>
205 E. 42nd Street,
New York, New York 10017

Dear Sir:

The entry-level Trade book sales position briefly outlined in your May 5th <u>PW</u> advertisement is very appealing to me. Please accept this letter and the attached resume as my application for this position.

While majoring in journalism (with a marketing emphasis) at Stein University, I worked on a number of projects which required the communication skills you specified in your ad. In addition, as advertising director for the <u>Daily Planet,</u> and a summer intern for a local advertising agency, I demonstrated the sales and interpersonal skills such a position requires.

I am especially excited about the possibility of covering the Midwest region , as your ad indicates this new employee would. As I was born and raised in Indiana, I am already familiar with and enjoy Chicago, St. Louis, Minneapolis, and the other major cities this territory encompasses.

I would like to meet with you at your convenience to discuss this position and my qualifications for it in more detail. I will be in Chicago for other interviews the week of May 27th. I will call you the week of May 14th, to see if we can set up an appointment for that week.

Thank you for your time. I look forward to meeting with you.

Sincerely yours,

Bill Killpatrick

COVER LETTER 2

May 6, 1987

Tim Carhart
44 Overview Circle,
Fargo, North Dakota
(718)888-0101

Ms. Pamela Cummings
Advertising Director
Print 'Em & Sell 'Em Publications, Inc.
2435 Dyer Street,
Kokomo, IN 46254

Dear Ms. Cummings:

I recently met your colleague, Arthur Hyman, at a seminar sponsored by <u>Publishers Weekly</u> magazine. He mentioned you were considering hiring two or three entry-level people for your Marketing/Sales Training Program and suggested I contact you.

Ms. Cummings, it has been my dream to work at a major publisher on a respectedconsumer publication. If at all possible, I had hoped to be accepted in a well-respected, formal advertising sales training program.Your training program is the best in the industry.

And I'm the right person for you to hire. While majoring in journalism (with a marketing emphasis) at University State, I worked on a number of projects, two of which simulated marketing problems you had to solve for your recent publication of I<u>Lose 100 Lbs. and Make a Million Dollars in Just 18 Days!</u>In addition, as ad director for the <u>Centennial</u> and, this past summer, working as an account services intern for a local agency, I clearly demonstrated my sales, communication and interpersonal skills.

Ms. Cummings, I will be returning home to Indiana in one week and would like to meet with you soon thereafter to discuss this opportunity in more detail. I will call you on May 14th to schedule an appointment. I look forward to talking with you then.

Sincerely yours,

Tim Carhart

CHAPTER 21

Playing The Interview Game To Win

Well, the days of research, preparation, chart-making, form-filling, and resume-printing worked. They're lining up to meet you! So it's time to prepare once again -- for the interviewing process that will inevitably determine the job offers you actually get.

Start by setting up a calendar on which you can enter and track all your scheduled appointments. When you schedule an interview with a publisher, ask them how much time you should allow for the appointment. Some companies require all new applicants to fill out numerous forms and/or complete a battery of intelligence or psychological tests -- all before the first interview. If you've only allowed an hour for the interview -- and scheduled another at a nearby house ten minutes later -- the first time you confront a three-hour test series will effectively destroy any schedule.

Some companies, especially if the first interview is very positive, like to keep applicants around to talk to other executives. This process may be planned or, in a lot of cases, a spontaneous decision by an interviewer who likes you and wants you to meet some other key decision-makers. Other companies will tend to schedule such a series of second interviews on a separate day. Find out, if you can, how the publisher you're planning to visit generally operates. Otherwise, especially if you've traveled to New York or another city to interview with a number of companies in a short period of time, a schedule that's too tight will fall apart in no time at all.

If you need to travel out-of-state to interview with a publisher, be sure to ask if they will be paying some or all of your travel expenses. (It's generally expected that you'll be paying your own way to companies within your home state.) If the publisher doesn't offer -- and you don't ask -- presume you're paying the freight.

Even if the publisher agrees to reimburse you, make sure you have enough money to pay all the expenses yourself. While some companies may reimburse you immediately, handing you a check as you leave the building, the majority may take from a week to a month to forward you an expense check.

PRE-INTERVIEW RESEARCH

The research you did to find these publishing companies is nothing compared to the research you need to do now that you're beginning to narrow your search. If you followed our detailed suggestions when you started targeting these publishers in the first place, you've already amassed a lot of information about them. If you didn't bother to do the research *then*, you sure better decide to do it *now*. Study each publishing company as if you were going to be tested on your detailed knowledge of their organization and operations. Here's a complete checklist of the facts you should try to know about each company you plan to visit for a job interview:

The Basics

1. The address of (and directions to) the office you're visiting.
2. Headquarters location (if different).
3. Some idea of domestic and international branches.
4. Relative size (compared to other houses.
5. Annual sales and income (last two years).
6. Subsidiary companies; specialized divisions.
7. Departments (overall company structure).
8. Number of books in print; number of new titles (last two years)

The Subtleties

1. The history of the company (including specialties, honors and awards, famous names, etc.).
2. Names, titles and backgrounds of top management.
3. Major authors associated with the house.
4. Existence (and type) of training program.
5. Relocation policy.
6. Relative salaries (compared to other publishers).
7. Recent developments concerning the company or its major authors (from your trade magazine and newspaper reading).
8. Everything you can learn about the career, likes and dislikes of the person(s) interviewing you.

The amount of time and work necessary to be *this* well-prepared for an interview is considerable. It will not be accomplished the day before the interview. You may even find some of the information you need to be unavailable on short notice. (Is it really so important to do all this? Well, *some*body out there is going to. And if you happen to be interviewing for the same job as that other, well-prepared, knowledgeable candidate, who do *you* think will impress the interview more?)

If you give yourself enough time, most of this information is surprisingly easy to obtain. In addition to the detailed information in the Job Opportunities Databank (Section VII) of this Career Directory and the other reference sources we covered in the earlier chapters of this job search section, the publishing company itself can supply you with a great deal of data. A company's Annual Report -- which all publicly-owned companies must publish yearly for their stockholders -- is a virtual treasure trove of information. Write each house and request copies of their last two Annual Reports. A comparison of sales, income, and

164

other data over this period may enable you to infer some interesting things about the company's overall financial health and growth potential. Many libraries also have collections of annual reports from major corporations. Also, each house has a <u>catalogue</u> that it prepares (primarily) for its wholesalers and retail book buyers, sometimes as often as quarterly. These will help you be current on big-name authors, new releases, best-sellers in the works, etc.

Attempting to learn about your interviewer is a chore, the importance of which is underestimated by most applicants (who then, of course, don't bother to do it). Being one of the exceptions may get you a job. Use the biographical references mentioned earlier in this section. If he is listed in any of these sources, you'll be able to learn an awful lot about his background. In addition, find out if he's written any articles that have appeared in the trade press or, even better, books on his area(s) of expertise. Referring to his own writings during the course of an interview, without making it *too* obvious a compliment, can be very effective. We all have egos and we all like people to talk about us. The interviewer is no different from the rest of us. You might also check to see if any of your networking contacts worked with him at his current (or a previous) house and can help "fill you in."

QUESTIONS EVERY INTERVIEWER KNOWS...AND MOST USE

Preparing for your interviews by learning about the publishing company is a key first step. Preparing to deal with the questions the interviewer will throw at you is a necessary second one. Don't go in "cold," oblivious to what's going to occur when you walk into his office. There are certain questions we can almost guarantee will be asked during any first interview. Study the list of questions (and hints) that follow, and prepare at least one solid, concise answer that you can trot out on cue. Practice with a friend until your answers to these most-asked questions sound intelligent, professional and, most important, unmemorized and unrehearsed.

1. "Why do you want to be in book publishing?"

Using your knowledge and understanding of the book industry, explain why you find the business exciting, and where and how you see yourself fitting in.

2. "Why do you think you'll be successful in this business?"

Using the information from your self-evaluation and the research you did on that particular company, formulate an answer which marries your strengths to theirs and to the characteristics of the position for which you're applying.

3. "Why did you choose our company?"

This is an excellent opportunity to explain the extensive process of research and education you've undertaken. Tell them about your strengths and how you match up with their company. Emphasize specific things about their firm that led you to seek an interview. Be a salesperson -- be convincing.

4. "What can you do for us?"

Construct an answer that essentially lists your strengths, the experience you have which will contribute to your job performance, and any other unique qualifications that will place you at the head of the applicant pack. Be careful: This is a question specifically designed to _eliminate_ some of that pack. Sell yourself. Be one of the few called back for a second interview.

5. "What position here interests you?"

If you're interviewing for a specific position, answer accordingly. If you want to make sure you don't close the door on other opportunities of which you might be unaware, you can follow up with your own question: "I'm here to apply for your Editorial Training Program. Is there another position open for which you feel I'm qualified?"

If you've arranged an interview with a house without knowing of any specific openings, use the answer to this question to describe the kind of work you'd like to do and why you're qualified to do it. Avoid a specific job title, since they will tend to vary from company to company.

If you're on a first interview with the personnel department, just answer the question. They only want to figure out where to send you.

6. "What are your strengths and weaknesses?" and

7. "What are your hobbies (or outside interests)?"

Both questions can be easily answered using the data you gathered to complete the self-evaluation process. Be wary of being too forthcoming about your glaring faults (nobody expects you to volunteer every weakness and mistake), but do _not_ reply, "I don't have any." They won't believe you and, what's worse, _you_ won't believe you. After all, you did the evaluation -- you know it's a lie!

8. "What are your career goals?"

. . .Which is why we suggested you prepare a Five year Game Plan. Quote from the form.

9. "What jobs have you held and why did you leave them?"

Or the direct approach, "Have you ever been fired?" Take the opportunity to expand on your resume, rather than precisely answering the question by merely recapping your job experiences. In discussing each job, point out what you liked about it, what factors led to your leaving, and how the next job added to your continuing professional education. If you have been fired, say so. It's very easy to check.

10. "What are your salary requirements?"

If they are at all interested in you, this question will probably come up. The danger, of course, is that you may price yourself too low or, even worse, right out of a job you want. Since you will have a general idea of industry figures for that position (and may even have an idea of what that house tends to pay new people for the position), why not refer to a *range* of salaries, such as "$16,000 - $19,000?"

If the interviewer doesn't bring up salary at all, it's doubtful you're being seriously considered, so you probably don't need to even bring the subject up. (If you know you aren't getting the job or aren't interested in it if offered, you may try to nail down a salary figure in order to be better prepared for the next publisher interview).

11. "Tell me about yourself."

Watch out for this one! It's often one of the first questions asked. If you falter here, the rest of the interview could quickly become a downward slide to nowhere. Be prepared, and consider it an opportunity to combine your answers to many of the previous questions into one concise description of who you are, what you want to be, and why that publisher should take a chance on you. Summarize your resume -- briefly -- and expand on particular courses or experiences relevant to the company or position. Do not go on about your hobbies or personal life, your dog, where you spent your summer vacation, etc. None of that is particularly relevant to securing that job. You may explain how that particular job fits in with your long-range career goals and talk specifically about what attracted you to their company in the first place.

The not-so-obvious questions

Every interviewer is different and, unfortunately, there are no rules saying he has to use all or any of the "basic" questions. But we think the odds are against his avoiding *all* of them. Whichever of these he includes, be assured most interviewers do like to come up with questions that are "uniquely theirs." It may be just one or a whole series -- questions he's developed over the years that he feels help separate the wheat from the chaff.

You can't exactly prepare yourself for questions like, "What would you do if...(fill in the blank with some obscure occurrence)?," "Tell me about your father," or "What's your favorite ice cream flavor?" Every interviewer we know has his or her favorites and all of these questions seem to come out of left field. Just stay relaxed, grit your teeth (quietly), and take a few seconds to frame a reasonably intelligent reply.

Some questions may be downright inappropriate. Young women, for example, may be asked about their plans for marriage and children. Don't call the interviewer a chauvinist (or worse). And don't point out that the question may be a little outside the law. (The nonprofessional interviewer may not realize such questions are illegal, and a huffy response may confuse -- and anger -- him.) Whenever any questions are raised about your personal life -- and this question surely qualifies -- it is much more effective to respond that you are very interested in the position and have no reason to believe that your personal life will preclude you from doing an excellent job.

"Do you have any questions?"

It's the fatal twelfth question on our list -- often the last one an interviewer throws at you -- after an hour or two of grilling. Unless the interview has been very long and unusually thorough, you probably *should* have questions about the job, the company, or even the industry. Unfortunately, by the time this question off-handedly hits the floor, you, sensing you're almost out of the "hot seat" and looking forward to leaving, may have absolutely nothing to say.

Preparing yourself for an interview means more than having answers for some of the questions an interviewer may ask. It means having your *own* set of questions -- at least five or six -- for the interviewer. The interviewer is trying to find the right person for the job. *You're* trying to find the right job. So you should be just as curious about him and his company as he is about you. Here's a short list of questions you may consider asking on any interview:

1. What will my typical day be like?

2. What happened to the last person who had this job?

3. Given my attitude and qualifications, how would you estimate my chances for career advancement at your company?

4. Why did you come to work here? What keeps you here?

5. If you were I, would you start here again?

6. How would you characterize the management philosophy of your firm?

7. What characteristics do the successful_____ at your company have in common (fill in the blank with an appropriate title, such as "editors," "sales reps," etc.)?

8. What's the best (and worst) thing about working here?

9. On a scale of 1 to 10, how would you rate your company in terms of salaries, benefits, and employee satisfaction, in comparison to others your size?

Other questions about the company or position will be obvious -- they're the areas your research hasn't been able to fill in. Ask the interviewer. But be careful and use common sense. No one is going to answer highly personal, rude or indiscreet questions. Even innocent questions might be misconstrued if you don't think about the best way to pose them -- *before* they come trippingly off your tongue.

Unless you're interviewing with the Personnel (or Human Resources) department, remember that most, if not all, of the executives you'll be meeting will *not* be professional interviewers. Which means they might well spend more time talking about themselves than the company, the position or you. If that happens, use it as an opportunity to create an informal dialogue. Such a "conversational approach" is often a more productive way of finding out important information, and selling yourself, than a straightforward question and answer session anyway.

THE DAY OF THE INTERVIEW

The preparation's done. "I-Day" is at hand.

On the day of the interview, wear a conservative business suit (not a sports coat, not a "nice" blouse and skirt).

It's not unusual for resumes and cover letters to head in different directions when a company starts passing them around to a number of executives. If you sent them, both may even be long-gone. So bring along extra copies of your resume and your own copy of the cover letter that originally accompanied it. Whether or not you make them available, we suggest you prepare a neatly-typed list of references (including the name, title, company, address and phone number of each person). You may want to bring along a copy of your college transcript, especially if it's something to brag about. (Once you get your first job, you'll probably never use it -- or be asked for it -- again, so enjoy it while you can!) And, if appropriate or required, make sure you bring samples of your work (e.g., your art portfolio or "clippings file").

Plan to arrive fifteen minutes before your scheduled appointment. If you're in an unfamiliar city, or have a long drive to the company, allow extra time for the unexpected delays that seem to occur with mind-numbing regularity on days like this.

Arriving early will give you some time to check your appearance, catch your breath, check in with the receptionist, learn how to correctly pronounce the interviewer's name, and get yourself organized and battle-ready.

Arriving late does not make a sterling first impression. If you are only a few minutes late, it's probably best not to mention it or even excuse yourself. With a little luck, everybody else is behind schedule and no one will notice. However, if you're more than fifteen minutes late, have an honest (or serviceable) explanation ready and offer it at your first opportunity. Then drop the subject as quickly as possible and move on to the interview.

When you meet the interviewer, shake hands firmly. People pay attention to handshakes. Ask for a business card. This will make sure you get the name and title right when you write your follow-up letter. You can staple it to the company file for easy reference as you continue your networking.

Try to maintain eye contact with the interviewer as you talk. This will indicate you're interested in what he has to say. Sit straight. Keep your voice at a comfortable level, and try to sound enthusiastic (without imitating a high school cheerleader). Be confident and poised, and provide direct, accurate and honest answers to his trickiest questions. And, as you try to remember all this, just be yourself and try to act like you're comfortable and almost enjoying yourself!

Interviews are sometimes conducted over lunch, though this is not usually the case with entry-level people. If it does happen to you, though, try to order something in the middle price range, neither filet mignon nor a cheeseburger. Do not order alcohol. If your interviewer orders a carafe of wine, you may share it. Otherwise, alcohol should be considered *verboten*, under any and all circumstances. Then hope your mother taught you the correct way to eat and talk at the same time. If not, just do your best to maintain your poise.

There are some things interviewers will always view with displeasure -- street language, complete lack of eye contact, insufficient or vague explanations or answers, a noticeable lack of energy, poor interpersonal skills (i.e., not listening or the basic inability to carry on an intelligent conversation), and a demonstrable lack of motivation.

Small oversights can cost you a job. Phil Mushnick, a regular sports columnist for the *New York Post*, describes the seemingly insignificant incident that, legend has it, made Joe Namath the quarterback for the New York Jets football team:

> If not for one rainy night in 1964, Namath might never have become a Jet. On that evening, (Jets owner) Sonny and Mrs. Werblin were entertaining Tulsa University quarterback Jerry Rhome at a Manhattan restaurant. Werblin was also entertaining plans to draft Rhome and build the franchise around him, much the way he would with Namath.
>
> Legend has it that, following dinner, Rhome made a solo dash for Werblin's car, which was waiting outside in the rain, leaving the Werblins to soak while he climbed in first. Friends of Werblin say that episode convinced him that Rhome wasn't the (quarterback) he wanted to lead his team. Shortly afterwards, the Jets traded Rhome's draft rights to Houston for a No. 1 pick, which they used to select Namath.

As the above story demonstrates, even if it's more legend than fact, every impression may count. And the very *last* impression an interviewer has may outweigh everything else. So, before you allow an interview to end, summarize why you want the job, why you are qualified, and what, in particular, you can offer their company.

Then, take some action. If the interviewer hasn't told you about the rest of the interview process and/or where you stand, ask him. Will you be seeing other people that day? If so, ask him for some background on the other people with whom you'll be interviewing. If there are no other meetings that day, what's the next step? When can you expect to hear from them about coming back?

When you return home, file all the business cards, copies of correspondence, and notes from the interview(s) with each company in the appropriate files. If you obtained some new information, be sure to update your Command Chart. Finally, but most importantly, ask yourself which publishers you really want to work for and which you are no longer interested in. This will quickly determine how far you want the process at each house to develop before you politely tell them to stop considering you for the job.

Immediately send a thank-you letter to each executive you met. These should, of course, be neatly-typed business letters, not handwritten notes (unless you are most friendly, indeed, with the interviewer and want to *stress* the "informal" nature of your note). If you are still interested in pursuing a position at their company, tell them in no uncertain terms. Reiterate why you feel you're the best candidate and tell each of the executives when you hope (expect?) to hear from them.

FIELDING THE JOB OFFERS

You may face a dilemma after all the interviewing is finished and you're just sitting and waiting for the offers. What if you're offered a job at House B -- your second, fifth or eighteenth choice -- but still haven't heard from House A -- your first choice? Worse, what if House B wants an answer before you expect to hear from A?

Well, you can call A, tell them you want to work there, but have received a good offer from another publisher. Do they have any idea how soon they expect to make a decision? You can even ask the interviewer to "rate your chances." Then, if he indicates the chances are good that you'll be offered a job within a week or so, you can hopefully buy that much time from B.

Of course, it rarely works out so neatly. If you find yourself with too many secondary choices making job offers, while the two or three publishers you really like continue to procrastinate, you probably should accept another offer. None of the "first choice" publishers might come through, and you certainly don't want to wind up without any job at all!

If your first or second choice *does* finally come through with an offer you want to accept, you can always call the other publisher, apologize, and tell them you won't be able to start working for them after all. It is not immoral. In fact, many employment counselors will tell you to accept every job offer. But companies do expect a certain percentage of hirees to wind up with other jobs before they're scheduled to start.

So, in general, accept a job offer unless you are positive you don't want it. This will give you at least a semblance of security in case no other offer materializes.

FINDING A SCHOOL YEAR OR SUMMER INTERNSHIP

There are less internships than entry-level jobs, so expect even stiffer competition. Utilizing the same steps outlined for finding an entry-level job, start preparing your search for a summer internship *the summer before*. Many publishers fill their quota of interns by early Spring, so you need to get a jump on the competition.

Internships are rarely, if ever, advertised and, until now, details on most of them were unpublished. In Section VII, we've included a list of major publishers that offer internships -- salaried, unsalaried or some of each -- and the specific person to contact at each company. In addition, some large publishers contact the career placement offices at a number of colleges as internship positions become available, so check with your counselor. Also, be sure to read the excellent chapter on book publishing internships and training programs that follows, by Chet Logan, VP-Personnel at Harper & Row.

How important is getting an internship to your post-graduation job search? In a word -- very. Nearly every contributor has stressed such experience. And, of the publishers we surveyed, most cited "publishing experience" -- meaning some kind of internship -- when asked to list requirements for their entry-level positions.

Should you choose a large, prestigious publisher, like Doubleday, Simon & Schuster or Random House, or the small, scholarly publisher near your home or college? The former will be an impressive addition to your resume, but may limit your exposure to a single department or function. The latter may offer you "hands-on" experience in a number of areas but add little luster to the resume. While we tend to value actual experience over "names," you have to make your own decision.

Given the scramble for any internship, however, we would even more strongly recommend accepting the first one that comes your way, whether it is the one you want or not. You will probably *not* have a number to choose from!

No job search is an easy one. They all require time, energy, research and more than a modicum of luck. And jobs at "big name" publishing companies are never easy to get. The detailed job search process we've outlined in these chapters is complicated, time-consuming and, we expect, far more involved than most of you will like. None of you will precisely follow each recommended step. But, hopefully, you will come to understand why we've made each recommendations and find them helpful in your own search.

Because the extra work you do now *will* pay off in the long run. The more time and effort you put into your career *now* -- as you're just starting out -- the more likely you'll end up at the right publisher, in the right department, heading in the right direction, and well on your way to achieving the personal goals you set.

Good luck!

CHAPTER 22

Internships And Training Programs In Book Publishing

By

Chester S. Logan, Vice President - Personnel
Harper & Row, Publishers, Inc.

If you want an accounting job in a publishing company, by all means get a good degree in accounting and try to acquire some experience in a leading public accounting firm.

If you aspire to a job in book production, some education and experience in the printing trades will improve your chances.

But if you're aiming at a job in the editorial or marketing functions of book publishing, your best credentials will be a good liberal arts education at the bachelor's degree level, some basic office skills, and a good measure of energy and curiosity.

What accounts for this difference? Publishers call it the <u>apprenticeship system</u>.

Traditionally, book publishers have considered hands-on, on-the-job experience the best way for neophytes to learn many of the basic functions of the business -- particularly in editorial, design, and marketing. This apprenticeship system may seem old-fashioned compared to many other businesses, and in some ways it *is* inefficient, but no one has yet found a better way. Perhaps the survival of the apprenticeship tradition can be attributed to the fact that successful publishing depends so much on subjective judgment and taste, intuitive qualities that cannot be taught, but *can* be sharpened by experience. Of course, success in publishing also requires technical skills. Many of these skills can be learned on-the-job, but may be learned more quickly through structured training programs.

With all this in mind, let's look at the wide variety of training resources available to would-be and beginning publishers, and the internships that can speed up the process.

FORMAL TRAINING

Educational programs in publishing abound, and many of them provide valuable information and some technical training in the process and business of publishing. Some offer an overview of the industry, coupled with hands-on workshop experience. Examples of this are the summer institutes at several universities across the country (Radcliffe, Stanford, Howard, N.Y.U., University of Denver) and the Coalition of Publishers for Employment (COPE) course in New York City.

The university summer institutes introduce prospective publishing employees to the business as a whole. Students learn about the different kinds of book publishing and the work each requires. Many discover for the first time that there is more to publishing than editing fiction and non-fiction for the general reader. Summer institute students are better able to focus their job searches, because they have a better sense of where their own interests and abilities are likely to fit (as marketing assistants, editorial assistants, design trainees, etc.). A few learn that publishing isn't the business for them and thereby avoid future frustration and disappointment. Probably the greatest benefit these students gain is the opportunity to develop valuable contacts with the visiting lecturers, who are experienced professionals from the industry.

Several colleges have introduced degree programs in book publishing in recent years. They offer special bachelor's degrees or post-graduate certificates. These programs usually take an approach similar to the summer institutes, but cover these same topics in much greater depth. While it is too soon to know whether graduates of these programs fare better in their publishing careers than those with less specific education, the former certainly gain a perspective that can only help their future career decisions.

Many colleges offer non-credit courses on publishing subjects. Among these are general overviews of editorial or marketing processes, and technical instruction in topics such as copywriting and copy editing. These types of courses are especially useful for publishing employees who wish to enhance the knowledge and skills they are learning on the job. They are also helpful to those exploring career changes within the industry. Most publishing companies encourage employees to take such courses by providing tuition assistance.

TRAINING WITHIN THE COMPANY

Training and education within the company is usually called "in-house" training. The two main components of this kind of training are <u>structured lectures and workshops</u> and <u>informal, day-by-day instruction</u> from supervisors.

A few book publishing companies offer courses and seminars on a regular basis, but most offer them "as needed." In either case, the speakers and instructors are usually drawn from the ranks of professional employees in the company. They generally address the issues and practices that are most relevant to their own organizations. Some of these in-house courses may be very specific: how to prepare a manuscript for production, how to develop an advertising campaign, or how to prepare a budget and monitor results. However, the courses are more likely to be general, addressed to employees who want to understand better how the company operates and what goes on in other departments. Frequently the more general courses serve as orientation for new employees. In-house education of this sort varies widely from company to company, from much to none, and from structured to casual.

As with any other apprenticeship system, the most important training in publishing comes from the daily interaction of employees with their supervisors and colleagues. Much depends on the experience and style of the supervisors. Formal education outside and informal programs within the company are valuable supplements to the learning process, but most publishers agree that there is no substitute for learning by doing. More often than not, supervisors in publishing are willing to give new employees a considerable amount of independence to expand their range of responsibilities.

INTERNSHIPS

If you can get one, take it.

Internships vary widely. However, the one thing they have in common is the opportunity to work in a company and get firsthand exposure to the real world of publishing. As you'll see from the listings in the Job Opportunities Databank in the back of this volume, a number of book publishing companies offer internships, some regularly, others only occasionally. Some are formally organized to give the interns hands-on experience in a variety of basic functions. Others are less structured, giving interns the opportunity to assist professional managers and observe what goes on. Internships in the industry are *not* commonplace and there are many applicants for the limited number available. So how do you get one? The following four steps will give you a better shot:

Step #1: Start early. Don't wait until the end of the academic year, by which time most openings will have been filled.

Step #2: Write directly to the companies that interest you most. Start with the listings in the back of this <u>Career Directory</u>. To get information not listed here -- or to find information on smaller publishers not included in this volume -- use <u>Literary Marketplace</u>. Approach the people in charge of the publishing divisions that attract you. It is always a good idea to write to personnel departments, too -- they may know of internships of which others in the company are unaware.

Step #3: Work with your college's career placement office. Find out about whether intern experience counts for degree credits. This is particularly important for unpaid internships because of federal employment regulations.

Step #4: Investigate foundations and independent intern programs. Some foundations have special programs for interns. For example, the Morehead Foundation sponsors a scholarship program at the University of North Carolina that features internships in a variety of industries, including publishing. The INROADS program for minorities has a very effective intern sponsorship program in a wide range of industries which, in the past few years, has included publishing. College and school career offices are the best source of information about these.

SO WHAT DO YOU DO?

There may be no substitute for the apprenticeship approach to careers in book publishing. Few people have achieved promotion or advancement because of degrees or certificates of learning. Nevertheless, the most successful people in publishing are those who add to their innate abilities a curiosity and knowledge of the complete process. This is where training and outside courses can add much to one's hands-on experience. This is also where those who have had college-level orientation education have a head start. And it is where those who have been so fortunate as to have some sort of internship experience are at a particular advantage.

The "Accidental Profession" welcomes you warmly. The next steps are up to you.

* * *

Mr. Logan began his publishing career as a college textbook sales representative with the Oxford University Press after his 1951 graduation from Princeton. Since then, he has held editorial and marketing management positions at Oxford, Reinhold Publishing Corp. (now Van Nostrand-Reinhold), and Harper & Row. He assumed his present position at Harper in 1973.

He has been active in the Association of American Publishers (AAP), including membership in the Education for Publishing Committee in 1977, and chairmanship of the College Division in 1969.

He has been president and chairman of COPE (Coalition of Publishers for Education), is a member of the advisory board of the American Reading Council, and has lectured in publishing courses at the University of Denver, Howard University and New York University.

Mr. Logan's writings include contributions to The Accidental Profession (AAP, 1977) and The Business of Book Publishing (Westview Press, 1985).

SECTION VII

Job Opportunities Databank

CHAPTER 23

Entry-Level Job Listings

There are two chapters in this section. This one includes information on the book publishers we surveyed regarding entry-level job opportunities. (Chapter 24 includes internship and training program information). The vast majority of this information was compiled by our staff through direct mail questionnaires and telephone calls -- it is simply not available anywhere else but in this Career Directory.

Use the information here as a guide: It isn't hard to see that the majority of entry-level opportunities are at the biggest publishers -- those with a lot more than 20 titles in. print or 3 employees. But there are also a surprising number of smaller publishers -- with just a few titles in print and a few employees -- that are ready to hire a surprising number of recent college graduates. With these firms as a guide, you should be able to get a better feel for the possibilities out there. You can then use a reference book like *Literary Marketplace* (from R.R. Bowker) to find other book publishers that match those listed here in size or location.

Most of the information should be self-explanatory.

Where we had some pertinent information, we've included details on U.S. and international branch offices, including breakdowns of employment at each level (head-quarters, U.S. offices, International offices).

The information following "Entry-level hiring in 1986" lists the *total* number of entry-level people hired in 1986, followed by, if available, a breakdown -- how many grad students, college grads, high school students, career changers, and "others." Hiring from a single group is simply noted in the form "College-1."

"(Anticipated) Entry-level hiring in 1987" is that publisher's best estimate of anticipated need for new people. How accurate is it? Not very. For example, in the first edition of this volume, published in 1986, Addison-Wesley indicated they would be hiring 10 entry-level people in 1986. You'll note from their current listing that they actually hired 76 **entry-level people!** And are now indicating 20 to be hired in 1987. Similarly, Harry Abrams predicted **0** entry-level hiring for 1986, and wound up hiring 6 college grads. So use this fig-ure (and the one showing 1986 hiring) as an *indicator* at best.

You can probably consider the entries conerning 1987 hiring plans conserva-tive -- as far as we can tell, if any publisher indicated they would be hiring entry-level people in 1986 (in the first edition of this Career Directory), they tended to *underestimate* their needs, not *overestimate* them. So even if they say they're hiring "1," they should be considered a distinct possibility.

Two important points: 1) A "?" following the "(Anticipated) Entry-level hiring in 1987" entry means *they intend to hire entry-level people in 1987* ; they were just unable to come up with any specific number. 2) If the publisher indicates they do not plan to hire any entry-level people (and, especially, if they don't seem to have a history of hiring them), they may still have listed "Opportunities." In this case, these should not be considered actual jobs, merely the positions they consider entry-level...whether or not they currently have openings.

If the publishers themselves had any specific suggestions or comments, we've included them. These will help you get a head start on other applicants -- you'll know what the companies want you to do!

Whenever we couldn't confirm the accuracy of an entry, we merely entered "NA," -- Not Available.

Lastly, we asked each publisher to assess their feeling about the overall atmosphere for entry-level hiring in 1987. These assessments are their best guesses *for the industry as a whole* . . .not just for their own house. This is just another of our attempts to give you some information that you might be able to use to gauge your chances out there.

Oh, and don't forget the second chapter of this section -- it lists all of the publishers we've identified that offer internships and/or training programs.

HARRY N. ABRAMS, INC.
A Division of The Times Mirror Company
100 Fifth Avenue
New York, NY 10011
212-206-7715
EMPLOYMENT CONTACT: Elvira Giannasca, Personnel Manager
TYPES OF PUBLISHING: Trade (Hardcover)
TITLES IN PRINT: 400
TITLES PUBLISHED IN 1985: 80
TITLES PUBLISHED IN 1986: 100
TOTAL EMPLOYEES: 133 (18 international)
ENTRY-LEVEL HIRING IN 1986: College-6
(ANTICIPATED) ENTRY-LEVEL HIRING IN 1987: 0
ENTRY-LEVEL OPPORTUNITIES: Editorial Asst. - College degree; typing, filing, knowledge of publishing. Marketing Asst. - College degree; clerical skills, publishing background. Publicity Asst. - College degree; clerical skills, good phone contact. Production Asst. - College degree; typing, filing, secretarial background.
OUTLOOK FOR 1987 ENTRY-LEVEL EMPLOYMENT: Same as last year.

ADDISON-WESLEY PUBLISHING COMPANY, INC.
Jacob Way
Reading, MA 01867
617-944-3700
EMPLOYMENT CONTACT: Roger L. Drumm, Corporate Recruiter
TYPES OF PUBLISHING: Audio/Visual, College Text, Elhi, Professional, Reference, Scholarly, Scientific/Technical, Software, Trade (Hardcover) Trade (Paperbound), Training.
TITLES IN PRINT: 5,700
TITLES PUBLISHED IN 1985: 400
TITLES PUBLISHED IN 1986: 420
TOTAL EMPLOYEES: 1,292 (Headquarters-623, U.S. offices-625, International offices-244)
ENTRY-LEVEL HIRING IN 1986: 76 (Grad students-3, College-25, High school-30, Career changers-18)
(ANTICIPATED) ENTRY-LEVEL HIRING IN 1987: 20
ENTRY-LEVEL OPPORTUNITIES: All of the following positions require a college degree or equivalent experience, preferably with a liberal arts major, plus those other skills specified: College Field Sales - Leadership, verbal communications skills. Editorial Asst. or Promotion Asst. - Word processing, organization. Telemarketing Sales or Sales Asst. - Strong communication skills, organization, minimal production experience. Marketing Asst. - Word processing, written and verbal communication skills.
SUGGESTIONS: "Conduct extensive research before contacting publishers. Use local sources (i.e., on-campus authors, faculty, bookstore managers, trade buyers, design schools). Also consult publisher's catalog to determine the nature of its publishing programs. Contact Publishing Institutes (e.g., Stanford, Howard University, UC Berkeley, Denver, Radcliffe, Rice, CUNY, Hofstra, etc.) Visit trade shows, academic conventions." - Mr. Drumm
OUTLOOK FOR 1987 ENTRY-LEVEL EMPLOYMENT: Same as last year.

AD-LIB PUBLICATIONS

61 N Fifth St, PO Box #1102
Fairfield, IA 52666-1102
515-472-6617
EMPLOYMENT CONTACT: John Kremer, Publisher
TYPES OF PUBLISHING: Professional, Reference, Software, Trade (Hardcover), Trade (Paperbound).
TITLES IN PRINT: 6
TITLES PUBLISHED IN 1985: 3
TITLES PUBLISHED IN 1986: 6
TOTAL EMPLOYEES: 3
ENTRY-LEVEL HIRING IN 1986: 2 (College-1, Career changers-1)
(ANTICIPATED) ENTRY-LEVEL HIRING IN 1987: 6
ENTRY-LEVEL OPPORTUNITIES: Data Entry - High school graduate; typing. Database Managers/Editors - College degree; typing, detail oriented. Publicist - College degree; writing.
OUTLOOK FOR 1987 ENTRY-LEVEL EMPLOYMENT: Somewhat better than last year.

AFIPS PRESS

1899 Preston White Drive
Reston, VA 22091
EMPLOYMENT CONTACT: Chris Hoelzel, Director
TYPES OF PUBLISHING: College Text, Professional, Scientific/Technical.
TITLES IN PRINT: 100
TITLES PUBLISHED IN 1985: 6
TITLES PUBLISHED IN 1986: 6
TOTAL EMPLOYEES: 9
ENTRY-LEVEL HIRING IN 1986: NA
(ANTICIPATED) ENTRY-LEVEL HIRING IN 1987: 0

ALASKA NORTHWEST PUBLISHING COMPANY

130 Second Ave South
Edmonds, WA 98020
EMPLOYMENT CONTACT: Rick Paul, Associate Publisher
TYPES OF PUBLISHING: Audio/Visual, Trade (Hardcover), Trade (Paperbound) (plus monthly consumer magazine, annual travel guides.)
TITLES IN PRINT: 100
TITLES PUBLISHED IN 1985: 12
TITLES PUBLISHED IN 1986: 20
TOTAL EMPLOYEES: 45
ENTRY-LEVEL HIRING IN 1986: High school-4
(ANTICIPATED) ENTRY-LEVEL HIRING IN 1987: 0
ENTRY-LEVEL OPPORTUNITIES: Editorial Asst - Proper language usage, typing, strong writing ability, organized manner. News Release Writer - Newswriting basics, proper language usage, typing, strong writing ability, organized manner. Assistant to Publisher - All of the above qualifications plus general business acumen, knowledge of industry dynamics, ability to handle a myriad of jobs as the publisher's "gopher."
SUGGESTIONS: "Send letters with resumes first. No calls please."
OUTLOOK FOR 1987 ENTRY-LEVEL EMPLOYMENT: Same as last year

AMERICAN PHILOSOPHICAL SOCIETY
104 South Fifth St
Philadelphia, PA 19106
215-627-0706
EMPLOYMENT CONTACT: Carole N. Le Faivre, Associate Editor
TYPES OF PUBLISHING: Scholarly.
TITLES PUBLISHED IN 1985: 14
TITLES PUBLISHED IN 1986: 14
TOTAL EMPLOYEES: 3
ENTRY-LEVEL HIRING IN 1986: 0
(ANTICIPATED) ENTRY-LEVEL HIRING IN 1987: 1 (part-time)
ENTRY-LEVEL OPPORTUNITIES: Word Processing/Secretary - College degree; able to
read/write French and/or German.
OUTLOOK FOR 1987 ENTRY-LEVEL EMPLOYMENT: Same as last year

ASHLEY BOOKS, INC.
30 Main St
Port Washington, NY 11050
516-883-2221
EMPLOYMENT CONTACT: Joan Calder, Vice President
TYPES OF PUBLISHING: College Text, Elhi, Professional, Religious, Scholarly,
Scientific/Technical, Trade (Hardcover), Trade (Paperbound), (Health field fiction & non-
fiction)
TITLES IN PRINT: 375
TITLES PUBLISHED IN 1985: 30
TITLES PUBLISHED IN 1986: 50
TOTAL EMPLOYEES: 10
ENTRY-LEVEL HIRING IN 1986: 3 (Grad students-l, College-2)
(ANTICIPATED) ENTRY-LEVEL HIRING IN 1987: 3
ENTRY-LEVEL OPPORTUNITIES: Assistants in all Departments - English or History major
helpful (however all majors will be considered if person can apply themselves with
enthusiasm and really wishes to learn publishing), writing and typing skills. "Any applicant
must be a self-starter and a well organized person."
SUGGESTIONS: "Call and make an appointment to see Joan Calder. It would be helpful to
bring a resume."
OUTLOOK FOR 1987 ENTRY-LEVEL EMPLOYMENT: Much better than last year

BANTAM BOOKS, INC.
666 Fifth Avenue
New York, NY 10103
212-765-6500
EMPLOYMENT CONTACT: Terri Gioia, Director of Personnel

183

BEEKMAN PUBLISHERS, INC.
PO Box #888
Woodstock, NY 12498
914-679-2300
EMPLOYMENT CONTACT: Joanne Michaels, Vice President
TYPES OF PUBLISHING: Professional, Reference, Scientific/Technical, Reprints
TITLES PUBLISHED IN 1985: 3
TITLES PUBLISHED IN 1986: 5
TOTAL EMPLOYEES: 5
ENTRY-LEVEL HIRING IN 1986: 0
(ANTICIPATED) ENTRY-LEVEL HIRING IN 1987: 1
ENTRY-LEVEL OPPORTUNITIES: Rights Manager Asst - College degree; typing 60 wpm.
OUTLOOK FOR 1987 ENTRY-LEVEL EMPLOYMENT: Somewhat better than last year

ROBERT BENTLEY, INC.
1000 Massachusetts Ave
Cambridge, MA 02138
EMPLOYMENT CONTACT: Michael Bentley, VP/Executive Editor
TYPES OF PUBLISHING: College Text, Professional, Reference, Scientific/Technical.
TITLES IN PRINT: 135
TITLES PUBLISHED IN 1985: 10
TITLES PUBLISHED IN 1986: 11
TOTAL EMPLOYEES: 11
ENTRY-LEVEL HIRING IN 1986: 4 (College-3, Career changers-1)
(ANTICIPATED) ENTRY-LEVEL HIRING IN 1987: 2
ENTRY-LEVEL OPPORTUNITIES: Asst Production Editor - College degree. No other
requirements specified.
COMMENTS: "Interest and organizing ability are important."
OUTLOOK FOR 1987 ENTRY-LEVEL EMPLOYMENT: Same as last year.

BERKLEY PUBLISHING GROUP
A Division of Putnam Publishing Group
200 Madison Ave
New York, NY 10016
212-676-8900
EMPLOYMENT CONTACT: Terri Schaeffer, Personnel Recruiter
TYPES OF PUBLISHING: Mass Market Paperback, Trade (Paperbound), General fiction & non-
fiction, science-fiction, romance, westerns, inspirational, etc.
TOTAL EMPLOYEES: 150
ENTRY-LEVEL HIRING IN 1986: NA
(ANTICIPATED) ENTRY-LEVEL HIRING IN 1987: ?
ENTRY-LEVEL OPPORTUNITIES: Editorial Asst, Publicity Asst, Sales Asst, Sub Rights Asst,
Contracts Asst, Production Asst. - All require a college degree, good typing and office skills,
light office experience preferred. Art Asst. - Art school or college degree; above requirements
plus mechanical or board skills.
OUTLOOK FOR 1987 ENTRY-LEVEL EMPLOYMENT: Same as last year

BIRCH TREE GROUP LTD
PO Box #2072. 180 Alexander St
Princeton, NJ 08540
609-683-0090
EMPLOYMENT CONTACT: Catherine Yanzeck, Personnel Department
TYPES OF PUBLISHING: Educational Music Methods
TITLES IN PRINT: 300
TITLES PUBLISHED IN 1985: 26
TITLES PUBLISHED IN 1986: 25
TOTAL EMPLOYEES: 25-30 (including 5 international)
ENTRY-LEVEL HIRING IN 1986: 5 (College-2, High school-1, Career changers-2)
(ANTICIPATED) ENTRY-LEVEL HIRING IN 1987: 5
ENTRY-LEVEL OPPORTUNITIES: All openings are possible - Advertising/Promotion,
Publicity, Production/Editorial, Subsidiary Rights, Legal, Distribution, Personnel/Office
Services.
OUTLOOK FOR 1987 ENTRY-LEVEL EMPLOYMENT: Same as last year

BRANDEN PUBLISHING COMPANY
17 Station St, Box #843
Brookline Village, MA 02147
617-734-204@
EMPLOYMENT CONTACT: Adolph Caso, President
TYPES OF PUBLISHING: Children's,College Text, Professional, Reference, Religious, Scholarly
Scientific/Technical, Software, Trade (Hardcover), Trade (Paperbound).
TITLES IN PRINT: 250
TITLES PUBLISHED IN 1985: 10
TITLES PUBLISHED IN 1986: 16
TOTAL EMPLOYEES: 8
ENTRY-LEVEL HIRING IN 1986: 2 (Grad students-1, College-1)
(ANTICIPATED) ENTRY-LEVEL HIRING IN 1987: 2
ENTRY-LEVEL OPPORTUNITIES: Business Plan - Graduate student; marketing. coursework
and skills. Marketing Plan - Graduate student; sales ability.
SUGGESTIONS: "We look for well-prepared individuals with (above) criteria and initiative".
OUTLOOK FOR 1987 ENTRY-LEVEL EMPLOYMENT: Somewhat better than last year.

BRUNNER/MAZEL, INC.
19 Union Square West
New York, NY 10003
212-924-3344
EMPLOYMENT CONTACT: Mark Tracten, President
TYPES OF PUBLISHING: Scientific/Technical
TITLES IN PRINT: 20
TITLES PUBLISHED IN 1985: 27
TITLES PUBLISHED IN 1986: 32
TOTAL EMPLOYEES: 28
ENTRY-LEVEL HIRING IN 1986: College-1
(ANTICIPATED) ENTRY-LEVEL HIRING IN 1987: 0
OUTLOOK FOR 1987 ENTRY-LEVEL EMPLOYMENT: Same as last year.

CAMBRIDGE UNIVERSITY PRESS
32 E 57th St
New York, NY 10022
212-688-8885
EMPLOYMENT CONTACT: Carol D. New, Personnel Manager
TYPES OF PUBLISHING: Children's, College Text, Professional, Reference, Religious, Scholarly, Scientific/Technical, Software.
TITLES IN PRINT: 8,000
TITLES PUBLISHED IN 1985: 887
TITLES PUBLISHED IN 1986: 880
TOTAL EMPLOYEES: 834 (Headquarters-60, U.S. offices-80, International offices-696)
ENTRY-LEVEL HIRING IN 1986: College-10
(ANTICIPATED) ENTRY-LEVEL HIRING IN 1987: 10
ENTRY-LEVEL OPPORTUNITIES: Editorial Asst, Marketing Asst, Production Asst - All require a college degree, 60 WPM typing, and computer skills.
COMMENTS: "Applicants are tested for typing skills, spelling and grammar."
OUTLOOK FOR 1987 ENTRY-LEVEL EMPLOYMENT: Same as last year.

THE CAREER PRESS INC.
62 Beverly Rd., PO Box 34
Hawthorne, NJ 07507
201-427-0229
EMPLOYMENT CONTACT: Richard Start, Asst. to the President
TYPES OF PUBLISHING: Reference (Hardcover and Paperbound)
TITLES IN PRINT: 10
TITLES PUBLISHED IN 1985:0
TITLES PUBLISHED IN 1986: 4 (1987=10)
ENTRY-LEVEL HIRING IN 1986: 1
ANTICIPATED ENTRY-LEVEL HIRING IN 1987: 1
ENTRY-LEVEL OPPORTUNITIES: Assistant editor - College degree (major unimportant), excellent typing (50 wpm absolute minimum), good organizational, communication, grammar, spelling, composition skills. Good "team spirit." Hard worker. Word processing experience and knowledge of publishing business preferred (any college publication experience a plus); PC experience a definite plus.
COMMENTS: Cover letters and resumes only, no phone calls.

CAROLRHODA BOOKS, INC.
241 First Avenue North
Minneapolis, MN 55401
612-332-3344
EMPLOYMENT CONTACT: Beverly Charette, Editorial Director
TYPES OF PUBLISHING: Children's, Trade (School & Library editions)
(Anticipated) entry-level hiring in 1987: 0

CATHOLIC UNIVERSITY OF AMERICA PRESS
620 Michigan Ave NE
Washington, DC 20715
202-635-5052
TYPES OF PUBLISHING: Professional, Reference, Religious, Scholarly
TITLES IN PRINT: 194
TITLES PUBLISHED IN 1985: 10
TITLES PUBLISHED IN 1986: 16
TOTAL EMPLOYEES: 8
ENTRY-LEVEL HIRING IN 1986: NA
(ANTICIPATED) ENTRY-LEVEL HIRING IN 1987: 0
OUTLOOK FOR 1987 ENTRY-LEVEL EMPLOYMENT: Same as last year.

CBS EDUCATIONAL & PROFESSIONAL PUBLISHING
A Division of CBS Inc.
500 Summit Lake Dr
Valhalla, NY 10595
EMPLOYMENT CONTACT: John Buzzeo, Director of Personnel
TYPES OF PUBLISHING: College Text, Elhi, Scientific/Technical, Software, Medical
TOTAL EMPLOYEES: 2,100 (Headquarters-600, U.S. offices-1,250, International offices-350)
ENTRY-LEVEL HIRING IN 1986: NA
(ANTICIPATED) ENTRY-LEVEL HIRING IN 1987: ?
ENTRY-LEVEL OPPORTUNITIES: Editorial As@t., Marketing Asst., Sales Asst., Advertising Asst., Sales Representative, Junior Copywriter, Production Asst. - All these positions require a college degree. Junior Financial Analyst - College degree (BA accounting or finance). Junior Accountant - College degree (BA accounting). Secretary - High school or college graduate. No other requirements specified.

CHILDRENS PRESS
A Division of Regensteiner Publishing. Enterprises.
1224 West Van Buren
Chicago, IL 60607
312-666-4200
EMPLOYMENT CONTACT: Roy Spahr, VP & General Manager
TYPES OF PUBLISHING: Children's, El/Hi, Trade (Paperbound).
TITLES IN PRINT: 1,500
TITLES PUBLISHED IN 1985: 165
TITLES PUBLISHED IN 1986: 165
TOTAL EMPLOYEES: 150
ENTRY-LEVEL HIRING IN 1986: 9 (College-3, High school-6)
(ANTICIPATED) ENTRY-LEVEL HIRING IN 1987: 4-10
ENTRY-LEVEL OPPORTUNITIES: Both of the following positions require a 4 year college degree: Photo Editor, Junior Editor. No other requirements specified.
OUTLOOK FOR 1987 ENTRY-LEVEL EMPLOYMENT: Somewhat better than last year.

CLYMER PUBLICATIONS
12860 Muscatine St
Arleta, CA 91333-4520
818-767-7660
EMPLOYMENT CONTACT: Production Manager or Managing Editor
TYPES OF PUBLISHING: Do-it yourself repair manuals
TITLES IN PRINT: 200
TITLES PUBLISHED IN 1985: 10
TITLES PUBLISHED IN 1986: 15
TOTAL EMPLOYEES: 35
ENTRY-LEVEL HIRING IN 1986: 7 (College-5, High school-1, Career changers-1)
(ANTICIPATED) ENTRY-LEVEL HIRING IN 1987: 5
ENTRY-LEVEL OPPORTUNITIES: Production Coordinator - Some college, strong interest in book production. Editorial Assistant - Some college, strong knowledge of engine mechanics, basic editorial skills.
OUTLOOK FOR 1987 ENTRY-LEVEL EMPLOYMENT: Same as last year

COLEMAN PUBLISHING
99 Milbar Blvd
Farmingdale, NY 11735
516-293-0383
EMPLOYMENT CONTACT: Saul Steinberg, Director
TYPES OF PUBLISHING: Audio/Visual, Children's Reference, Religious
TITLES IN PRINT: 200
TITLES PUBLISHED IN 1985: 35
TITLES PUBLISHED IN 1986: 40
TOTAL EMPLOYEES: 25
ENTRY-LEVEL HIRING IN 1986: College-6
(ANTICIPATED) ENTRY-LEVEL HIRING IN 1987: 2

CPI (CONTEMPORARY PERSPECTIVES, INC.)
145 E 49th St
New York, NY 10017
212-763-3800
TYPES OF PUBLISHING: Elhi, Software.
TITLES IN PRINT: 150
TOTAL EMPLOYEES: NA
ENTRY-LEVEL HIRING IN 1986: College-1
(ANTICIPATED) ENTRY-LEVEL HIRING IN 1987: ?
ENTRY-LEVEL OPPORTUNITIES: "CPI is a small educational publishing developer, hiring on an as-needed basis for various editorial/production positions." No specific titles/positions described."
OUTLOOK FOR 1987 ENTRY-LEVEL EMPLOYMENT: Same as last year.

CRAIN BOOKS
4255 W. Touhy Avenue
Lincolnwood, IL 60646
3122-679-5500
EMPLOYMENT CONTACT: Don Van Dyke, Personnel Director
TYPES OF PUBLISHING: Professional, Reference, Scientific/Technical

CROSSROAD/UNGAR/CONTINUUM
370 Lexington Ave
New York, NY 10580
212-532-3650
TYPES OF PUBLISHING: College Text, Professional, Reference, Religious, Scholarly, Trade
(Hardcover), Trade (Paperbound)
TITLES IN PRINT: 1,000
TITLES PUBLISHED IN 1985: 50
TITLES PUBLISHED IN 1986: 75
TOTAL EMPLOYEES: 20
ENTRY-LEVEL HIRING IN 1986: 4 (College-2, High school-2)
(ANTICIPATED) ENTRY-LEVEL HIRING IN 1987: NA
ENTRY-LEVEL OPPORTUNITIES: Editorial Asst, Promotion Asst, Sales Asst, Production Asst,
Administrative Asst - All require a college degree, typing and word processing skills.
OUTLOOK FOR 1987 ENTRY-LEVEL EMPLOYMENT: Same as last year.

CROWN PUBLISHERS, INC.
226 Park Avenue South
New York, NY 10003
212-254-1600
EMPLOYMENT CONTACT: Cherly Kidd, Employment Representative
TYPES OF PUBLISHING: Audio/Visual, Children's, Software, Trade (Hardcover).
TITLES PUBLISHED IN 1985: 170
TITLES PUBLISHED IN 1986: 200
TOTAL EMPLOYEES: 1,200
ENTRY-LEVEL HIRING IN 1986: 24-29 (Grad students-2, College-20-25, High school-2)
(ANTICIPATED) ENTRY-LEVEL HIRING IN 1987: 20
ENTRY-LEVEL OPPORTUNITIES: All of the following require a college degree (BA preferred)
plus typing (30-40 wpm). PC or CRT familiarity a plus, prior office experience or intern
program helpful: Publicity Asst., Editorial Asst., Marketing/Production Asst., Production
Asst., Sales Asst.
OUTLOOK FOR 1987 ENTRY-LEVEL EMPLOYMENT: Same as last year

HARRY CUFF PUBLICATIONS LTD
1 Dorset St
St. John's, Newfoundland, Canada A1B 1W8
709-726-6590
TYPES OF PUBLISHING: Children's, College Text, Professional, Scholarly, Trade
(Paperbound).
TITLES IN PRINT: 50
TITLES PUBLISHED IN 1985: 15
TITLES PUBLISHED IN 1986: 10
TOTAL EMPLOYEES: 6
ENTRY-LEVEL HIRING IN 1986: NA
(ANTICIPATED) ENTRY-LEVEL HIRING IN 1987: 0
OUTLOOK FOR 1987 ENTRY-LEVEL EMPLOYMENT: Same as last year.

MARCEL DEKKER, INC.
270 Madison Ave
New York, NY 10016
212-696-9000
EMPLOYMENT CONTACT: Stacey Miller, Personnel Recruiter
TYPES OF PUBLISHING: College Text, Elhi, Professional, Reference, Scholarly,
Scientific/Technical, Software, Trade (Hardcover), Trade (Paperbound).
TITLES IN PRINT: 2,215
TITLES PUBLISHED IN 1985: 172
TITLES PUBLISHED IN 1986: 175
TOTAL EMPLOYEES: 216 (Headquarters-176, U.S. offices-30, International offices-10)
ENTRY-LEVEL HIRING IN 1986: 15 (College-10, High school-3, Career changers-2)
(ANTICIPATED) ENTRY-LEVEL HIRING IN 1987: 15-20
ENTRY-LEVEL OPPORTUNITIES: Editorial Asst. - College degree; experience on school
publication, P/T office background. Production Asst or Journal Production Editor - College
degree; P/T office experience, typing (40 wpm) and work on school publication a plus.
Promotion Asst. - College degree (English preferred); 6O wpm, P/T office experience.
Administrative Asst. - College degree or Secretarial School; 60 wpm, P/T office experience.
Art Asst. - Some college, art school a must; paste-up experience and portfolio. Marketing
Asst.- College degree (BA Liberal Arts preferred); 50 wpm, p/t office experience.
SUGGESTIONS: "Please send cover letter with salary requirements and resume."
OUTLOOK FOR 1987 ENTRY-LEVEL EMPLOYMENT: Same as last year.

DELL PUBLISHING COMPANY, INC.
One Dag Hammarskjold Plaza
New York, NY 10017
212-605-3000
EMPLOYMENT CONTACT: Cathy Adams, Employment Manager

DEVIN-ADAIR, PUBLISHERS INC.

6 N Water St
Greenwich, CT 06830
203-531-7755
EMPLOYMENT CONTACT: Roger H. Lourie, Managing Director
TYPES OF PUBLISHING: Professional, Trade (Hardcover), Trade (Paperbound)
TITLES IN PRINT: 500+
TITLES PUBLISHED IN 1985: 30
TITLES PUBLISHED IN 1986: 25
TOTAL EMPLOYEES: 10 (including 2 international)
ENTRY-LEVEL HIRING IN 1986: College-1
(ANTICIPATED) ENTRY-LEVEL HIRING IN 1987: 1
OUTLOOK FOR 1987 ENTRY-LEVEL EMPLOYMENT: Not quite as good as last year.

DIMENSION BOOKS INC.

1 Summit St
Rockaway, NJ 07866
201-627-44334
EMPLOYMENT CONTACT: Thomas P. Coffey, President
TYPES OF PUBLISHING: Mass Market Paperback, Professional, Religious, Trade (Hardcover), Trade (Paperbound).
TITLES IN PRINT: 450
TITLES PUBLISHED IN 1985: 40
TITLES PUBLISHED IN 1986: 40
TOTAL EMPLOYEES: 12

DOUBLEDAY & COMPANY, INC.

245 PARK AVE.
NEW YORK, NY 10167
212-984-7561
EMPLOYMENT CONTACT: Dick Strowbridge, Personnel Manager
TYPES OF PUBLISHING: Children's, General Trade (Hardcover), Mystery, Religious, Science Fiction.
TITLES IN PRINT: 4,000+
TOTAL EMPLOYEES: 325
ENTRY-LEVEL HIRING IN 1986: NA
(ANTICIPATED) ENTRY-LEVEL HIRING IN 1987: ?
ENTRY-LEVEL OPPORTUNITIES: Editorial secretary - BA or BS, typing 50 wpm. Publicity Secretary - BA or BS, typing 50 wpm. Marketing Secretary - Business degree, typing 50 wpm. Production clerk - BA or BS, typing 50 wpm. Media Assistant - Business degree, light typing.

DUNDURN PRESS LTD
1558 Queen St E
Toronto, Ontario, Canada   M4L 1E8
416-461-1881
EMPLOYMENT CONTACT: Kirk Howard, President
TYPES OF PUBLISHING: Reference, Scholarly, Trade (Hardcover), Trade (Paperbound).
TITLES IN PRINT: 125
TITLES PUBLISHED IN 1985: 15
TITLES PUBLISHED IN 1986: 20
TOTAL EMPLOYEES: 6
ENTRY-LEVEL HIRING IN 1986: Grad students-3
(ANTICIPATED) ENTRY-LEVEL HIRING IN 1987: 1
OUTLOOK FOR 1987 ENTRY-LEVEL EMPLOYMENT: Same as last year

THE DUSHKIN PUBLISHING GROUP, INC.
Sluice Dock
Guilford, CT 06437
203-453-4351
EMPLOYMENT CONTACT: Don Young, Administrative Manager
TYPES OF PUBLISHING: College Text, El/Hi, Reference.
TITLES IN PRINT: 80
TITLES PUBLISHED IN 1985: 7
TITLES PUBLISHED IN 1986: 10
TOTAL EMPLOYEES: 50
ENTRY-LEVEL HIRING IN 1986: 4 (College-1, High school-3)
(ANTICIPATED) ENTRY-LEVEL HIRING IN 1987: 3-4
ENTRY-LEVEL OPPORTUNITIES: Word Processor - High school graduate. Order Entry Clerk - High school graduate. Telemarketing Representative - College degree . Editorial Asst. - College degree. Paste-up Artist - Design school graduate. No other requirements specified.
OUTLOOK FOR 1987 ENTRY-LEVEL EMPLOYMENT: Same as last year.

EDITION FIDES
5710 Ave Decelles
Montreal, Quebec Canada H3S 2C5
514-735-6406
EMPLOYMENT CONTACT: Mr. Raymond Lapres
TYPES OF PUBLISHING: Children's, College Text, Elhi, Mass Market Paperback, Professional, Reference, Religious, Scientific/Technical, Trade (Hardcover), Trade (Paperbound).
TITLES PUBLISHED IN 1985: 40
TITLES PUBLISHED IN 1986: 40
TOTAL EMPLOYEES: 18
ENTRY-LEVEL HIRING IN 1986: 4 (Grad students-2, High school-2)
(ANTICIPATED) ENTRY-LEVEL HIRING IN 1987: 1-2
ENTRY-LEVEL OPPORTUNITIES: PR Religious Sector - College degree; knowledge of religious studies, good PR. Publishing Asst - College degree; very good knowledge of French and religious studies.
OUTLOOK FOR 1987 ENTRY-LEVEL EMPLOYMENT: Same as last year.

ENCYCLOPAEDIA BRITANNICA
310 South Michigan Ave
Chicago, IL 60604
312-347-7284
EMPLOYMENT CONTACT: Joan K. Downey, Personnel Manager
TYPES OF PUBLISHING: Reference
TOTAL EMPLOYEES: 1,031 (Headquarters-727, U.S. offices-294, International offices-10)
ENTRY-LEVEL HIRING IN 1986: 32 (Grad students-5, college-5, High school-20, Other-some college-2)
(ANTICIPATED) ENTRY-LEVEL HIRING IN 1987: ?
ENTRY-LEVEL OPPORTUNITIES: Asst. Copy Editor Trainee - Some college, proofreading experience on student publications. Research Specialist - College degree (Science), research ability, excellent reading skills, knowledge of library procedures & computer searching. Editorial Asst.- College degree,proofreading experience on student publication, typing (45 wpm). Asst. Librarian - MLS Degree; familiarity with AACR2, OCLC, NEXIS essential, reading knowledge of at least one foreign language. Many clerical (business) positions, too numerous to list.
OUTLOOK FOR 1987 ENTRY-LEVEL EMPLOYMENT: Same as last year

FABER & FABER, INC.
50 Cross St
Winchester, MA 01890
617-721-1427
EMPLOYMENT CONTACT: Susan Nash, Vice President
TYPES OF PUBLISHING: Children's, Trade (Hardcover), Trade (Paperbound).
TITLES IN PRINT: 800
TITLES PUBLISHED IN 1985: 125
TITLES PUBLISHED IN 1986: 165
EMPLOYEES: 12

F & W PUBLICATIONS INC.
9933 Alliance Rd
Cincinnati, OH 45242
813-984-0717
EMPLOYMENT CONTACT: Kathy Schneider, Personnel Manager
TYPES OF PUBLISHING: Reference, Trade (Hardcover), Trade (Paperbound). TITLES IN PRINT: 166
TITLES PUBLISHED IN 1985: 59
TITLES PUBLISHED IN 1986: 49
TOTAL EMPLOYEES: 126
ENTRY-LEVEL HIRING IN 1986: 12-16 (College - 6-8, High school - 6-8)
(ANTICIPATED) ENTRY-LEVEL HIRING IN 1987: 4-6
ENTRY-LEVEL OPPORTUNITIES: Assistant Editor - College degree; Art related background, including slides of work. Marketing/Public Relations - College degree; Strong writer. Marketing Assistant - Some college; clerical, quantitative skills.
SUGGESTIONS: "Send work/writing samples, when appropriate, with resume."
OUTLOOK FOR 1987 ENTRY-LEVEL EMPLOYMENT: Somewhat better than last year.

FARRAR, STRAUS & GIROUX, INC.
19 Union Square W
New York, NY 10003
212-741-6900
EMPLOYMENT CONTACT: Peggy Miller, Office Manager
TYPES OF PUBLISHING: Children's, Trade (hardcover), Trade (Paperbound)
TITLES PUBLISHED IN 1985: 100
TITLES PUBLISHED IN 1986: NA
TOTAL EMPLOYEES: 80
ENTRY-LEVEL HIRING IN 1986: 0
(ANTICIPATED) ENTRY-LEVEL HIRING IN 1987: 0

GARDEN WAY/STOREY PUBLISHING
A Division of Storey Communications, Inc
Schoolhouse Rd
Pownal, VT 05261
802-823-5871
EMPLOYMENT CONTACT: Maribeth Casey, Assistant Sales Manager
TYPES OF PUBLISHING: Trade (Paperbound)
TITLES IN PRINT: 200
TITLES PUBLISHED IN 1985: 15
TITLES PUBLISHED IN 1986: 13
TOTAL EMPLOYEES: 23
ENTRY-LEVEL HIRING IN 1986: NA
(ANTICIPATED) ENTRY-LEVEL HIRING IN 1987: 0
ENTRY-LEVEL OPPORTUNITIES: Asst Editor - College degree (BA preferred); typing.
Production - Paste-up experience. Business Office Asst - general accounting.
OUTLOOK FOR 1987 ENTRY-LEVEL EMPLOYMENT: Same as last year

GARLAND PUBLISHING
136 Madison Avenue
New York, NY 10016
212-686-7492
EMPLOYMENT CONTACT: Personnel Department
TYPES OF PUBLISHING: College Text, Professional, Reference, Religious, Scholarly.
TITLES IN PRINT: 5,000
TITLES PUBLISHED IN 1985: 800
TITLES PUBLISHED IN 1986: 1,000
TOTAL EMPLOYEES: 81 (1 international)
ENTRY-LEVEL HIRING IN 1986: 9 (Grad student-1, College-5, High school-1, Career changers-2)
(ANTICIPATED) ENTRY-LEVEL HIRING IN 1987: 0
OUTLOOK FOR 1987 ENTRY-LEVEL EMPLOYMENT: Somewhat better than last year

WARREN H. GREEN, INC.
8356 Olive Blvd
St. Louis, MO 63132
314-991-1335
EMPLOYMENT CONTACT: Warren H. Green, President
TYPES OF PUBLISHING: Professional, Scholarly.
TITLES IN PRINT: 260
TITLES PUBLISHED IN 1985: 38
TITLES PUBLISHED IN 1986: 42
TOTAL EMPLOYEES: 6
ENTRY-LEVEL HIRING IN 1986: 0
(ANTICIPATED) ENTRY-LEVEL HIRING IN 1987: 0
COMMENTS: "We publish clinical medicine and medical research books. This requires B.S. or
M.S. degrees AND publishing experience and strength in medical terminology, physics,
chemistry, math and statistics."

GUERNICA EDITIONS
PO Box #633, Station N.D.G.
Montreal, Quebec, Canada H4A 3R1
514-256-5599
EMPLOYMENT CONTACT: Antonio D'Alfonso, Director
Types of publishing: Children's, College Text, Mass Market Paperback, Reference, Scholarly,
Trade (Hardcover), Trade (Paperbound)
TITLES IN PRINT: 50
TITLES PUBLISHED IN 1985: 11
TITLES PUBLISHED IN 1986: 8
TOTAL EMPLOYEES: 16
ENTRY-LEVEL HIRING IN 1986: 10
(ANTICIPATED) ENTRY-LEVEL HIRING IN 1987: 0
ENTRY-LEVEL OPPORTUNITIES: University student with literary background
OUTLOOK FOR 1987 ENTRY-LEVEL EMPLOYMENT: Same as last year

HARCOURT BRACE JOVANOVICH, INC.
1250 Sixth Avenue
San Diego, CA 92101
619-231-6616
EMPLOYMENT CONTACT: Marilyn Bailan, Director of Personnel

HARPER & ROW PUBLISHERS, INC.
10 E 53rd St
New York, NY 10022
212-207-7000
EMPLOYMENT CONTACT: Joan Maniscalco, Assistant Personnel Manager
TYPES OF PUBLISHING: Children's College Text, Mass Market Paperback, Professional, Reference, Religious, Scientific/Technical, Trade (Hardcover) Trade (Paperbound).
TITLES PUBLISHED IN 1985: 1,200
TITLES PUBLISHED IN 1986: 1,200
TOTAL EMPLOYEES: 1,800 (500 in headquarters office)
ENTRY-LEVEL HIRING IN 1986: NA
(ANTICIPATED) ENTRY-LEVEL HIRING IN 1987: 50
ENTRY-LEVEL OPPORTUNITIES: Secretary, Secretary Asst., Production Asst. - Good typing, excellent English skills. Copywriters - Portfolio to show. Clerks - Good typing, good English skills. Contract Asst - College degree; good typing, good English skills.
OUTLOOK FOR 1987 ENTRY-LEVEL EMPLOYMENT: Same as last year

D.C. HEATH & COMPANY
A Division of Raytheon Company
126 Spring St
Lexington, MA 02173
617-862-6650
EMPLOYMENT CONTACT: Janet Kenneally or Mary Fraser, Personnel
TYPES OF PUBLISHING: College Text, Elhi, Professional, Scholarly, Trade (Hardcover), Trade (Paperbound).
TITLES PUBLISHED IN 1985: 400+
TITLES PUBLISHED IN 1986: 400+
TOTAL EMPLOYEES: 775
ENTRY-LEVEL HIRING IN 1986: College-4
(ANTICIPATED) ENTRY-LEVEL HIRING IN 1987: 3-4
ENTRY-LEVEL OPPORTUNITIES: Sales Representatives - College degree; sales experience helpful. Editorial Asst. - College degree. Asst. Editors - College degree; teaching experience in specific fields or publishing experience.
OUTLOOK FOR 1987 ENTRY-LEVEL EMPLOYMENT: Somewhat better than last year.

HOUGHTON MIFFLIN COMPANY
1 Beacon St
Boston, MA 02108
617-726-5000
EMPLOYMENT CONTACT: Personnel Office
TYPES OF PUBLISHING: Children's, College Text, Elhi, Reference, Software, Trade (Hardcover), Trade (Paperbound).
TITLES PUBLISHED IN 1985: 466
TITLES PUBLISHED IN 1986: 986
TOTAL EMPLOYEES: 694
ENTRY-LEVEL HIRING IN 1986: 42
(ANTICIPATED) ENTRY-LEVEL HIRING IN 1987: ?

ENTRY-LEVEL OPPORTUNITIES: Administrative Secretary - High school graduate (business/secretarial courses); typing, filing, organizational skills, willingness to learn word processing and/or dictaphone, 1 year office experience. Administrative Asst. - High school graduate (advanced business/secretarial courses); typing, filing, organizational skills, willingness to learn word processing and/or dictaphone. Editorial Asst. - College degree (BA, BS or equivalent); previous publishing experience. Associate Editor - College degree (BA/BS or equivalent required; MA/MS or equivalent preferred); teaching experience.

COMMENTS: "Of the 42 entry-level hires, half of these employees were hired for straight secretarial positions. The balance of the positions is split between non-editorial assistant and support positions and associate or assistant editorial slots. These latter are often filled by those with some publishing experience or career changers, in spite of the "entry-level" status. There is no defined entry-level as such with the exception of one or two editing assistant job titles. All positions that do function as entry-level do so because of unplanned opportunity with the job, but made possible by the location of the position in an editorial or production department. The incumbent's academic preparation and/or prior experience in positions such as teaching is often a contributing factor."

HUMAN KINETICS PUBLISHERS
1607 North Market St., PO Box #5076
Champaign, IL 61820
217-361-5076
EMPLOYMENT CONTACT: Mary T. Krzysik, CPS, Executive Secretary
TYPES OF PUBLISHING: Audio/Visual, College Text, Professional, Reference, Scholarly, Scientific/Technical, Trade (Hardcover), Trade (Paperbound) TITLES IN PRINT: 250
TITLES PUBLISHED IN 1986: 30
TITLES PUBLISHED IN 1986: 60
TOTAL EMPLOYEES: 55
ENTRY-LEVEL HIRING IN 1986: 21 (Grad students-5, College-5, High school-8, Career changers - 3)
(ANTICIPATED) ENTRY-LEVEL HIRING IN 1987: 10
ENTRY-LEVEL OPPORTUNITIES: Asst Editor - College degree (BS Journalism or English); excellent organizational and interpersonal skills, knowledge of copy editing and proofreading procedures. Receptionist/Typist - High school graduate; initiative, typing 50-60 wpm, word processing, good communication skills. Mail Clerk/Errands - High school graduate; previous mailroom experience, organizational skills, initiative. Asst Bookkeeper - High school graduate; education or experience in accounts receivable, computer experience. Paste-Up Artist - High school graduate, BS in Art & Design; understanding of graphic arts techniques, standards and procedures, attention to detail. Typesetter - High school graduate; knowledge of typesetting and graphic arts techniques. ACEP Services Asst. - High school graduate, BS or attendance at college; excellent organizational, computer communication, & secretarial skills. Packing Clerk - High school graduate. Invoice/Fulfillment Clerk -- High school graduate; communication, organizational and typing skills; math ability. Marketing Assistant-Special Sales - B.S. degree in Physical Education; experience in marketing, communication and interpersonal skills.

COMMENTS: "The positions listed above are what we consider entry-level positions. Other positions that may become available require an M.S. or Ph.D degree in the fields of physical education and sports medicine. We hire only non-smokers. All applicants should submit a resume and a cover letter."

HUMAN SCIENCES PRESS, INC.
72 Fifth Ave
New York, NY 10011
212-243-6000
EMPLOYMENT CONTACT: Sheldon R. Roen Ph.D., Chairman
TYPES OF PUBLISHING: Children's, College Text, Professional, Religious, Scholarly, Trade (Hardcover), Trade (Paperbound), Professional Journals.
TITLES IN PRINT: 575
TITLES PUBLISHED IN 1985: 40
TITLES PUBLISHED IN 1986: 35
TOTAL EMPLOYEES: NA
ENTRY-LEVEL HIRING IN 1986: 7 (College-3, High school-4)
(ANTICIPATED) ENTRY-LEVEL HIRING IN 1987: 3
ENTRY-LEVEL OPPORTUNITIES: Marketing - College degree; typing, ambitious. Data Entry - High school graduate; fast typing, dedication.
OUTLOOK FOR 1987 ENTRY-LEVEL EMPLOYMENT: Much better than last year

RICHARD D. IRWIN, INC.
A Subsidiary of Dow Jones & Co, Inc.
1818 Ridge Rd
Homewood, IL 60430
312-798-6000
EMPLOYMENT CONTACT: Steven R. Hardardt, Staff Development Coordinator or Diane P. King, VP Staff Development)
TYPES OF PUBLISHING: College Text, Professional, Trade (Hardcover).
TITLES IN PRINT: 750
TITLES PUBLISHED IN 1985: 230
TITLES PUBLISHED IN 1986: 250
TOTAL EMPLOYEES: 375 (Headquarters-225, Other U.S. offices-150)
ENTRY-LEVEL HIRING IN 1986: 9 (Grad students-1, College-8)
(ANTICIPATED) ENTRY-LEVEL HIRING IN 1987: 12
ENTRY-LEVEL OPPORTUNITIES: Sales - College degree (but MBA preferred); strong people skills, self-starters. Production Editor - College degree (English or Journalism): strong writing style; sensitivity. Advertising Copywriter - Same requirements.
SUGGESTIONS: "A cover letter describing interest in book publishing, resume and work samples if appropriate."
OUTLOOK FOR 1987 ENTRY-LEVEL EMPLOYMENT: Somewhat better than last year.

JOHN KNOX PRESS
A subsidiary of Presbyterian Publishing House
341 Ponce de Leon Ave, NE
Atlanta, GA   30365
404-873-1549
EMPLOYMENT CONTACT: Vicki Miller, Personnel Officer
TYPES OF PUBLISHING: College Text, Professional, Reference, Religious, Scholarly, Trade
(Hardcover), Trade (Paperbound).
TITLES IN PRINT: 226
TITLES PUBLISHED IN 1985: 15
TITLES PUBLISHED IN 1988: 15-16
TOTAL EMPLOYEES: 9
ENTRY-LEVEL HIRING IN 1986: 0
(ANTICIPATED) ENTRY-LEVEL HIRING IN 1987: 1-2*
ENTRY-LEVEL OPPORTUNITIES: Copy editor(free lance) - College degree; graduate
work/degree (especially in Religion), copy editing/proofreading experience. *There is also a
chance we will need freelancers from time to time.
COMMENTS: "Turnover in John Knox Press is very low; I last recruited for a position there in
1983; openings are more frequent in other divisions of the Publishing House, and an entry-
level person might do better to apply to one of these." - Vicki Miller, Personnel Officer,
Presbyterian Publishing House.

LEA & FEBIGER
600 S Washington Square
Philadelphia, PA   19106
215-922-1330
EMPLOYMENT CONTACT: Robert N. Spahr, Partner
TYPES OF PUBLISHING: Medical.
TITLES IN PRINT: 310
TITLES PUBLISHED IN 1985: 52
TITLES PUBLISHED IN 1986: 56
TOTAL EMPLOYEES: 52
ENTRY-LEVEL HIRING IN 1986: 6 (Grad student-1, College-1, High school-1, Career changers-3)
(ANTICIPATED) ENTRY-LEVEL HIRING IN 1987: 1-2
ENTRY-LEVEL OPPORTUNITIES: Copy Editor - College degree (B.A. English preferred); good
language skills & excellent grasp of grammar, basic elements of style and composition.
Secretary (Advertising Department) - College degree (preferred); typing skills. Order Clerk -
High school graduate; typing skills.
OUTLOOK FOR 1987 ENTRY-LEVEL EMPLOYMENT: Same as last year

LERNER PUBLICATIONS COMPANY
241 First Ave N
Minneapolis, MN 55401
612-332-3344
EMPLOYMENT CONTACT: Nancy Campbell, Editor
TYPES OF PUBLISHING: Children's.
TITLES IN PRINT: 800
TITLES PUBLISHED IN 1986: 66
TITLES PUBLISHED IN 1986: 100
TOTAL EMPLOYEES: 55
ENTRY-LEVEL HIRING IN 1986: College-4
(ANTICIPATED) ENTRY-LEVEL HIRING IN 1987: 4
ENTRY-LEVEL OPPORTUNITIES: Editorial Assistant - College degree; critical thinker.
Marketing Assistant - College degree; critical thinker, enthusiastic.
OUTLOOK FOR 1987 ENTRY-LEVEL EMPLOYMENT: Somewhat better than last year.

LITTLE, BROWN AND COMPANY
A Subsidiary of Time Inc.
34 Beacon Street
Boston, MA 02106
617-227-0730
EMPLOYMENT CONTACT: Lydia Kenlaw, Human Resources Representative
TYPES OF PUBLISHING: Children's, College Text, Professional, Reference, Trade (Hardcover), Trade (Paperbound).
TOTAL EMPLOYEES: 645
ENTRY-LEVEL HIRING IN 1986: 90
(ANTICIPATED) ENTRY-LEVEL HIRING IN 1987: 90
ENTRY-LEVEL OPPORTUNITIES: All of the following positions require previous office experience (including 45-65 wpm) and a demonstrated interest in publishing. The level of position would be commensurate with experience of candidate. There are no educational requirements for these office positions: Department Secretary, Secretary/Assistant/Customer Service Rep., Editorial Asst./Production Asst., Administrative Asst., Executive Asst.
Sales Rep.- College degree (BA or BS); good interpersonal, selling skills. SUGGESTIONS: "A letter of inquiry, along with a resume, should initially be forwarded to the Human Resources Dept. Special areas of interest, typing (and other special skills), and salary history/or requirements should be included.
OUTLOOK FOR 1987 ENTRY-LEVEL EMPLOYMENT: Same as last year.

LONGMAN, INC.
95 Church St.
White Plains, NY 10601
914-993-5000
EMPLOYMENT CONTACT: Karen O'Brien, Personnel Director
TYPES OF PUBLISHING: College, Children's, Elhi, Professional, Reference, Scientific/Technical.
TOTAL EMPLOYEES: 108

LOUISIANA STATE UNIVERSITY PRESS
Baton Rouge, LA 70893
504-388-6294
EMPLOYMENT CONTACT: Personnel Manager
TYPES OF PUBLISHING: Scholarly, Trade (Hardcover), Trade (Paperbound).
TITLES IN PRINT: 800
TITLES PUBLISHED IN 1985: 60
TITLES PUBLISHED IN 1986: 60
TOTAL EMPLOYEES: 30
ENTRY-LEVEL HIRING IN 1986: Grad students-2
(ANTICIPATED) ENTRY-LEVEL HIRING IN 1987: 0
OUTLOOK FOR 1987 ENTRY-LEVEL EMPLOYMENT: Same as last year.

McDOUGAL, LITTELL & COMPANY
1 American Plaza, PO Box #1667
Evanston, IL 60204
312-860-2300
EMPLOYMENT CONTACT: Kathy Mattox, Personnel Director
TYPES OF PUBLISHING: Children's, Elhi
TITLES IN PRINT: 842
TITLES PUBLISHED IN 1985: 10 series
TITLES PUBLISHED IN 1986: 4 series
TOTAL EMPLOYEES: 275 (Headquarters-175, other U.S. offices-100)
ENTRY-LEVEL HIRING IN 1986: 35 (College-15, High school-10, Career changers-10)
(ANTICIPATED) ENTRY-LEVEL HIRING IN 1987: 26
ENTRY-LEVEL OPPORTUNITIES: Personnel Clerical - High school graduate (minimum); typing, general office skills. Production Asst. - High school graduate (minimum); organizational skills, figure aptitude. Sales Asst. - College degree; communication skills. Accountant - College degree (or high school plus experience). Administrative Asst. - High school graduate (minimum); office experience. Advertising Asst. - College degree; communication skills. Asst. Editor - College degree; teaching experience.
SUGGESTIONS: "Send resume"
OUTLOOK FOR 1987 ENTRY-LEVEL EMPLOYMENT: Same as last year.

McGRAW-HILL BOOK COMPANY
1221 Avenue of the Americas
New York, NY 10280
212-512-3333
EMPLOYMENT CONTACT: William Leonard, Manager of Corporate Recruitment
TYPES OF PUBLISHING: Children's, College Text, Elhi, Mass Market Paperback, Professional, Reference, Religious, Scholarly, Scientific/Technical, Software, Trade (Hardcover), Trade (Paperbound).
TITLES IN PRINT: 20,808
TITLES PUBLISHED IN 1985: 750
TITLES PUBLISHED IN 1986: 800

(Continued on overleaf)

McGRAW-HILL BOOK COMPANY (Continued)
TOTAL EMPLOYEES: 4,107 (Headquarters-625, U.S. offices-2,542, International offices-940)
ENTRY-LEVEL HIRING IN 1986: 75 (College-25, High school-30, Career changers-10, Other-10)
(ANTICIPATED) ENTRY-LEVEL HIRING IN 1987: 100
ENTRY-LEVEL OPPORTUNITIES: Clerical - H.S./Business School graduate; math aptitude.
Entry Secretary - H.S./College/Business School graduate; typing, steno, word processing.
OUTLOOK FOR 1987 ENTRY-LEVEL EMPLOYMENT: Not quite as good as last year

MACMILLAN PUBLISHING COMPANY
A subsidiary of MacMillan, Inc.
866 Third Avenue
New York, NY 10022
212-702-2000
EMPLOYMENT CONTACT: Personnel Recruiter, 2nd Floor Personnel Department.
TYPES OF PUBLISHING: Children's, College Text, Elhi, Mass Market Paperback, Professional, Reference, Religious, Scholarly, Scientific/Technical, Software, Trade (Hardcover), Trade (Paperbound), and Music Books.
TITLES IN PRINT: 26,000
TITLES PUBLISHED IN 1985 2,000
TITLES PUBLISHED IN 1986: 2,800
TOTAL EMPLOYEES: 2,300
ENTRY-LEVEL HIRING IN 1986: 50 (Grad students-11, College-20, High school-10, Career changers-4, Other-5)
(ANTICIPATED) ENTRY-LEVEL HIRING IN 1987: 60
ENTRY-LEVEL OPPORTUNITIES: Assistantships in Editorial, Production, Marketing, Subsidiary Rights, Publicity, Contracts and Permissions. All positions require a college degree and some prior general office experience (or an equivalent combination of education and experience), excellent organizational, communication and written skills (grammar, punctuation, spelling, etc.), accurate typing (minimum 45 wpm). Exposure to personal computers always a plus. Recommended areas of study: English, Communications, History, Journalism, Marketing, Advertising, Art/Design. Some entry-level assistantships are titled "Secretary," depending on the department. Some positions may require good figure aptitude and/or bookkeeping skills.
OUTLOOK FOR 1987 ENTRY-LEVEL EMPLOYMENT: Same as last year.

MASTERY EDUCATION
85 Main St
Watertown, MA 02172
617-926-0329
EMPLOYMENT CONTACT: Elena Wright, Managing Editor
TYPES OF PUBLISHING: Elhi
TITLES IN PRINT: 107
TITLES PUBLISHED IN 1985: 25
TITLES PUBLISHED IN 1986: 15
ENTRY-LEVEL HIRING IN 1986: High school-2
(ANTICIPATED) ENTRY-LEVEL HIRING IN 1987: 2
ENTRY-LEVEL OPPORTUNITIES: Trainee or Work/study opportunities for experienced paste-up/layout, word processor and proofing asst. - coursework or experience required.

MAYFIELD PUBLISHING COMPANY
285 Hamilton Ave
Palo Alto, CA 94022
415-326-1640
EMPLOYMENT CONTACT: Pamela Trainer
TYPES OF PUBLISHING: College Text.
TITLES IN PRINT: 140
TITLES PUBLISHED IN 1985: 20
TITLES PUBLISHED IN 1986: 12
TOTAL EMPLOYEES: 32
ENTRY-LEVEL HIRING IN 1986: College-5
(ANTICIPATED) ENTRY-LEVEL HIRING IN 1987: 1-2
ENTRY-LEVEL OPPORTUNITIES: Editorial Asst - College degree; good English language skills, typing (50 wpm), word processing skills helpful, but not mandatory.
OUTLOOK FOR 1987 ENTRY-LEVEL EMPLOYMENT: Not nearly as good as last year.

MERRIAM-WEBSTER INC.
A Subsidiary of Encyclopaedia Britannica
47 Federal St, PO Box #281
Springfield, MA 01102
413-734-3134
EMPLOYMENT CONTACT: Dr. Frederick C. Mish, Editorial Director
TYPES OF PUBLISHING: Reference.
TITLES IN PRINT: 30
TITLES PUBLISHED IN 1985: 2
TITLES PUBLISHED IN 1986: 2
TOTAL EMPLOYEES: 59
ENTRY-LEVEL HIRING IN 1986: College-1
(ANTICIPATED) ENTRY-LEVEL HIRING IN 1987: 0
ENTRY-LEVEL OPPORTUNITIES: Editorial Asst. - College degree (Bachelor's with excellent academic record); native speaker of English, strong interest in English and language generally, well-developed writing skills.
OUTLOOK FOR 1987 ENTRY-LEVEL EMPLOYMENT: Same as last year

MERRILL PUBLISHING COMPANY
A subsidiary of Bell & Howell Company
936 Eastwind Drive
Westerville, OH 43081
614-890-1111
EMPLOYMENT CONTACT: Maureen L. Cox, Employment Manager
TYPES OF PUBLISHING: College Text, Elhi
TITLES IN PRINT: 4,000
TITLES PUBLISHED IN 1985: 600
TITLES PUBLISHED IN 1986: 700
TOTAL EMPLOYEES: 580 (Headquarters-460, Other U.S. offices-120)

(Continued on overleaf)

MERRILL PUBLISHING COMPANY (Continued)
ENTRY-LEVEL HIRING IN 1986: High school-10
(ANTICIPATED) ENTRY-LEVEL HIRING IN 1987: 5
ENTRY-LEVEL OPPORTUNITIES: Associate Editorial Asst., Customer Service Clerks,
Microfilm Clerks - High school graduate; typing, grammar, spelling. Warehouse Workers -
No specific education or experience required.

WILLIAM MORROW & CO, INC.
A subsidiary of the Hearst Corporation
105 Madison Ave
New York, NY 10016
212-889-3050
EMPLOYMENT CONTACT: Barbara Spence, Personnel Director
TYPES OF PUBLISHING: Children's, Trade (Hardcover).
TITLES IN PRINT: 2,317
TITLES PUBLISHED IN 1985: 234
TITLES PUBLISHED IN 1986: 210
TOTAL EMPLOYEES: 150
ENTRY-LEVEL HIRING IN 1986: 15 (College-10, High school-5)
(ANTICIPATED) ENTRY-LEVEL HIRING IN 1987: 7
ENTRY-LEVEL OPPORTUNITIES: Editorial Asst./Secretary - College degree; typing.
Department Aide - High school graduate; typing. Clerk/Typist - H.S. grad typing. Design Asst.
- Art school graduate; good mechanical skills, typography knowledge. Mail Clerk - H.S. grad.
SUGGESTIONS: "Send resume and cover letter - call for an interview.
OUTLOOK FOR 1987 ENTRY-LEVEL EMPLOYMENT: Same as last year

THE C.V. MOSBY COMPANY
A Subsidiary of Times Mirror
11830 Westline Industrial Drive
St. Louis, MO 63108
314-872-8370
EMPLOYMENT CONTACT: Amanda Shapiro, Personnel Associate
TYPES OF PUBLISHING: College Text, Professional, Reference, Scientific/Technical, Software.
TITLES IN PRINT: 2,000
TOTAL EMPLOYEES: 600 (Headquarters-500, U.S. offices-60, INternational offices-40)
ENTRY-LEVEL HIRING IN 1986: 100 (Grad students-10, College-30, High school-35, Career
changers-10, Other-15)
ANTICIPATED) ENTRY-LEVEL HIRING IN 1987: ?
ENTRY-LEVEL OPPORTUNITIES: Editorial Asst - College degree (preferred)in English or
Sciences; clerical skills & phone communication skills. Asst Editor - College degree (English
or Sciences preferred), basic knowledge of publishing, specialized (i.e., nursing) knowledge.
Production Editor trainee - College degree (English), prefer technical editing certificate;
editing and production skills. Customer Service Representative - Some college; extensive
phone experience. Sales Service Representative, TelemarketIng Representative - College
degree (preferred); sales background preferred. Bookkeeping - High school graduate; CRT,
typing, adding machine. Credit Collection Rep. - High school graduate; bookkeeping or credit
training required.
OUTLOOK FOR 1987 ENTRY-LEVEL EMPLOYMENT: Same as last year.

THOMAS NELSON PUBLISHERS
Elm Hill Pike at Nelson Place
Nashville, TN 37214
615-889-9000
EMPLOYMENT CONTACT: Christy Clark, Personnel Assistant.
TYPES OF PUBLISHING: Audio/Visual, Children's, Mass Market Paperback, Paperback Trade,
Reference,. Religious, Romance novels.
TOTAL EMPLOYEES: 400

NELSON-HALL PUBLISHERS
111 N Canal St
Chicago, IL 60606
312-930-9446
EMPLOYMENT CONTACT: Stephen Ferrara, Vice President-Personnel
TYPES OF PUBLISHING: Audio/Visual, College Text, Elhi, Professional, Reference, Religious,
Scholarly, Scientific/Technical, Software, Trade (Hardcover), Trade (Paperbound)
TITLES IN PRINT: 1,400
TITLES PUBLISHED IN 1985: 103
TITLES PUBLISHED IN 1986: 106
TOTAL EMPLOYEES: 56
ENTRY-LEVEL HIRING IN 1986: 7 (Grad students-2, College-5)
(ANTICIPATED) ENTRY-LEVEL HIRING IN 1987: 4
ENTRY-LEVEL OPPORTUNITIES: "College degree a minimum requirement for candidates."
OUTLOOK FOR 1987 ENTRY-LEVEL EMPLOYMENT: Somewhat better than last year.

NEW DIRECTIONS PUBLISHING CORP
80 Eighth Ave
New York, NY 10011
212-255-2030
EMPLOYMENT CONTACT: Personnel
TYPES OF PUBLISHING: Trade (Hardcover), Trade (Paperbound).
TITLES IN PRINT: 528
TITLES PUBLISHED IN 1985: 24
TITLES PUBLISHED IN 1986: 27
TOTAL EMPLOYEES: 6 (plus 1 part-time)
ENTRY-LEVEL HIRING IN 1986: 1 (part-time)
(ANTICIPATED) ENTRY-LEVEL HIRING IN 1987: 0
OUTLOOK FOR 1987 ENTRY-LEVEL EMPLOYMENT: Not quite as good as last year.

NEW YORK UNIVERSITY PRESS
7O Washington Square South
New York, NY 10012
212-598-2886
EMPLOYMENT CONTACT: Colin Jones, Director
TYPES OF PUBLISHING: College Text, Professional, Reference, Scholarly
TITLES IN PRINT: 550
TITLES PUBLISHED IN 1985: 80
TITLES PUBLISHED IN 1986: 100
TOTAL EMPLOYEES: 4
ENTRY-LEVEL HIRING IN 1986: College-1
(ANTICIPATED) ENTRY-LEVEL HIRING IN 1987: 2
ENTRY-LEVEL OPPORTUNITIES: Acquisition Editor - College degree (BA or MA preferred); three years publishing experience, not necessarily editorial. Editorial Asst. - College degree (BA preferred); fast typist, no experience in publishing.
OUTLOOK FOR 1987 ENTRY-LEVEL EMPLOYMENT: Same as last year.

NORTH-SOUTH INSTITUTE
185 Rideau St,
Ottawa, Canada K1N 5X8
EMPLOYMENT CONTACT: Max Brem, Senior Editor
TYPES OF PUBLISHING: Professional, Trade (Paperbound).
TITLES IN PRINT: 27
TITLES PUBLISHED IN 1985: 1
TITLES PUBLISHED IN 1986: 3
TOTAL EMPLOYEES: NA
ENTRY-LEVEL HIRING IN 1986: NA
(ANTICIPATED) ENTRY-LEVEL HIRING IN 1987: 0

W.W. NORTON & COMPANY, INC.
600 Fifth Avenue
New York, NY 10110
212-354-5500
EMPLOYMENT CONTACT: Marc W. Spaeth
TYPES OF PUBLISHING: College Text, Professional, Trade (Hardcover), Trade (Paperbound).
TITLES IN PRINT: 3,187
TITLES PUBLISHED IN 1985: 320
TITLES PUBLISHED IN 1986: 325
TOTAL EMPLOYEES: 260
ENTRY-LEVEL HIRING IN 1986: 16 (Grad students-1, College-10, High school-2, Career changers-1)
(ANTICIPATED) ENTRY-LEVEL HIRING IN 1987: 4
ENTRY-LEVEL OPPORTUNITIES: College Sales - College degree; driving. Editorial Asst. - College degree; typing. Accounting/Clerical - High school or college degree; typing, bookkeeping. Trade Sales - College degree; retail bookstore experience or sales experience with another publisher.
SUGGESTIONS: "Send resume -- if no response follow up with a phone call."
OUTLOOK FOR 1987 ENTRY-LEVEL EMPLOYMENT: Same as last year

THE ORYX PRESS
2214 N Central at Encanto
Phoenix, AZ 85004
602-254-6156
EMPLOYMENT CONTACT: Department heads
TYPES OF PUBLISHING: Professional, Reference, Scholarly, Scientific/Technical, Software.
TITLES IN PRINT: 260
TITLES PUBLISHED IN 1985: 35
TITLES PUBLISHED IN 1986: 55
TOTAL EMPLOYEES: 41
ENTRY-LEVEL HIRING IN 1986: College-5
(ANTICIPATED) ENTRY-LEVEL HIRING IN 1987: 0
OUTLOOK FOR 1987 ENTRY-LEVEL EMPLOYMENT: Same as last year

OXFORD UNIVERSITY PRESS
200 Madison Ave
New York, NY 10016
212-679-7300
EMPLOYMENT CONTACT: Nancy O'Connor, Personnel Manager
TYPES OF PUBLISHING: College Text, Professional, Reference, Scholarly, Trade (Hardcover), Trade (Paperbound), and ESL.
TOTAL EMPLOYEES: 280
ENTRY-LEVEL HIRING IN 1986: 14 (College-12, High school-2)
(ANTICIPATED) ENTRY-LEVEL HIRING IN 1987: 8
ENTRY-LEVEL OPPORTUNITIES: Editorial Asst. - College degree: typing, PC. Marketing Asst. - College degree; typing, PC.
COMMENTS: "Typing (min 45/50 wpm), PC/word processing experience definitely a plus."
OUTLOOK FOR 1987 ENTRY-LEVEL EMPLOYMENT: Same as last year.

PANTHEON BOOKS
A Subsidiary of Random House
201 E 50th St, Ste #4
New York, NY 10022
212-751-2600
EMPLOYMENT CONTACT: Diane Wachtell, Assistant to the Managing Director
TYPES OF PUBLISHING: Trade (Hardcover), Trade (Paperbound).
TITLES IN PRINT: 500
TITLES PUBLISHED IN 1985: 50
TITLES PUBLISHED IN 1986: 50
TOTAL EMPLOYEES: 22
ENTRY-LEVEL HIRING IN 1986: College-3
(ANTICIPATED) ENTRY-LEVEL HIRING IN 1987: 0
ENTRY-LEVEL OPPORTUNITIES: Editorial Rights or Publicity Asst. - College degree; typing, organization, experience, editorial interest.
OUTLOOK FOR 1987 ENTRY-LEVEL EMPLOYMENT: Same as last year.

PERGAMON PRESS
Fairview Park
Elmsford, NY 10523
914-592-7700
EMPLOYMENT CONTACT: D. Pappalardo, Personnel
TYPES OF PUBLISHING: Scholarly, Scientific/Technical, Software.
TITLES IN PRINT: 2,000
TITLES PUBLISHED IN 1985: 70
TITLES PUBLISHED IN 1986: 75
TOTAL EMPLOYEES: 275 (Headquarters-200, Other U.S. offices-75)
ENTRY-LEVEL HIRING IN 1986: College-20
(ANTICIPATED) ENTRY-LEVEL HIRING IN 1987: 20
ENTRY-LEVEL OPPORTUNITIES: All of the following must have knowledge of word processing or personal computers: Editorial Asst - College degree (BA preferred). Production Asst. - College degree (BA preferred). Entry Accountant - College degree (BBA preferred). Secretary - Associate's degree.
OUTLOOK FOR 1987 ENTRY-LEVEL EMPLOYMENT: Same as last year.

PRENTICE HALL, INC.
A subsidiary of Simon & Schuster, Inc.
Route 9W
Englewood Cliffs, NJ 07632
201-592-2000
EMPLOYMENT CONTACT: Donald Caldwell, Personnel Manager
TOTAL EMPLOYEES: 2,700
ENTRY-LEVEL HIRING IN 1986: NA
(ANTICIPATED ENTRY-LEVEL HIRING IN 1987: ?
ENTRY-LEVEL JOB OPPORTUNITIES: Editorial trainee - College degree; excellent English skills.
OUTLOOK FOR 1987 ENTRY-LEVEL EMPLOYMENT: Same as last year.

PRICE/STERN/SLOAN PUBLISHERS, INC.
410 N. La cienega Blvd
Los Angeles, CA 90048
213-657-6100
EMPLOYMENT CONTACT: Department heads
TYPES OF PUBLISHING: Children's, Trade (Hardcover), Trade (Paperbound)
TITLES IN PRINT: 1,200+
TOTAL EMPLOYEES: 150

THE PUTNAM PUBLISHING GROUP
200 Madison Ave
New York, NY 10016
212-576-8900
EMPLOYMENT CONTACT: Terri Schaeffer, Personnel Recruiter
TYPES OF PUBLISHING: Children's, Trade (Hardcover), Trade (Paperbound), (General Fiction and Non-Fiction).
TOTAL EMPLOYEES: 200
ENTRY-LEVEL HIRING IN 1986: NA
(ANTICIPATED) ENTRY-LEVEL HIRING IN 1987: ?
ENTRY-LEVEL OPPORTUNITIES: Editorial Asst., Publicity Asst., Sales Asst., Sub Rights Asst., Contracts Asst., Production Asst. - College degree; good typing and office skills, light office experience preferred. Art Asst. - Art school or college degree; above requirements, plus mechanical or board skills.
OUTLOOK FOR 1987 ENTRY-LEVEL EMPLOYMENT: Same as last year.

RAND McNALLY & COMPANY
8255 Central Park Avenue
Skokie, IL 60076
3122-673-9100
EMPLOYMENT CONTACT: Paul Conti, Employment Manager

RANDOM HOUSE, INC.
201-E. 50th St
New York, NY 10022
212-572-2698
EMPLOYMENT CONTACT: Shari Garfinkel, Senior Personnel Recruiter
TYPES OF PUBLISHING: Audio/Visual, Children's College Text, Elhi, Mass Market Paperback, Professional, Reference, Religious, Software, Trade (Hardcover), Trade (Paperbound)
TITLES PUBLISHED IN 1985: 1,728
TITLES PUBLISHED IN 1986: 1,736
TOTAL EMPLOYEES: 2,050 (Headquarters-1,129; Westminster, MD-Distribution Center-921)
ENTRY-LEVEL HIRING IN 1986: 165 (Grad students-30, College-100, High school-20, Career changers-15)
(ANTICIPATED) ENTRY-LEVEL HIRING IN 1987: 150
ENTRY-LEVEL OPPORTUNITIES: Editorial Asst. - College degree (or equivalent experience); writing skills, typing. Production Asst. - College degree (or equivalent experience); good with numbers, organized and detail-oriented, accurate typing (35 wpm). Publicity Asst. - College degree (or equivalent experience); written and oral communication skills, sales orientation, typing (50 wpm). Sub-Rights Asst. - College degree (or equivalent experience); Sales "personality" and negotiating skills, typing 50 wpm. Secretary - Some college and/or office experience; typing (50-70 wpm), strong English language skills, organized and detailed oriented. Sales Assistant -- College degree or equivalent experience; comfort with numbers, sales orientation, typing (50 wpm), strong people skills.
OUTLOOK FOR 1987 ENTRY-LEVEL EMPLOYMENT: Same as last year.

ST. MARTIN'S PRESS
175 Fifth Avenue
New York, NY 10010
212-674-5151
EMPLOYMENT CONTACT: Randy Essner, Asst. Director of Personnel or Maria Fornario, Director of Personnel.
TYPES OF PUBLISHING: College, Mass Market Paperback, Reference, Trade (Hardcover), Trade (paperbound).
TITLES IN PRINT: 3,100
TITLES PUBLISHED IN 1986: 1,200
TOTAL EMPLOYEES: 250
ENTRY-LEVEL HIRING IN 1986: 25
(ANTICIPATED ENTRY-LEVEL HIRING IN 1987: 15
ENTRY-LEVEL OPPORTUNITIES: Assistants in Editorial, Production, Subsidiary Rights, Publicity, Sales/Marketing, Advertising, Contracts, Design - All require a B.A. in Liberal Arts or the Social Sciences, plus some related experience (on campus or an internship); excellent written and verbal communications skills; the ability to deal with detailed information; copywriting, editing, proofreading skills, where appropriate; a strong commitment to the book publishing industry; office procedure skills (i.e., typing, recordkeeping, etc.).
OUTLOOK FOR 1987 ENTRY-LEVEL EMPLOYMENT: Somewhat better than last year

W.B. SAUNDERS COMPANY
A Division of CBS Educational & Professional Publishing
210 W Washington Square
Philadelphia, PA 19105
215-574-4951
EMPLOYMENT CONTACT: Andrea Krimins, Personnel Director
TYPES OF PUBLISHING: Professional, Scientific/Technical, Software, (Medical Books & Periodicals)
TITLES IN PRINT: 800
TITLES PUBLISHED IN 1985: 110
TITLES PUBLISHED IN 1986: 110
TOTAL EMPLOYEES: 400
ENTRY-LEVEL HIRING IN 1986: College-2
(ANTICIPATED) ENTRY-LEVEL HIRING IN 1987: 0
ENTRY-LEVEL OPPORTUNITIES: Production Editor Trainee - College degree; copy editing/proofreading. Proofreader - College degree; proofreading technical language (medical preferred). Textbook Sales - College degree; communication skills, prior sales experience.
OUTLOOK FOR 1987 ENTRY-LEVEL EMPLOYMENT: Same as last year.

SCHOLASTIC, INC.
730 Broadway
New York, NY 10003
212-505-3000
EMPLOYMENT CONTACT: Barbara Wachtel, Employment Manager or Julius James, Recruiter.
TYPES OF PUBLISHING: Children's, Elhi, Software, Trade (Paperbound)
TOTAL EMPLOYEES: 1,500

SIMON & SCHUSTER, INC.
1230 Avenue of the Americas
New York, NY 10016
212-698-7000
EMPLOYMENT CONTACT: Cathy Williams, Employee Relations Manager
TYPES OF PUBLISHING: Audio/Visual, Children's, College, Elhi, Mass Market Paperback,
Professional, Reference, Scientific/Technical, Trade (Hardcover), Trade (Paperbound).
TOTAL EMPLOYEES: 7,000

W.H. SMITH PUBLISHERS INC.
A Subsidiary of W.H. Smith & Son Holdings
112 Madison Avenue
New York, NY 10016
212-532-6600
EMPLOYMENT CONTACT: Shannon A. White, Administrative Assistant to the President
TYPES OF PUBLISHING: Software, Trade (Hardcover), Promotional.
TITLES IN PRINT: 2,000
TITLES PUBLISHED IN 1985: 200
TITLES PUBLISHED IN 1986: 200
TOTAL EMPLOYEES: 120
ENTRY-LEVEL HIRING IN 1986: 1
(ANTICIPATED) ENTRY-LEVEL HIRING IN 1987: 6
ENTRY-LEVEL OPPORTUNITIES: Invoice Control Clerk - High school graduate; mature-
mInded, filing experience. Customer Service Representative - High school graduate (B.A. or
B.S. preferred); previous customer service experience, CRT experience. Credit Analyst -
College degree (preferred); customer service/accounts receivable experience. Accounting
Clerk - Accounting courses (degree preferred); PC experience. Data Entry Clerk - High school
graduate: CRT input experience. Assistant to the Publisher -
College degree: typing, PC input, experience with publishing industry.
SUGGESTIONS: "Send resumes first."

SOUTH-WESTERN PUBLISHING COMPANY
5101 Madison Rd
Cincinnati, OH 45227
513-271-8811
EMPLOYMENT CONTACT: Lloyd B. Combs, Sr VP Human Resources
TYPES OF PUBLISHING: Audio/Visual, College Text, Elhi, Professional, Software.
TITLES IN PRINT: 600
TITLES PUBLISHED IN 1985: 90
TITLES PUBLISHED IN 1986: 120
TOTAL EMPLOYEES: 660 (Headquarters-460, Other U.S. offices-200)
ENTRY-LEVEL HIRING IN 1986: College-20
(ANTICIPATED) ENTRY-LEVEL HIRING IN 1987: 10
ENTRY-LEVEL OPPORTUNITIES: Editorial Associate - College degree (business, economics,
English or journalism, B grade average): 30 wpm typing, personal computer experience.
SUGGESTIONS: "Written application including collegiate transcript."

SPRINGER-VERLAG NEW YORK, INC.
175 Fifth Ave
New York, NY 10010
212-460-1500
EMPLOYMENT CONTACT: Rebecca Bleiman, Personnel Asst
TYPES OF PUBLISHING: College Text, Reference, Scientific/Technical
TITLES PUBLISHED IN 1985: 159
TITLES PUBLISHED IN 1986: 180
TOTAL EMPLOYEES: 1,200 (Headquarters-200, International offices-1,000)
ENTRY-LEVEL HIRING IN 1986: 12-17 (Grad students-2, College-10 to 15.
(ANTICIPATED) ENTRY-LEVEL HIRING IN 1987: 10-15
ENTRY-LEVEL OPPORTUNITIES: Promotion Asst, Production Asst, Editorial Secretary, Administrative Asst, Documentation Clerk in Sales - College degree; good communication skills, knowledge of German is always a plus, good organization skills, prior office experience a plus.
SUGGESTIONS: "We like applicants to send resumes before a decision is made to interview them. We like people to specify the area of publishing they are in interested in.
OUTLOOK FOR 1987 ENTRY-LEVEL EMPLOYMENT: Same as last year.

STEMMER HOUSE PUBLISHERS, INC.
2627 Caves Rd
Owings Mills, MD 21117
301-363-3690
EMPLOYMENT CONTACT: Barbara Holdridge, President
TYPES OF PUBLISHING: Audio/Visual, Children's, Trade (Hardcover), Trade (Paperbound).
TITLES IN PRINT: 156
TITLES PUBLISHED IN 1985: 15
TITLES PUBLISHED IN 1986: 10
TOTAL EMPLOYEES: 6
ENTRY-LEVEL HIRING IN 1986: College-1
(ANTICIPATED) ENTRY-LEVEL HIRING IN 1987: 2
ENTRY-LEVEL OPPORTUNITIES: Editorial - College degree; proofreading. Art - College degree (A.B or B.F.A required); interest in books. Clerical - College or business school degree; data processing experience
SUGGESTIONS: "Send letter; no phone calls please."
OUTLOOK FOR 1987 ENTRY-LEVEL EMPLOYMENT: Same as last year.

STERLING PUBLISHING COMPANY. INC.
2 Park Avenue
New York, NY 10016
212-532-7160
TYPES OF PUBLISHING: Children's, Reference, Trade (Hardcover), Trade (Paperbound).
TITLES IN PRINT: 500
TITLES PUBLISHED IN 1985: 100
TITLES PUBLISHED IN 1986: 100
TOTAL EMPLOYEES: 60

ENTRY-LEVEL HIRING IN 1986: College-1
(ANTICIPATED) ENTRY-LEVEL HIRING IN 1987: 0
OUTLOOK FOR 1987 ENTRY-LEVEL EMPLOYMENT: Somewhat better than last year.

JEREMY P. TARCHER, INC.
9110 Sunset Blvd
Los Angeles, CA 90069
213-273-3274
EMPLOYMENT CONTACT: Janice Gallagher
TYPES OF PUBLISHING: Trade (Hardcover), Trade (Paperbound).
TITLES PUBLISHED IN 1985: 20
TITLES PUBLISHED IN 1986: 24
TOTAL EMPLOYEES: 12
ENTRY-LEVEL HIRING IN 1986: College-2
(ANTICIPATED) ENTRY-LEVEL HIRING IN 1987: 1
ENTRY-LEVEL OPPORTUNITIES: Editorial Asst. - College degree. No other requirements specified.
OUTLOOK FOR 1987 ENTRY-LEVEL EMPLOYMENT: Same as last year.

TIME-LIFE BOOKS, INC.
777 Duke St
Alexandria, VA 22314
703-838-7000
EMPLOYMENT CONTACT: Tom Swiger, Director of Personnel Administration

TRANSACTION PUBLISHERS
Rutgers University
New Brunswick, NJ 08903
201-932-2280
EMPLOYMENT CONTACT: Scott Bramson, Vice President
TYPES OF PUBLISHING: Professional, Reference, Scholarly, Social Scientific/Technical.
TITLES IN PRINT: 1,450
TITLES PUBLISHED IN 1985: 110
TITLES PUBLISHED IN 1986: 118
TOTAL EMPLOYEES: 32
ENTRY-LEVEL HIRING IN 1986: 5 (Grad students-3, Career changers-2)
(ANTICIPATED) ENTRY-LEVEL HIRING IN 1987: 4
ENTRY-LEVEL OPPORTUNITIES: Copy-Editing, Asst. Book Editor - College degree; preferably major in social science or communication. Proofreader - College degree; languages or English major.
OUTLOOK FOR 1987 ENTRY-LEVEL EMPLOYMENT: Somewhat better than last year.

UNIVERSITY OF HAWAII PRESS
2840 Kolowalu St
Honolulu, HI 96822
808-948-8255
EMPLOYMENT CONTACT: Robert Sparks, Director
TYPES OF PUBLISHING: Children's, College Text, Reference, Scholarly, Trade (Hardcover),
Trade (Paperbound).
TITLES IN PRINT: 700
TITLES PUBLISHED IN 1985: 40
TITLES PUBLISHED IN 1986: 40
TOTAL EMPLOYEES: 26
ENTRY-LEVEL HIRING IN 1986: 2 (College-1, High school-1)
(ANTICIPATED) ENTRY-LEVEL HIRING IN 1987: 2
ENTRY-LEVEL OPPORTUNITIES: Editor I - College degree (or equivalent); better than average
knowledge of English usage, knowledge of publication procedures, familiarity with
computers. Production Asst. - College degree (or equivalent); familiarity with production
procedures.
OUTLOOK FOR 1987 ENTRY-LEVEL EMPLOYMENT: Same as last year

UNIVERSITY OF ILLINOIS PRESS
54 E Gregory Dr
Champaign, IL 61820
217-333-0950
EMPLOYMENT CONTACT: Elizabeth Dulany, Asst Director @ Managing Editor
TYPES OF PUBLISHING: Scholarly, Trade (Hardcover), Trade (Paperbound).
TITLES IN PRINT: 810
TITLES PUBLISHED IN 1985: 60
TITLES PUBLISHED IN 1986: 70
TOTAL EMPLOYEES: 40
ENTRY-LEVEL HIRING IN 1986: College-1
(ANTICIPATED) ENTRY-LEVEL HIRING IN 1987: 0
ENTRY-LEVEL OPPORTUNITIES: Copy Editor - College degree: 2-3 years editorial experience.
OUTLOOK FOR 1987 ENTRY-LEVEL EMPLOYMENT: Same as last year.

UNIVERSITY OF NEW MEXICO PRESS
Journalism Building
Albuquerque, NM 87131
505-277-2346
EMPLOYMENT CONTACT: David V. Holtby, Associate Director
TYPES OF PUBLISHING: Professional, Scholarly.
TITLES IN PRINT: 372
TITLES PUBLISHED IN 1985: 56
TITLES PUBLISHED IN 1986: 57
TOTAL EMPLOYEES: 20
ENTRY-LEVEL HIRING IN 1986: College-2
(ANTICIPATED) ENTRY-LEVEL HIRING IN 1987: ?

ENTRY-LEVEL OPPORTUNITIES: Production Asst - College degree (graphic or fine Arts); experience in paste-up. Marketing Asst - College degree (journalism or advertising). Editorial Asst. - College degree (liberal arts); experience in copy editing. Sales Asst. - College degree (liberal arts or business); sales or bookstore experience. Order Fulfillment Asst - College (2-year) degree (liberal arts or business); sales or bookstore experience.
OUTLOOK FOR 1987 ENTRY-LEVEL EMPLOYMENT: Not quite as good as last year.

UNIVERSITY OF NORTH CAROLINA PRESS
Box 2288
Chapel Hill, NC 27514
919-916-3561
EMPLOYMENT CONTACT: Matthew Hodgson, Director
TYPES OF PUBLISHING: University press
TITLES IN PRINT: 500
TOTAL EMPLOYEES: 50

UNIVERSITY OF OKLAHOMA PRESS
1005 Asp Ave
Norman, OK 73019
405-325-5111
EMPLOYMENT CONTACT: Department heads
TYPES OF PUBLISHING: College Text, Elhi, Scholarly, Trade (Hardcover), Trade (Paperbound)
TITLES IN PRINT: 743
TITLES PUBLISHED IN 1985: 54
TITLES PUBLISHED IN 1986: 55
TOTAL EMPLOYEES: 23
ENTRY-LEVEL HIRING IN 1986: NA
(ANTICIPATED) ENTRY-LEVEL HIRING IN 1987: 0
Outlook for 1987 Entry-level employment: Somewhat better than last year.

UNIVERSITY OF WASHINGTON PRESS
PO Box #50096
Seattle, WA 98145
206-543-4050
EMPLOYMENT CONTACT: Juanita B. Pike, Program Manager
TYPES OF PUBLISHING: Audio/Visual, Reference, Scholarly, Trade (Hardcover) Trade (Paperbound)
TITLES IN PRINT: 1,300
TITLES PUBLISHED IN 1985: 91
TITLES PUBLISHED IN 1986: 95
TOTAL EMPLOYEES: 30
ENTRY-LEVEL HIRING IN 1986: NA
(ANTICIPATED) ENTRY-LEVEL HIRING IN 1987: 0
COMMENTS: "We employ students on a regular basis."

UNIVERSITY PRESS OF AMERICA, INC.
4720 Boston Way
Lanham, MD 20706
301-459-3366
EMPLOYMENT CONTACT: Department heads
TYPES OF PUBLISHING: College, professional
TITLES IN PRINT: 3,500
TITLES PUBLISHED IN 1985: 450
TITLES PUBLISHED IN 1986: 500
TOTAL EMPLOYEES: 50
ENTRY-LEVEL HIRING IN 1986: NA
(ANTICIPATED) ENTRY-LEVEL HIRING IN 1987: ?
OUTLOOK FOR 1987 ENTRY-LEVEL EMPLOYMENT: Somewhat better than last year.

UNIVERSITY PRESS OF NEW ENGLAND
3 Lebanon St
Hanover, NH 03755
603-646-3349
EMPLOYMENT CONTACT: Thomas McFarland, Director
TYPES OF PUBLISHING: Scholarly, Trade (Hardcover), Trade (Paperbound). TITLES IN PRINT:
250
TITLES PUBLISHED IN 1985: 28
TITLES PUBLISHED IN 1986: 31
TOTAL EMPLOYEES: 12
ENTRY-LEVEL HIRING IN 1986: Grad students-1
(ANTICIPATED) ENTRY-LEVEL HIRING IN 1987: 1
OUTLOOK FOR 1987 ENTRY-LEVEL EMPLOYMENT: Same as last year.

UNIVERSITY PRESS OF VIRGINIA
PO Box #3608 University Station
Charlottesville, VA 22903
804-924-3468
EMPLOYMENT CONTACT: Walker Cowen, Director
TYPES OF PUBLISHING: Scholarly.
TITLES IN PRINT: 703
TITLES PUBLISHED IN 1985: 58
TITLES PUBLISHED IN 1986: 50
TOTAL EMPLOYEES: 14
ENTRY-LEVEL HIRING IN 1986: 0
(ANTICIPATED) ENTRY-LEVEL HIRING IN 1987: 0
OUTLOOK FOR 1987 ENTRY-LEVEL EMPLOYMENT: Same as last year.

VAN NOSTRAND REINHOLD
115 Fifth Avenue
New York, NY 10003
212-254-3232
EMPLOYMENT CONTACT: Linda Watson, Personnel Manager
TYPES OF PUBLISHING: College, Professional, Reference, Scientific/Technical.
TITLES IN PRINT: 2,100
TITLES PUBLISHED IN 1986: 150
(ANTICIPATED ENTRY-LEVEL HIRING IN 1987: NA
ENTRY-LEVEL OPPORTUNITIES: Junior copywriter - BA; creative writing and research abilities; one year experience. Junior Manuscript Editor (Technical) - BS; proficient in English; meticulous eyes for detail; 6 months-1 year prior book publishing experience; knowledgeable in subject area. Editorial Assistant High school or BA; good command of English language; detail-minded; 6 months-1 year experience desired, but not required. Promotion Assistant - High school or BS; prior advertising/promotion experience required; some knowledge of space sales/mailing lists essential. Junior Designer - Art degree; knowledge of type, specs, design, art production required. Junior Accountant - 6 months-1 year experience with bank reconciliations, posting, journal entries, etc. Production Assistant - High school (plus some college, preferred); general; clerical skills; detail-oriented. Accounts Payable Clerk - High school (plus some college preferred); good figure aptitude; strong clerical background; detail-oriented; familiar with computerized AP system; 1-2 years experience required. Inventory Assistant - High school grad; general clerical, typing, light bookkeeping; 6 months-1 year experience required. Junior Editor - BA; proficient in English; meticulous eyes for detail; must have knowledge of subject area. Clerk-Typist - High school grad; typing; good command of English language; knowledge of general office procedures; Art Assistant - High school grad; general clerical, typing, basic knowledge of art production.

VIKING PENGUIN INC.
40 W 23rd St
New York, NY 10010
212-337-5200
EMPLOYMENT CONTACT: Eileen O'Rourke, Personnel Manager
TYPES OF PUBLISHING: Children's, Mass Market Paperback, Trade (Hardcover), Trade (Paperbound).
TITLES IN PRINT: 3,470
TITLES PUBLISHED IN 1985: 582
TITLES PUBLISHED IN 1986: 575
TOTAL EMPLOYEES: 400 (Headquarters-160, Other U.S. offices-240)
ENTRY-LEVEL HIRING IN 1986: 31 (College-30, High school-1)
(ANTICIPATED) ENTRY-LEVEL HIRING IN 1987: 15
ENTRY-LEVEL OPPORTUNITIES: Editorial Asst - College degree (English or related); good typing, internship a plus. Advertising & Promotion Asst. - College degree: typing, writing skills and/or some experience in graphics or layout (i.e. school newspaper). Production Asst - High school or College degree; typing, math skills. Contracts Asst - College degree; good typing, office experience helpful. Publicity Asst - College degree; good typing, writing skills. Children's Books Asst - College degree; good typing and writing skills; courses related to children's books helpful.
SUGGESTIONS: "We welcome resumes from interested applicants."

J. WESTON WALCH, PUBLISHER
PO Box #658
Portland, ME 04104
207-772-2846
EMPLOYMENT CONTACT: Richard S. Kimball, Managing Editor
TYPES OF PUBLISHING: Audio/Visual, Elhi.
TITLES IN PRINT: 1,000
TITLES PUBLISHED IN 1985: 100
TITLES PUBLISHED IN 1986: 100
TOTAL EMPLOYEES: 80
ENTRY-LEVEL HIRING IN 1986: College-3
(ANTICIPATED) ENTRY-LEVEL HIRING IN 1987: 0
ENTRY-LEVEL OPPORTUNITIES: Editorial Asst - College degree; education or experience in acquisitions, pre-press production, or computer software development.
OUTLOOK FOR 1987 ENTRY-LEVEL EMPLOYMENT: Same as last year.

WARNER BOOKS, INC.
A Division of Warner Publishing Inc.
666 Fifth Avenue
New York, NY 10103
212-246-6400
EMPLOYMENT CONTACT: Laura Tinio, Asst. Human Resources Manager
Types of publishing: Audio/Visual, Children's, Mass Market Paperback, Professional, Scholarly, Scientific/Technical, Trade (Hardcover), Trade (Paperbound).
TOTAL EMPLOYEES: 79
ENTRY-LEVEL HIRING IN 1986: 15 (College-13, High school-2)
(ANTICIPATED) ENTRY-LEVEL HIRING IN 1987: 6
ENTRY-LEVEL OPPORTUNITIES: Editorial Asst. - College degree (prefer BS in English); typing, clerical and phone skills. Secretary - High school or business school training preferred; some office experience, typing (50 wpm), good communication skills.
OUTLOOK FOR 1987 ENTRY-LEVEL EMPLOYMENT: Same as last year.

SAMUEL WEISER, INC.
PO Box #612
York Beach, ME 03910
207-363-4393
EMPLOYMENT CONTACT: B. Lundsted, Vice President
TYPES OF PUBLISHING: Trade (Paperbound), (new age books, oriental philosophy, alternative healing, and religions of the world)
TITLES IN PRINT: 350-400
TITLES PUBLISHED IN 1985: 20
TITLES PUBLISHED IN 1986: 20
TOTAL EMPLOYEES: 12-14
ENTRY-LEVEL HIRING IN 1986: 9 (College-2, High school-3, Career changers-4)
(ANTICIPATED) ENTRY-LEVEL HIRING IN 1987: 0

ENTRY-LEVEL OPPORTUNITIES: "We have no entry-level positions opening. However, I would say that production people could use a college degree, but the emphasis is on being able to write copy, spell, types quickly, and have some understanding of the material we publish. Understanding in this case does not mean that one has to specialize in knowing all facets of the occult, but an interest in the subject matter would certainly make the work more fun. New employees need to bring a willingness to learn to a new job. Most of them bring inflated resumes and then they become difficult to teach, for that can't start at the beginning when they start the job. Such people usually last from 3 to 6 months around here."
COMMENTS: "We accept letters and applications from people who have an interest in the material we publish, who can write, type and think Working for a small publishing firm is exciting, but it means that employees have to like the work. That's hard to find. Most people want to be stars.
OUTLOOK FOR 1987 ENTRY-LEVEL EMPLOYMENT: Same as last year

WILLIAMS & WILKINS
Waverly Press, Inc.
428 East Preston St
Baltimore, MD 21202
301-528-4212
EMPLOYMENT CONTACT: Richard Yochum, VP Human Resources
TYPES OF PUBLISHING: Medical, Allied Health, Nursing.
TITLES IN PRINT: 750
TITLES PUBLISHED IN 1985: 75
TITLES PUBLISHED IN 1986: 75
TOTAL EMPLOYEES: 78 (Headquarters-6, Other U.S. offices-67, International-5)
ENTRY-LEVEL HIRING IN 1986: College-7
(ANTICIPATED) ENTRY-LEVEL HIRING IN 1987: 0
ENTRY-LEVEL OPPORTUNITIES: Educational Sales Representative - College degree; selling experience. Associate Editors - College degree. Production Sponsors - College degree; manufacturing.
OUTLOOK FOR 1987 ENTRY-LEVEL EMPLOYMENT: Same as last year

WILLIAMSON PUBLISHING COMPANY
Church Hill Rd, Box 185
Charlotte, VT 05445
802-425-2102
EMPLOYMENT CONTACT: Jack Williamson, Publisher
TYPES OF PUBLISHING: Trade (Paperbound).
TITLES IN PRINT: 20
TITLES PUBLISHED IN 1985: 5
TITLES PUBLISHED IN 1986: 12
TOTAL EMPLOYEES: 6
ENTRY-LEVEL HIRING IN 1986: College-2
(ANTICIPATED) ENTRY-LEVEL HIRING IN 1987: 1-2
ENTRY-LEVEL OPPORTUNITIES: Sales & marketing - College degree; no other requirements specified.
OUTLOOK FOR 1987 ENTRY-LEVEL EMPLOYMENT: Somewhat better than last year.

CHAPTER 24

Internship & Training Program Listings

Many of the publishers listed in the previous chapter also provided us with information about internships and training programs at their houses. We have included that information in this chapter.

The listings are pretty self-explanatory. Following the name, address and telephone number of the publisher (different than the first edition -- we wanted to make it easier for you to use this information without having to constantly refer to the previous chapter), we listed the information as follows:

Internship contact The person in charge of internships, often *different* from the one indicated in the previous chapter as *employment contact*. If there are different contacts for different departments -- or for different offices -- we've indicated them.

Internships available: Salaried, non-salaried or some of each ("Both").

Approximate number expected in 1987: Just a note here -- a "?" means they have internships available, but couldn't (or wouldn't) hazard a guess as to an exact number.

Training available: Their own words -- what kinds of training they offer.

Departments: in which training is offered (not internships)

One final note: If any of the above entries is missing, that's because we were unable to confirm that entry with the company itself. Rather than give you wrong or misleading information, we simply omitted it.

ADDISON-WESLEY PUBLISHING COMPANY. INC.
Jacob Way
Reading, MA 01867
617-944-3700
TRAINING AVAILABLE: Training programs consist of specific one- or two-and-a-half-day audio/visual units on the topics of sales and time management techniques spread out over a year to supplement an intensive on-the-job training program.
DEPARTMENTS: Sales, Marketing

AD-LIB PUBLICATIONS
61 N Fifth St, PO Box #1102
Fairfield, IA 52556-1102
515-472-6617
TRAINING AVAILABLE: We incorporate our own three books about book marketing: 101 Ways to Market Your Books; Book Marketing Made Easier; and Book Marketing Opportunities: A Directory.
DEPARTMENTS: Marketing

AMERICAN PHILOSOPHICAL SOCIETY
104 South Fifth St
Philadelphia, PA 19106
215-627-0706
INTERNSHIP CONTACT: Carole N. Le Paivre, Associate Editor
TYPES OF INTERNSHIPS OFFERED: **Salaried**
ANTICIPATED NUMBER AVAILABLE IN 1987: NA

ASHLEY BOOKS, INC.
30 Main St
Port Washington, NY 11060
516-883-2221
INTERNSHIP CONTACT: Joan Calder, Vice President
TYPES OF INTERNSHIPS OFFERED: **Non-Salaried**
ANTICIPATED NUMBER AVAILABLE IN 1987: 5
TRAINING AVAILABLE: Interns learn publishing from every level -- editorial, publicity, promotion, marketing, writing copy, assisting in production, i.e., doing everything in the publishing spectrum.
DEPARTMENTS: All

BEEKMAN PUBLISHERS, INC.
PO Box #888
Woodstock, NY 12498
914-679-2300
INTERNSHIP CONTACT: Joanne Michaels, Vice President
TYPES OF INTERNSHIPS OFFERED: **Non-Salaried**
ANTICIPATED NUMBER AVAILABLE IN 1987: 1

ROBERT BENTLEY, INC.
1000 Massachusetts Ave
Cambridge, MA 02138
INTERNSHIP CONTACT: Michael Bentley, VP/Executive Editor
TYPES OF INTERNSHIPS OFFERED: **Both**
ANTICIPATED NUMBER AVAILABLE IN 1987: 1
TRAINING AVAILABLE: 1-2 trainee positions open per year. These positions are substantially more than on-the-job training, but do not usually involve off-site seminars.
DEPARTMENTS: Editorial/Production Dept

BERKLEY PUBLISHING GROUP
200 Madison Ave
New York, NY 10016
212-576-8900
INTERNSHIP CONTACT: Terri Schaeffer, Personnel Recruiter
TYPES OF INTERNSHIPS OFFERED: **Non-Salaried**
ANTICIPATED NUMBER AVAILABLE IN 1987: 1

BIRCH TREE GROUP LTD
PO Box #2072, 180 Alexander St
Princeton, NY 08540
609-683-0090
INTERNSHIP CONTACT: Catherine Yanzeck, Personnel Department
TYPES OF INTERNSHIPS OFFERED: **Both**
ANTICIPATED NUMBER AVAILABLE IN 1987: ?

BRANDEN PUBLISHING COMPANY
17 Station St, Box #843
Brookline Village, MA 02147
617-734-2045
INTERNSHIP CONTACT: Adolph Caso, President
TYPES OF INTERNSHIPS OFFERED: **Non-Salaried**
ANTICIPATED NUMBER AVAILABLE IN 1987: 2

CAMBRIDGE UNIVERSITY PRESS
32 E 57th St
New York, NY 10022
212-688-8885
INTERNSHIP CONTACT: Linda Saltsberg, Editorial Asst. or Helen Wheeler, Associate Editor
TYPES OF INTERNSHIPS OFFERED: **Non-Salaried**
ANTICIPATED NUMBER AVAILABLE IN 1987: 3-4

THE CAREER PRESS INC.
62 Beverly Rd, PO Box 34,
Hawthorne, NJ 07507
201-427-0229
Internship contact: Dick Start, Asst. to the President
TYPES OF INTERNSHIPS OFFERED: **Both**
ANTICIPATED NUMBER AVAILABLE IN 1987: 3-5
COMMENTS: Cover letters/resumes <u>only</u>. No phone calls, please. Apply by April 15 for Summer, 1987. Any time for school year internships.

CBS EDUCATIONAL & PROFESSIONAL PUBLISHING
A division of CBS Inc.
500 Summit Lake Dr
Valhalla, NY 10595
INTERNSHIP CONTACT: Jacqueline Lewis, Director, University Relations
TYPES OF INTERNSHIPS OFFERED: **Both**
ANTICIPATED NUMBER AVAILABLE IN 1987: 10-15

COLEMAN PUBLISHING
99 Milbar Blvd
Farmingdale, NY 11735
516-293-0383
INTERNSHIP CONTACT: Saul Steinberg, Director
TYPES OF INTERNSHIPS OFFERED: **Non-Salaried**
ANTICIPATED NUMBER AVAILABLE IN 1987: 2

CROWN PUBLISHERS, INC.
225 Park Avenue South
New York, NY 10003
212-254-1600
INTERNSHIP CONTACT: Linda Torraco, Employment Manager
TYPES OF INTERNSHIPS OFFERED: **Non-Salaried**
ANTICIPATED NUMBER AVAILABLE IN 1987: 6-8

MARCEL DEKKER, INC.
270 Madison Ave
New York, NY 10016
212-696-9000
INTERNSHIP CONTACT: Stacey Miller, Personnel Recruiter
TYPES OF INTERNSHIPS OFFERED: **Both**
ANTICIPATED NUMBER AVAILABLE IN 1987: 2
TRAINING AVAILABLE: High school executive internship program -- you must be a high school student.

DEVIN-ADAIR, PUBLISHERS INC.
6 N Water St
Greenwich, CT 06830
203-531-7755
INTERNSHIP CONTACT: Roger H. Lourie, Managing Director
TYPES OF INTERNSHIPS OFFERED: **Both**
ANTICIPATED NUMBER AVAILABLE IN 1987: 2
TRAINING AVAILABLE: Intern program covers the following - _Introduction_: Overall organization of a publishing enterprise, work flow, marketing overview, strategic planning. _Editorial Aspects_: Editorial activities, manuscripts, authors, testimonials, endorsements, authors' network. _Sales_: Retail trade sales, sales communications, bookstore promotion, special sales to organizations. Promotion to academic institutions and libraries, importance of reviews, middlemen (jobbers and wholesalers), direct mail sales, direct response advertising, Trade (bookstore) advertisements. _International Aspects_: Translations, English-language sales, rights, exhibits, USIA, foreign agents. Rights, permissions, royalties. Public relations, publicity, pre- and post-publication publicity. Role of reviewers. Book launch. _Operational Aspects_: Manufacturing and book production, typesetting, book design, cover creation. Warehousing and order fulfillment. Customer service. Responsiveness. Business, finance, accounting & bookkeeping, contracts, budgeting.
DEPARTMENTS: All

DUNDURN PRESS LTD
1558 Queen St E
Toronto, Ontario, Canada M4L 1E8
416-461-1881
INTERNSHIP CONTACT: Kirk Howard, President
TYPES OF INTERNSHIPS OFFERED: **Salaried**
ANTICIPATED NUMBER AVAILABLE IN 1987: 1

F & W PUBLICATIONS INC.
9933 Alliance Rd
Cincinnati, OH 45242
513-984-0717
INTERNSHIP CONTACT: Kathy Schneider, Personnel Manager
TYPES OF INTERNSHIPS OFFERED: **Salaried**
ANTICIPATED NUMBER AVAILABLE IN 1987: 2-3

FABER & FABER, INC.
50 Cross St.
Winchester, MA 01890
617-721-1427
INTERNSHIP CONTACT: Susan Nash, VP
"We haven't offered internships yet, but might in the future."

FARRAR, STRAUS & GIROUX, INC.
19 Union Square West
New York, NY 10003
212-741-6900
INTERNSHIP CONTACT: Peggy Miller, Office Manager
TYPES OF INTERNSHIPS AVAILABLE: **Non-Salaried**
ANTICIPATED NUMBER AVAILABLE IN 1987: NA

GARDEN WAY/STOREY PUBLISHING
Schoolhouse Rd
Pownal, VT 05261
802-823-5871
INTERNSHIP CONTACT: Martha M. Storey, Vice President
TYPES OF INTERNSHIPS OFFERED: **Both**
ANTICIPATED NUMBER AVAILABLE IN 1987: 2

D.C. HEATH & COMPANY
A division of Raytheon Company
125 Spring St
Lexington, MA 02173
617-862-6650
INTERNSHIP CONTACT: Janet Kenneally, Personnel
TYPES OF INTERNSHIPS OFFERED: **Non-Salaried**
ANTICIPATED NUMBER AVAILABLE IN 1987: 2

HUMAN KINETICS PUBLISHERS
1607 North Market St, PO Box #5076
Champaign, IL 61820
217-351-5076
INTERNSHIP CONTACT: Mary T. Krzysik, CPS, Executive Secretary
TYPES OF INTERNSHIPS OFFERED: **Salaried**
ANTICIPATED NUMBER AVAILABLE IN 1987: 2

RICHARD D. IRWIN, INC.
1818 Ridge Rd
Homewood, IL 60430
312-798-6000
INTERNSHIP CONTACT: Steven R. Hardardt, Staff Development Coordinator
TYPES OF INTERNSHIPS OFFERED: **Salaried**
ANTICIPATED NUMBER AVAILABLE IN 1987: 15-20

LEA & FEBIGER
600 S Washington Square
Philadelphia, PA 19106
215-922-1330
INTERNSHIP CONTACT: Ms. Dottie DiRienzi, Head of Copy Editing Department
TYPES OF INTERNSHIPS OFFERED: **Non-Salaried**
ANTICIPATED NUMBER AVAILABLE IN 1987: 1-2

LONGMAN, INC.
95 Church St
White Plains, NY 10601
914-993-5000
INTERNSHIP CONTACT: Karen O'Brien, Personnel Director
TYPES OF INTERNSHIPS AVAILABLE: **Non-Salaried**
ANTICIPATED NUMBER AVAILABLE IN 1987: NA

McDOUGAL, LITTELL & COMPANY
1 American Plaza, PO Box #1667
Evanston, IL 60204
312-860-2300
INTERNSHIP CONTACT: Kathy Mattox, Personnel Director
TYPES OF INTERNSHIPS OFFERED: **Non-Salaried**
ANTICIPATED NUMBER AVAILABLE IN 1987: 1

MACMILLAN PUBLISHING COMPANY
866 Third Avenue
New York, NY 10022
212-702-2000
INTERNSHIP CONTACT: Amryl W. Holloway, Manager-Staffing and Employee Relations
TYPES OF INTERNSHIPS OFFERED: **Non-Salaried**
ANTICIPATED NUMBER AVAILABLE IN 1987: 15

MASTERY EDUCATION
85 Main St
Watertown, MA 02172
617-926-0329
INTERNSHIP CONTACT: Elena Wright, Managing Editor
TYPES OF INTERNSHIPS OFFERED: **Non-Salaried**
ANTICIPATED NUMBER AVAILABLE IN 1987: 2

MERRIAM-WEBSTER INC.
47 Federal St, PO Box #281
Springfield, MA 01102
413-734-3134
TRAINING AVAILABLE: "Open-ended training covering various aspects of the dictionary-making process, such as reading for citations, defining, and cross-referencing.
DEPARTMENTS: Editorial

WILLIAM MORROW & COMPANY, INC.
105 Madison Ave
New York, NY 10016
212-889-3050
INTERNSHIP CONTACT: Barbara Spence, Personnel Director
TYPES OF INTERNSHIPS OFFERED: **Both**
ANTICIPATED NUMBER AVAILABLE IN 1987: NA

THE C.V. MOSBY COMPANY
11830 Westline Industrial Dr
St. Louis, MO 63108
314-872-8370
INTERNSHIP CONTACT: Jackie Parchman, Manager Internal Communications
TYPES OF INTERNSHIPS OFFERED: **Both**
ANTICIPATED NUMBER AVAILABLE IN 1987: 10
TRAINING AVAILABLE: In-house manual and product knowledge seminars DEPARTMENTS: Sales (Field)

NELSON-HALL PUBLISHERS
111 N Canal St
Chicago, IL 60606
312-930-9446
INTERNSHIP CONTACT: Steven Ferrara, Vice President-Personnel
TYPES OF INTERNSHIPS OFFERED: **Both**
ANTICIPATED NUMBER AVAILABLE IN 1987: 4

PANTHEON BOOKS
A subsidiary of Random House
201 E 50th St,
New York, NY 10022
212-751-2600
INTERNSHIP CONTACT: Diane Wachtell, Assistant to the Managing Director
TYPES OF INTERNSHIPS OFFERED: **Non-Salaried**
ANTICIPATED NUMBER AVAILABLE IN 1987: 1

PRENTICE-HALL, INC.
Route 9W
Englewood Cliffs, NJ 07632
201-592-2000
INTERNSHIP CONTACT: Donald Caldwell, Personnel Manager
TYPES OF INTERNSHIPS OFFERED: NA
ANTICIPATED NUMBER AVAILABLE IN 1987: ?
TRAINING AVAILABLE: Yes, but no details available.

PRICE/STERN/SLOAN,PUBLISHERS, INC.
410 North La Cienega Blvd
Los Angeles, CA 90048
213-657-6100
INTERNSHIP CONTACT: Claudia Sloan, Associate Editor
TYPES OF INTERNSHIPS OFFERED: **Both**
ANTICIPATED NUMBER AVAILABLE IN 1987: NA

THE PUTNAM PUBLISHING GROUP
200 Madison Ave
New York, NY 10016
212-576-8900
INTERNSHIP CONTACT: Terri Schaeffer, Personnel Recruiter
TYPES OF INTERNSHIPS OFFERED: **Non-Salaried**
ANTICIPATED NUMBER AVAILABLE IN 1987: 2

RANDOM HOUSE, INC.
See note at end of this chapter

ST. MARTIN'S PRESS
175 Fifth Avenue
New York, NY 10010
212-674-5151
INTERNSHIP CONTACT: Maria Fornario, Director of Personnel
TYPES OF INTERNSHIPS OFFERED: **Both**
ANTICIPATED NUMBER AVAILABLE IN 1987: NA

W.B. SAUNDERS COMPANY
210 W Washington Sq
Philadelphia, PA 19105
215-574-4951
INTERNSHIP CONTACT: Andrea Krimins, Personnel Director
TYPES OF INTERNSHIPS OFFERED: **Salaried**
ANTICIPATED NUMBER AVAILABLE IN 1987: 3
TRAINING AVAILABLE: Production Editor trainee position which leads to
Editorial/Production positions.
DEPARTMENTS: Periodicals

W.H. SMITH PUBLISHERS INC.
112 Madison Avenue
New York, NY 10016
212-532-6600
INTERNSHIP CONTACT: Wendy Friedman
TYPES OF INTERNSHIPS OFFERED: **Non-Salaried**
ANTICIPATED NUMBER AVAILABLE IN 1987: 1

STEMMER HOUSE PUBLISHERS, INC.
2627 Caves Rd
Owings Mills, MD 21117
301-363-3690
INTERNSHIP CONTACT: Barbara Holdridge, President
TYPES OF INTERNSHIPS OFFERED: **Both**
ANTICIPATED NUMBER AVAILABLE IN 1987: ?

JEREMY P. TARCHER, INC.
9110 Sunset Blvd
Los Angeles,CA 90069
213-273-3274
INTERNSHIP CONTACT: Janice Gallagher
TYPES OF INTERNSHIPS OFFERED: **Non-Salaried**
ANTICIPATED NUMBER AVAILABLE IN 1987: 2

TRANSACTION PUBLISHERS
Rutgers University
New Brunswick, NJ 08903
201-932-2280
INTERNSHIP CONTACT: Transaction/Rutgers Fellowship
TYPES OF INTERNSHIPS OFFERED: **Salaried**
ANTICIPATED NUMBER AVAILABLE IN 1987: ?

UNIVERSITY OF ILLINOIS PRESS
64 E Gregory Dr
Champaign, IL 61820
217-333-0950
INTERNSHIP CONTACT: Elizabeth Dulany, Asst Director & Managing Editor
TYPES OF INTERNSHIPS OFFERED: **Salaried**
ANTICIPATED NUMBER AVAILABLE IN 1987: ?

UNIVERSITY OF NEW MEXICO PRESS
Journalism Building
Albuquerque, NM 87131
505 277-2346
INTERNSHIP CONTACT: David V. Holtby, Associate Director
TYPES OF INTERNSHIPS OFFERED: **Non-Salaried**
ANTICIPATED NUMBER AVAILABLE IN 1987: 2

THE UNIVERSITY OF NORTH CAROLINA PRESS
Box 2288
Chapel Hill, NC 27514
919-966-3561
INTERNSHIP CONTACT: Matthew Hodgson, Director
TYPES OF INTERNSHIPS OFFERED: **Non-Salaried**
ANTICIPATED NUMBER AVAILABLE IN 1987: NA

UNIVERSITY PRESS OF AMERICA, INC.
4720 Boston Way,
Lanham, MD 20706
301-459-3366
INTERNSHIP CONTACT: James E. Lyons, Publisher
TYPES OF INTERNSHIPS OFFERED: **Both**
ANTICIPATED NUMBER AVAILABLE IN 1987: NA

VIKING PENGUIN INC.
40 W 23rd St
New York, NY 10010
212-337-5200
INTERNSHIP CONTACT: Department head in area of interest
TYPES OF INTERNSHIPS OFFERED: **Non-Salaried**
ANTICIPATED NUMBER AVAILABLE IN 1987: ?

WARNER BOOKS, INC.
See note at end of this chapter.

WILLIAMS & WILKINS
428 East Preston St
Baltimore, MD 21202
301-528-4212
INTERNSHIP CONTACT: Richard Yochum, VP Human Resources
TYPES OF INTERNSHIPS OFFERED: **Non-Salaried**
ANTICIPATED NUMBER AVAILABLE IN 1987: ?
TRAINING AVAILABLE: Overview of publishing functions, orientation to the particular department, specific task training for the job at hand.
DEPARTMENTS: All

Special Note: Two key publishers -- Random House and Warner Books -- indicated that although they did not currently offer an internship program, they were considering doing so in 1987. Inquire about details (when they are available) from the employment contacts at each company (see their entries in the previous chapter).

SECTION VIII

Appendices

APPENDIX A

Industry Trade Organizations

AMERICAN BOOKSELLERS ASSOCIATION
122 East 42nd Street, 14th floor
New York, NY 10168
(212)867-9060

The trade organization that represents retail booksellers nationwide (and publishers of *American Bookseller*), the ABA is not a primary association for a career in book <u>publishing</u> (as opposed to retail book<u>selling</u>). But their magazine and/or attendance at an ABA Convention -- the biggee for most publishers -- will give you a good feel for the business overall.

AMERICAN INSTITUTE OF GRAPHIC ARTS
1059 Third Avenue, 3rd floor
New York, NY 10021
(212)752-0813

Members from book and magazine publishing, plus some from the advertising community. Contact for book design workshops and clinics.

ASSOCIATION OF AMERICAN PUBLISHERS
220 East 23rd Street, 2nd floor
New York, NY 10010
(212)689-8920

Members include virtually all major (and not a few smaller) publishing houses. While their Education Department is long-defunct, they still welcome inquiries from newcomers and do their best to answer your questions and send pertinent literature. Still the primary organization to contact if you're interested in a book publishing career on any level, in any area.

ASSOCIATION OF AMERICAN UNIVERSITY PRESSES
One Park Avenue, Suite 1103,
New York, NY 10016
(212)889-6040

Similar to AAP (above); members include nearly 100 university presses in U.S. and abroad.

ASSOCIATION OF CANADIAN PUBLISHERS
70 The Esplanade East,
Toronto, Ontario, Canada M5E 1R2
(416)361-1408

Representing some 150-odd English-language publishers in Canada.

ASSOCIATION OF JEWISH BOOK PUBLISHERS
c/o Union of American Hebrew Congregations
838 Fifth Avenue,
New York, NY 10021
(212)249-0100

Members publish Jewish books, primarily for school use.

ASSOCIATION OF THE GRAPHIC ARTS
5 Penn Plaza, 12th floor,
New York, NY 10117-0305
(212)279-2100

Craft training and management seminars in graphic arts and production.

CHICAGO BOOK CLINIC
664 North Michigan Avenue,
Chicago, IL 60611
(312)951-8254

A nonprofit organization that offers seminars, courses and regular meetings for pros (and aspiring pros) in book publishing.

CHILDREN'S BOOK COUNCIL
67 Irving Place,
New York, NY 10003
(212)254-2666

Primarily a consumer/library educational association, but you may wish to contact if you're interested in children's book publishing.

CHRISTIAN BOOKSELLERS ASSOCIATION
PO Box 200, 2620 Venetucci Boulevard,
Colorado Springs, CO 80901
(303)576-7880

Like ABA, but involved with religious books.

COSMEP
PO Box 703
San Francisco, CA 94101

Primarily an organization of very small publishing houses, most individual self-publishers. No education programs, but perhaps the group to contact if you are considering starting your own publishing company.

NEW YORK RIGHTS AND PERMISSIONS GROUP
c/o Readers Digest General Books
750 Third Avenue,
New York, NY 10017
(212)850-7009

Sub rights professionals from some 70 publishing organizations.

PUBLISHERS AD CLUB
c/o Belle Blanchard
Doubleday and Company
245 Park Avenue,
New York, NY 10167
(212)953-4582

For aspiring book advertising pros. Monthly newsletter available.

PUBLISHERS PUBLICITY ASSOCIATION, INC.
c/o Putnam Publishing Group
200 Madison Avenue,
New York, NY 10016
(212)576-8850

For aspiring publicists. Holds monthly meetings and involved with planning the National Book Awards.

WOMEN IN COMMUNICATIONS, INC.
Box 9561,
Austin, TX 78766
(512)346-9875

Professional society for women in advertising, journalism and public relations. Chapters throughout the United States. Career information available for high school and college students. Publishes bi-monthly *Professional Communicator*.

WOMEN IN SCHOLARLY PUBLISHING
c/o Stanford University Press
Stanford, CA 94305
(415)497-9434

250 pros in scholarly publishing, primarily for university presses. Quarterly newsletter (free to members).

WOMEN'S NATIONAL BOOK ASSOCIATION, INC.
160 Fifth Avenue,
New York, NY 10010
(212)675-7804

Membership includes authors, editors, booksellers and librarians. A peripheral group, at best, for the aspiring professional, but may be useful to aggressive students.

APPENDIX B

Industry Trade Publications

There are, perhaps surprisingly, few magazines directly (or even *indirectly*) con-cerned with the business of book publishing. Even those we've listed below are primarily concerned either with book*selling*, primarily for libraries, or specialized publications on graphics, production, etc. Only one -- *Publishers Weekly* -- can claim to be really about book *publishing* (and publishers).

We've listed a number of publications that are peripheral -- those in the advertising and public relations areas for example. There are probably hundreds more depending on the specific area of publishing you decide to go into. These are the most important and will, at least, offer some initial advice.

ADVERTISING AGE
Crain Communications
740 North Rush Street,
Chicago, IL 60611
(312)649-5200

ADWEEK
A/S/M Communications
49 East 21 Street, 11th floor,
New York, NY 10010
(212)529-5500

AMERICAN BOOKSELLER
Booksellers Publishing, Inc.
122 East 42nd Street,
New York, NY 10168
(212)867-9060

AMERICAN PRINTER
MacLean Hunter Publishing Company
300 West Adams Street,
Chicago, IL 60606
(312)726-22802

ART DIRECTION
10 East 39th Street, 6th floor,
New York, NY 10016
(212)889-6500

ART PRODUCT NEWS
In-Art Publishing Company,
PO Box 117,
St. Petersburg, FL 33731
(813)821-6064

BOOKLIST
American Library Association
50 East Huron Street,
Chicago, IL 60611
(312)944-6780

BOOKSTORE JOURNAL
(Official publication of the Christian Booksellers Association)
CBA Service Group, Inc.
PO Box 200, 2620 Venetucci Boulevard,
Colorado Springs, CO 80901
(303)576-7880

CREATIVE
Magazines/Creative, Inc.
37 West 39th Street, Suite 604,
New York, NY 10018
(212)840-0160

GRAPHIC ARTS MONTHLY
Technical Publishing
875 Third Avenue,
New York, NY 10022
(212)605-9574

GRAPHIC DESIGN: USA
Kaye Publishing Corp.
120 East 56th Street, Suite 440,
New York, NY 10022
(212)759-8813

LIBRARY JOURNAL
SCHOOL LIBRARY JOURNAL
R.R. Bowker Company
245 West 17th Street,
New York, NY 10011
(212)645-9700

MAGAZINE AND BOOKSELLER
North American Publishing Company
322 Eighth Avenue,
New York, NY 10001
(212)620-7300

MARKETING NEWS
American Marketing Association
250 South Wacker Drive, Suite 22,
Chicago, IL 60606
(312)648-0536 (Association)
(312)993-9517 (Editorial)

PRINT
R.C. Publications, Inc.
355 Lexington Avenue, 17th floor,
New York, NY 10017
(212)682-0830

PUBLIC RELATIONS JOURNAL
Public Relations Society of America
845 Third Avenue, 12th floor,
New York, NY 10022
(212)826-1757

PUBLISHERS WEEKLY
R.R. Bowker Company
245 West 17th Street,
New York, NY 10011
(212)645-9700

UPPER AND LOWER CASE (U&lc)
International Typeface Corporation
2 Dag Hammarskjold Plaza, 3rd floor,
New York, NY 10017
(212)371-0699

THE WRITER
120 Boylston Street,
Boston, MA 02116
(617)423-3157

WRITERS DIGEST
9933 Alliance Road,
Cincinnati, OH 45242
(513)984-0717

ZIP/TARGET MARKETING
North American Publishing Company
401 North Broad Street,
Philadelphia, PA 19108
(215)238-5300

APPENDIX C

Book Publishing Courses

There are now quite a few courses available -- especially "summer institutes" -- for the aspiring book publishing professional. In this appendix, we have listed the most well-known/well-respected. We have also listed some (but ny no means all) of the best-known degree programs. For a more complete listing of the latter, consult Guide to Book Publishing Courses (Peterson's Guides, 1979). We have also omitted courses/programs primarily for writers. Where available, we have included the following information:

1. The name, address and phone number of the institution.

2. Who to contact (and/or the program director).

3. A brief description of the course/program offerings.

4. When the program or courses are offered.

5. Approximate length of each course/program.

6. Approximate costs.

7. Application procedure (including pertinent deadlines).

8. College credits awarded.

9. Whether the courses/program are primarily for entry-level people.

ASSOCIATION OF THE GRAPHIC ARTS
(formerly Printing Industries of Metropolitan New York)
5 Penn Plaza,
New York, NY 10001
(212)279-2100
Ed Murray, Director

Now in its 70th year, the AGA's Evening Schools (three campuses: New York City, Montclair, NJ and Hemstead, Long Island) offer some 40 courses per semester -- Spring and Fall. Spring classes begin in February, Fall in October. Most are 10 weeks, one night per week. Cost is around $125 (for members), $200 (for non-members) plus $15 registration fee. (They accept resumes to pass on to their 700+ corporate members.)

CITY UNIVERSITY OF NEW YORK, GRADUATE CENTER
Education in Publishing Program
33 West 42nd Street, Room 1206A,
New York, NY 10036
(212)575-1493
Barbara Heller, Director, Special Programs
Peg Rivers, Program Administrator

Offers some 25-odd publishing courses in the fall and spring semesters. Most courses are ten weeks (one evening per week) and are aimed at those with some experience in publishing. The entire program is developed from the basic curriculum drawn up by the Education for Publishing Committee of the Association of American Publishers. Application deadline: mid-September for fall (classes begin around October 1st); mid-February for spring (classes begin around March 1st). Certificate issued upon completion of course. Tuition works out to approximately $20 per night (so, for most courses, around $200).

GEORGE WASHINGTON UNIVERSITY
Publication Specialist Program
801 22nd Street, NW, Suite T-409
Washington, DC 20052
(202)994-7273 or 5766
Dee Buchanan, Program Director

Five sessions per year (primarily evenings, some Saturday mornings) covering all aspects of book, magazine and newsletter publishing. Each course last 8 weeks, costs from $290 - $305 and is noncredit. Full program -- consisting of 10, 20-hour courses (24 continuing education units) -- is $2,360. Certificate awarded upon completion of program. Spring program begins first week of February, Fall, last week of September.

HOWARD UNIVERSITY PRESS
Book Publishing Institute
2900 Van Ness St., NW
Washington, DC 20008
(202)686-6498
William S. Mayo, Acting Director

Intensive 5-week course, featuring top industry executives, is a good overview of the business, covering editorial, design, manufacturing, marketing and business aspects of book publishing. Accepts 30 students -- primarily recent college grads, but occasional college juniors or those changing careers -- for course running from May 27 to July 2 (1986 dates. Check for 1987). Cost is $1,500, plus a $35 nonrefundable application fee that must be received with an application no later than March 19th.

NEW YORK UNIVERSITY
School of Continuing Education
2 University Place, Room 21
New York, NY 10003
(212)598-3571 (Admissions)
Ronald W. Janoff, Director
Carol Myer, Program Coordinator

Offers approximately seven 10 or 12 week book publishing courses (plus courses and a degree program in magazine publishing), for both the entry-level and advanced student, plus occasional 1-day seminars. Courses available in three semesters -- Fall, Spring and Summer) and cost $240 each (plus $20 registration fee). Seminars, when offered, generally cost under $100. The Certificate in Book Publishing is awarded to those who successfully complete five courses with a minimum "B" grade point average.

NEW YORK UNIVERSITY'S SUMMER PUBLISHING INSTITUTE
Center for Publishing
48 Cooper Square,
New York, NY 10003
(212)477-9142
Ronald Janoff, Director
Carolyn Stark, Program Administrator

Highly respected course is offered each summer: 1987 dates are June 15-July 24. Application deadline is April 13. Cost is $2,500 (plus $35 application fee). Course limited to 60 students.

NORTHEASTERN UNIVERSITY
Center for Continuing Education
Graphic Arts Program
370 Common Street,
Dedham, MA 02026
(617)329-8000
Frank Trocki, Director

Courses in all aspects of book publishing, advertising, design, production and management. Courses are offered in all four quarters. Most are for 11 weeks and cost approximately $300 (which includes registration fee). "Hands-on" courses, such as Photo Typesetting, amy cost a bit more. Two different types of professional certificates are available. New this year: a *Graphic Arts Newsletter* available one month before the start of each quarter's classes, with details on courses, registration, etc.

PARSONS SCHOOL OF DESIGN
School of Continuing Education
66 West 12th Street,
New York, NY 10011
(212)741-8933
Donal Higgins, Dean

Approximately 50 courses in each of three semesters (plus half that in the summer quarter). Ten weeks per class -- once per week. In summer, twice a week for five weeks. Cost: $246 per credit; $220 per course noncredit. Applications accepted up to the beginning of each semester.

RADCLIFFE COLLEGE/HARVARD UNIVERSITY
Radcliffe Publishing Procedures Courses
6 Ash Street,
Cambridge, MA 02138
(617)495-8678
Frank Collins, Director

Radcliffe's 6 week course runs from late-June to early-August (1986 dates were June 23 to August 1). Application deadline is March 22nd; cost (including room and board) is $3,150. Course geared to entry-level candidates and includes both magazine and book publishing. Accepts approximately 85 students.

SCHOOL OF THE VISUAL ARTS
Division of Continuing Education
209 East 23rd Street,
New York, NY 10010
(212)679-7350 or 683-0600
Gene Daly, Director of Continuing Education

In addition to its highly respect B.F.A. and M.F.A. programs, the School offers 12-week courses in a number of areas -- book, newspaper and magazine design; advertising; production, etc for non-degree candidates. Programs begin in September, January and June. Cost approximately $230 per course (includes registration fee). From entry-level up.

STANFORD UNIVERSITY
Stanford Publishing Course
Stanford Alumni Association
Stanford, CA 94305
(415)497-2021
Della van Heyst, Director

Now eleven years old, this two-week course is available for either book or magazine publishing. 1986 dates were July 7th-19th. Aimed at publishing professionals: average age of participants is 36. Cost is $1,350.

UNIVERSITY OF CHICAGO
Publishing Program
Office of Continuing Education
5835 South Kimbark Avenue,
Chicago, IL 60637
(312)962-1722 or 1729
Joyce Feucht-Haviar, Director

Approximately one dozen courses offered each semester. Cost between $85 and $165. Geared to entry-level candidates.

UNIVERSITY OF DENVER
Publishing Institute
Graduate School of Librarianship
Denver, CO 80208
(303)871-2570
Elizabeth Geiser, Director

Four-week summer program accepts 85 students, most recent college graduates. Covers only book publishing (not magazines).

INDEX

TITLES AVAILABLE THROUGH CAREER PRESS

Ready to leave the ivy-covered walls and get a first job? Looking for an international career?

Stuck in a rut? Tired of a boss who's determined to block your next promotion?

Get the hard-hitting, practical, step-by-step advice you need to start a new career or get that promotion. Now, for the first time, four books originally published by Williamson Publishing* are available through The Career Press. Order your copies of these best-selling books today.

AFTER COLLEGE; The Business of Getting Jobs
By Jack Falvey 192 pages   ISBN 0-913589-17-9
Order Code 979 $11.95 postpaid.

Falvey explores contacts, resumes, on-campus interviews, qualifications and more. His recommendations are so well-founded, many readers may find this book more useful than a diploma!

"In a very readable style, Falvey explodes lots of the myths of getting a job...This book may well be the antidote called for in a society that is becoming increasingly specialized and over-educated."
         - *Library Journal,* May, 1986

WHAT'S NEXT?/Career Strategies After 35
By Jack Falvey 192 pages   ISBN 0-913589-26-8
Order Code 968 $11.95 postpaid.

Learn about your career mosaic, how to move your skills to the center of the action, how women can avoid dead-end jobs, how to renew your contact network and more.

Jack Falvey is a frequent contributor to the *Wall Street Journal* and *Inc.* magazine. He is a sought-after business and college speaker and has appeared on the *Today* show and numerous other television and radio programs.

TITLES AVAILABLE THROUGH CAREER PRESS

INTERNATIONAL CAREERS: An Insiders Guide
By David Rearwin 192 pages   ISBN 0-913589-28-4
Order Code 984 $11.95 postpaid.

International careers are the most sought after marketing and management careers of the '80s. People are frantically trying to acquire the elusive and magical credentials (over 24,000 U.S. students are currently studying Japanese!) in hopes of landing one of the coveted positions.

Enter David Rearwin. With an exciting, enviable and varied international career that spans 20 years, he presents an entire international career-building process, custom-tailored to the needs and demands of today's highly competitive international market.

THE TERMINATION TRAP: Best Strategies For A Job Going Sour
By Dr. Stephen Cohen 224 pages ISBN 0-913589-00-4

Order Code 904 $11.95 postpaid.

Learn about "in" groups and scapegoats, find out how to save a job if threatened, cope with losing a job, how to make a job a better one or move on to something better.

"...a first rate book...excellent organization, graphic examples and straight-from-the-shoulder analysis and advice. This is therapy as it should be."
         - *Vermont Sunday* Magazine

☎ Call Toll-Free 1-800-CAREER-1 ☎

For your convenience, we accept Mastercard or VISA. All books are available now. Or send a check or money order for $11.95 for each book to: THE CAREER PRESS, INC., 62 Beverly Road, P.O. Box 34, Hawthorne, N.J. 07507.